Addiction Di

Addiction Dilemmas

Family Experiences from Literature and Research and Their Challenges for Practice

Jim Orford

Alcohol, Drugs, Gambling and Addiction Research Group
School of Psychology
University of Birmingham
Birmingham, England

WILEY-BLACKWELL

A John Wiley & Sons, Ltd., Publication

This edition first published 2012
© 2012 John Wiley & Sons Ltd.

Wiley-Blackwell is an imprint of John Wiley & Sons, formed by the merger of Wiley's global Scientific, Technical and Medical business with Blackwell Publishing.

Registered Office
John Wiley & Sons Ltd, The Atrium, Southern Gate, Chichester, West Sussex, PO19 8SQ, UK

Editorial Offices
350 Main Street, Malden, MA 02148-5020, USA
9600 Garsington Road, Oxford, OX4 2DQ, UK
The Atrium, Southern Gate, Chichester, West Sussex, PO19 8SQ, UK

For details of our global editorial offices, for customer services, and for information about how to apply for permission to reuse the copyright material in this book please see our website at www.wiley.com/wiley-blackwell.

The right of Jim Orford to be identified as the author of this work has been asserted in accordance with the UK Copyright, Designs and Patents Act 1988.

Library of Congress Cataloging-in-Publication Data

Orford, Jim.
    Addiction dilemmas : family experiences from literature and research and their challenges for practice / Jim Orford.
        p. cm.
    Includes index.
    ISBN 978-0-470-97701-9 (cloth) – ISBN 978-0-470-97702-6 (pbk.)
1. Substance abuse–Psychological aspects. 2. Substance abuse–Social aspects. 3. Families. I. Title.
    RC564.O758 2012
    616.86–dc23   2011022724

A catalogue record for this book is available from the British Library.

This book is published in the following electronic formats: epdf: 9781119978831; Wiley Online Library online: 9781119978824; ePub: 9781119978695

Set in 10.5/13pt Minion by Aptara Inc., New Delhi, India.
Printed in Malaysia by Ho Printing (M) Sdn Bhd

1   2012

Contents

Preface

Addiction, in its various forms, is unfortunately extremely common. Because people who are themselves addicted usually experience a mixture of confusion, guilt, shame and depression about their addiction, and because they are often ambivalent about seeking help and changing, the problem is in large part a hidden one. The availability of treatment is at best patchy and in many parts of the world is virtually or completely absent. The hidden nature of the problem is further compounded when it comes to family members who are affected by the addiction of a close relative. It is those family members – the partners, parents, sons and daughters, sisters and brothers, grandmothers and others – who are the principal protagonists of the chapters of this book. Their problems come to light only with great difficulty. For them the barriers that stand in the way of obtaining help are multiplied by many factors. The latter include lack of awareness of any help that might be available to them, the sense of shame at having such a problem in the family, a fear of gossip, ridicule or criticism by others, a belief that such problems should be dealt with within the family, and a lack of trust in the services that do exist.

That fear of criticism and lack of trust in services may, sadly, have been well placed in the past. Even when services have been alert and responsive to problems of addiction they have tended to ignore the fact that addiction often profoundly affects the lives and health of close family members. Family members have mostly been on the periphery in addiction treatment services. Even worse, when professional attention has focused at all on family members, in the past it has often contributed to the very criticism that family members fear. Not only have family members been marginalized but they have also been misunderstood. For one thing it has often been presumed, or at least implied, that they are somehow to blame for the origin or perpetuation of their relatives' addiction.

Because the problems faced by the characters that appear in the chapters of this book are hidden and ill-defined it is almost impossible to put a figure on their prevalence with any accuracy. But, using figures for the prevalence of alcohol, drug and gambling problems in those countries where there has been research, and making very cautious estimates of the numbers of closely affected family members, my colleagues and I arrived at a minimum estimate of close to a hundred million adults worldwide seriously affected by the excessive drinking, drug use or gambling of close relatives (cited in our book Orford J. *et al.*, *Coping with Alcohol and Drug Problems: The Experiences of Family Members in Three Contrasting Cultures*). Indeed many would consider that to be a gross under-estimate. What this means is that every primary care medical practitioner or nurse, every social worker, teacher or community worker is certain to be in touch, whether they know it or not, with people who are experiencing the effects of living with someone who has a serious alcohol, drug or gambling problem.

It is towards the correction of the state of neglect, marginalization and misunderstanding of family members that the present book is aimed. For a number of years colleagues and I have been engaged in a programme of research and development designed to try to understand the experiences that family members face, and to develop and evaluate ways of helping family members. In the course of that research we have heard many family members tell their stories, and a number of the chapters in this book are based on those accounts (Chapters 1, 4, 6, 8, 10, 13, 17, 19 and 22). Those stories come from our work in England but also from other countries such as Mexico, Australia and Italy where we have collaborated in research on addiction and the family. The most common addiction that family members are concerned about is addiction to alcohol. Others are worried about their relatives' addiction to drugs. In a further set of stories it is addiction to gambling that is the cause of concern. The most frequently occurring relationship of affected family member to addicted relative is that of wife to husband, but other family members who tell their stories are mothers, fathers, husbands, daughters, sons, grandmothers and in-laws.

As that programme of work has progressed I have occasionally come across, usually by accident, biographies or autobiographies, written about or by people who themselves have experienced what it was like to live with someone suffering from an addiction problem. When such a writer has recognized the importance of addiction and has focused at some length on how it has affected the subject of the biography or autobiography, this gives us an incomparable opportunity to extend further our knowledge of how addiction affects family members. Several of the chapters in this book are therefore summaries of such works. One of the earliest I discovered was the autobiography of the writer Beverley Nichols who recounts his experiences in relation to his father's alcohol problem (Chapter 14). Only later did I find Virginia Ironside's book about her relationship with her mother who also had a drinking problem (Chapter 15). I was excited to discover Caitlin Thomas's co-authored book about her life with Dylan Thomas and I subsequently sought out a number of books written by or about her and her experience of Dylan Thomas's drinking (summarized in Chapter 11). It was only some time later that I discovered John Brinnin's book about his relationship with Dylan Thomas. That has a special role in this book because to my knowledge it is a unique account of the experience of being a close friend and colleague of someone with a drinking problem (Chapter 12). The other three chapters of this kind are constructed around Jacqueline Doherty's story of her experience of her son's drug dependence (Chapter 9); Molly Lefebure's biography of Sara Coleridge, the wife of the poet Samuel Taylor Coleridge who became dependent on opium – a biography that has the additional interest of having a lot to say about the effects of Coleridge's drug addiction, not only on his wife but also on his friends (Chapter 16); and Frank Hilton's biography of Baudelaire, highlighting his drug addiction, which is very relevant to the theme of this book because Baudelaire's mother is such an important figure in Hilton's book (Chapter 20).

The inclusion of five chapters reproducing short extracts from works of fiction may at first sight seem strange, but each has been included for a special reason. Chapter 2 is the only one that draws on a dramatic work – Eugene O'Neill's play *Long Day's Journey into Night*. I decided early on to include it, not only because of the powerful scene that I have included, which rang true to me as a student of addiction and the family, but also for the good reason that the play is widely recognized to be, and was offered by O'Neill himself as, autobiographical. The particular scene that figures in Chapter 2 concerns the mother, Mary, who, like O'Neill's own mother, has a morphine addiction. But O'Neill was also well acquainted with excessive drinking, which also featured in the play, since his father, himself and an elder brother, and two sons, all had problems with alcohol. Anne Brontë's

The Tenant of Wildfell Hall (Chapter 5) is one of two novels I have drawn on. The particular reason for including it lies in the peculiar structure of the book, a large part of which consists of the central character's diary in which she writes at unusual length about her perception of her husband's drinking problem and the changing ways in which she tries to cope with it. Coupled with the fact that there is good reason to believe that Anne Brontë was drawing on her experience of witnessing her elder brother's addiction, this insightful piece of, admittedly fictional, writing was always a strong candidate for inclusion. Chapter 7 consists of an extract from a film, *Nil by Mouth*. Once again we have here a work of fiction that draws on personal experience. The director, Gary Oldman, who wrote the script and produced, directed and partly financed the film, had himself experienced at first hand having a drinking problem. When it comes to gambling there are a number of relevant novels from the nineteenth century that I might have drawn on – notably Dostoevsky's autobiographical *The Gambler*, and from the first half of the twentieth century – for example Graham Greene's *Brighton Rock* and Walter Greenwood's *Love on the Dole*. But for Chapter 18 I have chosen to quote from a more modern novel, *A Chancer* by James Kelman. Although I have no reason to think that Kelman was drawing directly on personal experience, his reputation for accurate description of the hardships, often revolving around pubs and betting shops, in his native Glasgow, is a great one. The extract that appears in that chapter I chose because it seemed to me to capture so well what people have told my colleagues and myself about the tense family situations that can arise when addiction is present. The last of the fiction-based chapters returns to the medium of film, specifically the film *Fever Pitch* (Chapter 21). Again, although it is a work of fiction, it is much more than purely imaginative, based as it was on the advice of a number of expert technical advisers who knew about compulsive gambling.

The book is therefore based on a mix of personal accounts given to researchers, autobiographies and biographies, and well-informed works of fiction. In fact it was my slow discovery that the same themes about the way addiction affected the family were to be found repeatedly in these varied sources that inspired me to put together this collection. There is one further chapter that remains to be mentioned and which does not fit any one of those three categories. It appears as Chapter 3. It is built around a BBC television documentary about drug addiction and the family. It was an early entry. Indeed it was a strong influence on my decision to go ahead with the book. There have been many television documentaries since then on the subject of addiction but none has come so close to this book's central theme.

In the television studio, participants debated the very issue that parents had discussed with us in our research and which forms the central question for us here – how do family members respond in the face of a loved one's serious addiction problem?

I hope some members of families afflicted with addiction may find this book helpful. It might help them realize that, after all, they are not alone and completely misunderstood in their dilemmas; rather, that the difficulties they have been grappling with are very common and universal, and that many good people have been flummoxed and driven to despair about what to do. I hope it might help them think of new ideas about how to cope.

The audience that I most had in mind, however, consists of practitioners of one sort or another who are consulted by family members affected by addiction and who are often equally perplexed about how to advise or how to be of any help. I hope this book might provide additional understanding of the circumstances faced by families with an addicted member and might therefore usefully inform professional practice. In the process my hope is that it might contribute to reducing the misunderstanding that has existed about family members in these circumstances and add to an appreciation of what they are going through. Each chapter concludes with a commentary, drawing out what I believe are some of the most salient points, plus a number of questions and exercises that an individual or group of professionals or trainees might undertake. The separate chapters are each complete in themselves and can be used individually or in any order. The questions and exercises at the end of the chapters can be ignored if desired but my hope is that they will add to the value of the chapters, and the book as a whole, by serving as a training tool. They are designed to be challenging and to provoke debate and discussion on different aspects of a subject about which there are no simple answers. Just as family members themselves face dilemmas about how to cope, so do those who provide services for them face their own dilemmas about how to understand and how to respond. These personal and professional dilemmas are a reflection of the much wider societal dilemma about how to cope with highly prevalent addictions.

This is not a 'How to do it' book. Its aim, rather, is to aid better understanding by allowing readers to hear directly from family members – in literature or in research – and to critically reflect on what they are hearing. I believe that is a better route to knowledge and thence to constructive ways of helping. At the end of the book are some suggestions for further reading that might take that process further.

Sources and Acknowledgements

Chapter 1

Based on interviews with family members from several different families who took part in the English arm of a three-country study of family members affected by alcohol or drug problems, funded by the Mental Health Foundation. The results of that research are to be found in the books: *Coping with Alcohol and Drug Problems: The Experiences of Family Members in Three Contrasting Cultures* (Orford, J., Natera, G., Copello, A., Atkinson, C., Mora, J., Velleman, R., Crundall, I., Tiburcio, M., Templeton, L. and Walley, G., (2005), London: Routledge), *Living with Drink: Women who Live with Problem Drinkers* (Velleman, R., Copello, A. and Maslin, J. (1998), London: Longman), and *Risk and Resilience: Adults who were the Children of Problem Drinkers* (Velleman, R. and Orford, J. (1999), Amsterdam: Harwood); and in the following series of articles: Orford, J., Natera, G., Davies, J., Nava, A., Mora, J., Rigby, K., Bradbury, C., Copello, A. and Velleman, R. (1998) Stresses and strains for family members living with drinking or drug problems in England and Mexico, *Salud Mental*, 21:1–13; Orford, J., Natera, G., Davies, J., Nava, A., Mora, J., Rigby, K., Bradbury, C., Bowie, N., Copello, A. and Velleman, R. (1998) Tolerate, engage or withdraw: a study of the structure of family coping in England and Mexico, *Addiction*, 93:1799–1813; Orford, J., Natera, N., Davies, J., Nava, A., Mora, J., Rigby, K., Bradbury, C., Copello, A. and Velleman, R. (1998) Social support in coping with alcohol and drug problems at home: findings from Mexican and English families, *Addiction Research*, 6:395–420; and Orford, J., Natera, G., Velleman, R., Copello, A., Bowie, N., Bradbury, C., Davies, J. Mora, J., Nava, A., Rigby, K. and Tiburcio, M. (2001) Ways of coping and the health of relatives facing drug and alcohol problems in Mexico and England, *Addiction*, 96:761–74.

Chapter 2

Long Day's Journey into Night by Eugene O'Neill. The play was first published in Great Britain in 1956 and in paperback by Jonathan Cape in 1966. The quotations are from the 1990 reprinting of the paperback edition, from the character introductions on pages 10–11 and 16–17, and from Act 2, Scene 2, pages 64–6.

Chapter 3

Based on a BBC television documentary, *Tough Love*, in the Family Matters series, broadcast on 17 June 1991.

Chapter 4

Based on interviews with wives of men with gambling problems as part of a research project, funded by the Medical Research Council, and reported in Krishnan, M. and Orford, J. (2002) Gambling and the family from the stress-coping-support perspective, *International Gambling Studies*, 2:61–83.

Chapter 5

The Tenant of Wildfell Hall by Anne Brontë, first published in 1848. Quotations are from the 1996 Penguin classic edition, pages 202, 260, 267, 268–9, 322 and 339.

Chapter 6

Quotations taken from the paper: Ahuja, A., Orford, J. and Copello, A. (2003) Understanding how families cope with alcohol problems in the UK West Midlands Sikh community, *Contemporary Drug Problems*, 30:839–73, which was based on the unpublished PhD thesis, University of Birmingham, by Ahuja, A. (2000) entitled 'Understanding family coping with alcohol problems in the Sikh community'.

Chapter 7

From the film *Nil by Mouth*, directed by Gary Oldman (UK, 1997, 128 minutes, certificate 18).

Chapter 8

Based on interviews with family members in the Northern Territory, Australia, as part of a research project carried out in collaboration with the Northern Territory Health Department's Aboriginal Living with Alcohol Program. Results of the project can be found in the book, *Coping with Alcohol and Drug Problems: The Experiences of Family Members in Three Contrasting Cultures* (Orford, J., Natera, G., Copello, A., Atkinson, C., Mora, J., Velleman, R., Crundall, I., Tiburcio, M., Templeton, L. and Walley, G, (2005)); and in the report, *Worrying for Drinkers in the Family: An Interview Study with Indigenous Australians in Urban Areas and Remote Communities in the Northern Territory*, Final report to the Living with Alcohol Program, Territory Health Services, Northern Territory Government, Australia.

Chapter 9

Doherty, J. (2006) *Pete Doherty: My Prodigal Son*, London: Headline.

Chapter 10

Based on interviews with parents of young problem gamblers as part of a research project funded by the Medical Research Council and reported in Krishnan, M. and Orford, J. (2002) Gambling and the family from the stress-coping-support perspective, *International Gambling Studies*, 2:61–83.

Chapter 11

Thomas, C. and Tremlett, G. (1986) *Caitlin: Life with Dylan Thomas*, London: Secker and Warburg.

Thomas, C. (1957) *Leftover Life to Kill*, London: Putnam.

Thomas, C. (1998) *Double Drink Story: My Life with Dylan Thomas*, London: Virago Press.

Ferris, P. (1995) *Caitlin: The Life of Caitlin Thomas*, London: Pimlico (quotations with permission of the author).

Chapter 12

The main source is Brinnin, J.M. (1956) *Dylan Thomas in America*, London: Harborough (quotations are from the Ace Books paperback edition of 1957).

Brief reference is also made to: Nashold, J. and Tremlett, G. (1997) *The Death of Dylan Thomas*, Edinburgh: Mainstream Publishing.

Chapter 13

Based on extracts from the following sources:

Mora-Ríos, E.J. (1998) 'Salud mental en la mujer: una comparación transcultural en el campo de las adiciones.' Unpublished Masters in Clinical Psychology thesis, Universidad Nacional Autónoma de México.

Arcidiacono, C., Procentese, F., Velleman, R. and Albanesi, C. (2008) *Famiglie sotto stress: convivere con chi abusa di alcol o droghe*, Milano: Unicopli.

Yang, J. (1997) 'Culture, Family and Alcoholism in South Korea.' Unpublished PhD thesis, Goldsmiths College, University of London.

Velleman, R., Copello, A. and Maslin, J. (eds) (1998) *Living with Drink: Women who Live with Problem Drinkers*, London: Longman.

Chapter 14

Nichols, B. (1972) *Father Figure: An Uncensored Autobiography*, London: Heinemann.

Chapter 15

Ironside, V. (2003) *Janey and Me: Growing Up with My Mother*, London: Fourth Estate.

Chapter 16

The main source is: Lefebure, M. (1986) *The Bondage of Love: A Life of Mrs Samuel Taylor Coleridge*, London: Victor Gollancz (quotations with permission of the author).

The chapter also quotes from: Lefebure, M. (1977) *Samuel Taylor Coleridge: A Bondage of Opium*, London: Quartet Books (first published by Victor Gollancz in 1974) (quotations are from the 1977 Quartet Books edition).

Chapter 17

As for Chapter 1.

Chapter 18

Kelman, J. (1999) *A Chancer*, London: Vintage (originally published by Polygon Books in 1985) (the quotations in Chapter 18 are taken from the Vintage edition, pages 100–3 with the permission of the author).

Chapter 19

Of the four stories included in this chapter, three are based on interviews carried out as part of a study of the young adult sons and daughters of problem drinking parents, reported in: Velleman, R. and Orford, J. (1999) *Risk and Resilience: Adults who were the Children of Problem Drinkers*, Amsterdam: Harwood. The fourth is based on a case study published in: Arcidiacono, C., Procentese, F., Velleman, R. and Albanesi, C. (2008) *Famiglie sotto stress: convivere con chi abusa di alcol o droghe*, Milano: Unicopli.

Chapter 20

Hilton, F. (2004) *Baudelaire in Chains: A Portrait of the Artist as a Drug Addict*, London: Peter Owen (quotations with permission).

Chapter 21

From the film *Fever Pitch*, directed by Richard Brooks, 1985, cited by Dement, J.W. (1999) *Going for Broke: The Depiction of Compulsive Gambling in Film*, Lanham, Maryland: Scarecrow Press.

Chapter 22

The first example is adapted from an interview held as part of research into ways of helping family members in the general practice health service setting. The research was reported in Orford, J., Templeton, L., Patel, A., Copello, A. and Velleman, R. (2007) The 5-Step family intervention in primary care: I. Strengths and limitations according to family members, *Drugs: Education, Prevention and Policy*, 14:29–47.

All the other examples are taken, with permission, from: Barnard, M. (2007) *Drug Addiction and Families*, London: Jessica Kingsley.

The chapters for this book have been assembled over a number of years. During those years, and before, I have had the pleasure of working with many colleagues, notably at the Universities of Exeter and Birmingham and their local National Health Service Addiction Services where I have worked myself, and at the University of Bath and associated NHS Trust, at the Institute of Psychiatry in Mexico City and at the Living with Alcohol Program in Darwin, Australia. This book could only have been compiled with the help of that background and those colleagues. The people I have worked with on the various projects we have undertaken together during that time are far too many to list here, but they are all acknowledged in the various research articles and books referred to above. I would, however, like to mention by name my closest and longest standing colleagues Richard Velleman, Alex Copello and Lorna Templeton in England and Guillermina Natera in Mexico. I would also like to mention Pat Evans who has been our Research Group Secretary in Birmingham for a number of particularly happy years and who kindly prepared draft and final versions of the present manuscript.

1

We'll Be There for Him

A Family Responds to Relapse

In this chapter a number of members of one hypothetical family, and a doctor, speak in turn. Each states his or her view about how the family is responding, and should respond, to the excessive drinking of the main protagonist's husband. The latter has had a drinking problem for many years and has recently had a relapse after several months of encouraging improvement. This reversion to drinking has thrown into sharp relief the different ways in which family members have been coping, and might cope, with this problem. The family is closely based on the accounts given by a number of different family members, all living with drinking problems, who have taken part in the research I and my colleagues have carried out over a number of years with families affected by excessive drinking, drug-taking or gambling. The family is introduced through the medium of a series of monologues in which each person takes it in turn to express a view.

The cast in order of appearance:

Wendy. In her mid 50s and married to Bob, her second husband.
Karen. Wendy's daughter, Bob's stepdaughter. In her 20s, now married but still living nearby.

Addiction Dilemmas: Family Experiences from Literature and Research and their Challenges for Practice, First Edition. Jim Orford.

Bob. Also in his mid 50s, and also previously married. Has had a drinking problem for many years and has received treatment intermittently. Has not worked for some years.

David. In his early 20s. Karen's young brother, Wendy's son, Bob's stepson.

Doctor. Has been Wendy and Bob's GP for a number of years.

Ken. Bob's brother, who lives in the same town with his family, but who now sees little of Bob and Wendy.

Wendy. I feel mentally totally exhausted. I feel I've tried everything in the book and nothing has worked. It's as if I've been living for both of us these last umpteen years. This time I've given him an ultimatum, and I really mean it this time. If he carries on this way I shall leave. I was so angry this time I literally blew my top. But I can see both sides of it; he hasn't got much else to live for. Getting angry probably doesn't help. Sometimes I think I cope quite well. I'm not as soft on him as I once was, but on the other hand you can't be too hard. I try to make a joke out of it. I say, 'You know where the money is'. And it makes me feel guilty him not having anything. Should I give him money or not? It would make life easier, but then why should I watch him kill himself. But I'm not sure I have the energy to fight it any more. But if you love someone, you can't just walk away from the problem. It's a case of staying and coping or turning your back on someone.

Karen. I thought, 'Oh no, bloody hell, he's on the piss again'. I've been in the pub with him when he's been drinking and it's so embarrassing, sometimes I just wish the floor would open up. Mum gets so upset but she's very understanding. I've wondered sometimes why she's stayed, but I learnt to take my lead from her, not giving him sympathy, but being hard but not over-hard, saying 'Go on then' if he says he's going to the pub. He knows he can have a drink if he wants one. I think Mum's done pretty well and by and large the family copes well. She's firm and understanding and jokey. We have the same kind of ideas and attitudes, and we help each other. We both had a real go at him this last time, but it does worry me that being angry with him might provoke him into more drinking. I do go home feeling depressed sometimes, thinking there's nothing we can do for him. We both feel so frustrated that he won't talk about what the problem really is. I think there's something in his past that he's not talking about. I've also tipped his booze down the sink, watered his drink down, and marked the bottle, turning it upside down so he wouldn't realize. We really love him and will be there for him.

Bob. I do feel guilty over what I've done to Wendy. It was nice to see them pleased about my progress. They all got a bit angry over my recent slip-up and that made me angry. Why shouldn't I have a drink if I want one? I didn't really take much notice of them. I get angry when they try to talk to me about my problems. It's my problem, and I've got to sort it out. Wendy lets me get on with it, she's knows I'll fall asleep in the end. Sometimes she hides money from me or pours the drink away. She tells me in the morning that I've drunk it, but tells me the truth later when I'm sober. Karen's really good sometimes. She's motherly, slaps my wrists if I'm drinking and makes me feel guilty, but I always have a choice. David keeps out of the way, goes to his room, with a hurt, hangdog expression. The most useful thing I suppose was Wendy and David's hurt expression and Wendy starting to cry. She had a look of genuine hurt and told me I was killing myself. All the fun's gone out of it.

David. I don't know why Mum hasn't left him. She said she would. When he's not drinking too much I get on really well with him. We've been quite good friends. We've had some drinks together in the local pub. But then he drinks too much and asks me to buy drinks for him, which I refuse to do. I've actually been round to the local pubs asking them not to serve him spirits.

Doctor. I've been increasingly worried about their health, both of them. I've advised her to take a much stricter line with him. For example I've recommended that she has no drink at home at all, and makes it a rule not to allow drinking in the house, but she seems to find that very difficult.

Ken. I keep away now. I tried talking to Bob in the past, but it made no difference. I've literally cried to see what he was doing to himself. Goodness knows why Wendy stays with him.

Karen again. He was getting on much better. He seemed much happier, he wasn't saying nasty things about people like he used to, and I never saw him tipsy. We all thought we were coping well. David used to be rather aggressive in his attitude towards Bob but he had come round to the same way as Mum and I, giving him responsibility, making it clear to him that it was up to him. We didn't insist on him promising he wouldn't ever drink too much. That would just make him feel guilty, and there has to be room for a few mistakes. I do wish he would talk about things so we can get to the bottom of it. He switches off. Talking with him only gets so far and then he changes the subject. We are a bit stuck in a vicious circle now. Sometimes Mum and I think he doesn't really want our help, but I think he does. Mum and I probably talk to each other too much, when perhaps we should be talking to him instead.

Wendy again. The doctor says I should shut the door on him, but if you love them . . . I had this stupid idea that when he's home at least I know what he's drinking, and if he collapsed at least he'd collapse here. I'm sure the hospital staff are annoyed because they think I'm wasting their time – 'You're still with him' sort of thing. Other people, particularly his family, like to turn a blind eye to it, put the shutters down, or simply don't understand drink problems, perhaps they've not had much to do with drink. I try to understand what he's been going through. Talking about it and making no secret of it has helped. It's made us more tolerant, although sometimes I feel more like a mother to him than a wife. I've tried every trick in the book, hated him and loved him, mothered him, even joined in his drinking, which wasn't useful because it just gave him an excuse. I've shut myself in a room and cried, and gone through every emotion. I wonder if I've made things worse by encouraging him to drink at home rather than in the pub, but he now drinks spirits at home. I am tempted to let him drink because at least then you get half a conversation not just grunts and off to bed. In the long run when I thought I'd made things better I've actually made things worse. I wonder if I've pushed him away by not drinking with him, and with my sarcastic comments. But now it's sinking in that there is nothing I can do. It dawns on you somewhere along the line and you become resigned. But I've told him I'm not prepared to sit and watch him die. I love him too much for that. I've said to him, 'You know me, I like a fight'.

Bob. I sense when I'm in trouble. There's an electric atmosphere, the body language, the silence. I pretend it's not happening, I weather it out. It makes me feel guilty, and I think bugger it, I'm not going to be treated like a child. But Wendy, Karen and all their family have been very supportive, they're pleased with me, proud of me, although family support is tailing off a bit. Karen says she wouldn't bring her new baby round if I went back on the drink, but she's only joking. My family [i.e. his brother Ken, other siblings and their families] has a very bad attitude. They can't handle it at all. They treat me like a child. They're ashamed of me. They just think alcoholics are tramps, they don't realize.

Comments

There are many things about this family that are common to families where one of the members drinks, takes drugs or gambles to an extent that it is seriously stressful for the rest of the family. Notice that Wendy says she is mentally exhausted. She says she has gone through every emotion including anger and guilt. She has shut herself in a room and cried. She is now talking about leaving. Karen is now not so close to the action because she lives separately. But she spends a lot of time talking with her mother about her stepfather's drinking. She has felt embarrassed by the drinking in the past, is disappointed about the relapse, frustrated that he won't talk about what the real problem might be. She sometimes goes home feeling depressed about it. Karen's younger brother David, who still lives at home, doesn't say how he feels, but he does talk about how he has been put in the awkward situation of refusing to buy drinks for his stepfather, and has even gone to the lengths of going round to local pubs asking them not to serve his stepfather spirits. His sister says he was aggressive in his attitude to his stepfather, and Bob talks about noticing David's hurt expression. Even Bob's brother Ken, who has removed himself from the heat of the action by keeping away, says he has literally cried to see what his brother was doing to himself. The issue of Bob's drinking is clearly one that has caused a great deal of upset throughout the family. Bob himself, whose drinking is the focus of the concern, has felt guilty about what he has done to Wendy, and when his stepdaughter tells him off that makes him feel guilty again. He says he gets angry when they try to talk to him about his problems. He notices people's hurt expressions and senses the bad atmosphere. He says all the fun has gone out of his drinking. There are a lot of bad feelings around the issue of his drinking.

But there are good feelings as well. Both Wendy and Karen express love for Bob, and until the recent relapse they thought they had been coping quite well. Bob acknowledges the support he gets from them and was aware of how pleased they had been about his progress and that they had been proud of him.

A theme that we shall meet again and again in this book is the desperate search by family members for the best way of dealing with the problem. As Wendy says, she has tried every trick in the book. Like so many family members facing similar circumstances she worries that she may have done the wrong thing, and tends to blame herself if things don't work out. For example what should she do about drinking with him? At one stage she joined him in his drinking but found that wasn't useful because it simply gave him the excuse to carry on drinking. But she wonders now if she has pushed him away by not drinking with him. Karen in particular feels that there must be something in Bob's past that he is not talking about. She gets him on his own and tries to probe him about it, but it makes him angry and he doesn't open up. She has poured his drink away, watered it down, marked the bottle. These tactics, like David talking to local publicans, are common examples of the kinds of actions to which family members resort in their desperation to get a loved one's drinking under control.

Do such tactics work? And does it help if Wendy gets angry with Bob – probably not she thinks. Should she give him money or not? In some ways it would make life easier, but that might be aiding him in killing himself through carrying on drinking excessively. These are all common and agonizing dilemmas that family members face.

Many of the dilemmas collapse into one big question: should one be tough or tender towards the close relative whose drinking is so problematic? Should one err in the direction of being firm and controlling, in the process running the risk of alienating the very person one is trying to help, and thereby perhaps making the problem worse rather than better? Should one, on the other hand, err in the direction of being supportive and understanding, so running the risk of appearing to be over-tolerant of the drinking, even colluding with it, thereby helping to maintain it? Notice the way in which Wendy and Karen struggled with that central dilemma. Wendy says, 'I'm not as soft on him as I once was, but on the other hand you can't be too hard'. Karen says she has learned to take a lead from her mother, '... not giving him sympathy, but being hard but not over-hard'. She describes her mother's coping as, '... firm and understanding and jokey'. They are clearly both trying to strike a balance. Getting the problem into the open, making it clear they recognize it as a problem, but not being too harsh over it, trying to give Bob responsibility. Wendy thinks this policy has helped. She thinks it has made them more tolerant, although she admits that, '... sometimes I feel more like a mother to him than a wife'. She wonders if she may have made things worse by encouraging him to drink at home. There she at least knows where he is and what he is doing, but she regrets that he now drinks spirits at home.

A second general issue that commonly arises for family members faced with someone who is drinking, taking drugs or gambling excessively, is whether to go on struggling with those dilemmas at all. Would it not be preferable to separate, or at least to put some distance between oneself and the problem? Not surprisingly this is an issue that Wendy talks about. Following Bob's recent relapse, she has given him an ultimatum, saying that she will leave him if he carries on. It sounds as if this is not the first time she has threatened to leave since she says this time she really means it. Her energy to go on fighting the problem is reaching a low ebb. But, as she says, '... if you love someone, you can't just walk away from the problem. It's a case of staying and coping or turning your back on someone'. Both Wendy and Bob have negative things to say about Ken and other members of the family who have a 'bad attitude', who have turned their back, don't understand, and can't handle it.

How do other people respond to the position that Wendy is struggling to pursue? Not always, it seems, in a very understanding fashion. Again, this is a very common finding. Karen is close to her mother, is very supportive of her and tends to see eye to eye with her. She often uses the word 'we' when talking about the way they cope. Their doctor, on the other hand, thinks Wendy should be much stricter with Bob than she actually is, for example over the issue of drinking at home. There appears to be a misunderstanding between Wendy and her doctor. Wendy thinks the doctor is recommending that she should 'shut the door' on Bob, although that is not actually what the doctor is saying. For his part, the doctor construes the issue as a difficulty that Wendy has in being stricter with Bob, whereas Wendy herself portrays it as a difficult decision that she has come to, at least for the moment, over a difficult problem where there seems to be no very satisfactory solution. Both David and Ken express surprise that Wendy has not left Bob, apparently unsympathetic to Wendy's mixed feelings of love and frustration. Interestingly, although we do not hear directly from hospital staff, Wendy senses that they are annoyed with her for staying with him, and thinks that they think she is wasting their time.

Questions

1. Do you find yourself tending to 'take sides', feeling more sympathetic towards one or more people in that story, compared to others? Who do you sympathize with, and why? Is there anyone whose position you feel antagonistic towards? If so, why?
2. Do you think Wendy and Karen are getting the balance right between being tough and tender, strict or tolerant? Do you agree with the doctor

that Wendy should be stricter with Bob? Should Wendy, as their doctor believes, have a policy of not keeping alcohol at home at all?

3. Were Karen and David right to do things like pour his drink away or water it down, or have a word with local publicans?

4. What position should Wendy take when Bob needs money and she is not sure whether to give it to him?

5. What should Wendy's position be about leaving Bob?

6. Have you ever met someone, personally or professionally, who is in a situation similar to that of Wendy or Karen? What did you do? Did you give any advice?

7. If Wendy and Karen came to see you for help and advice, what would your goals be for them? How would you to try to achieve those goals?

Exercises

- Take Wendy's part. Take five minutes to explain to an imaginary counsellor how you feel about Bob's drinking and how you cope with it. You might speak this aloud to yourself, or to a friend who takes the part of the counsellor (but who need not respond in this exercise), or write up to 250 words if you would prefer. Then take Bob's part. This time talk (or write if you would prefer) about how you feel about your drinking and how members of the family react to it.

- This exercise needs two people. One to take Wendy's part, the other Bob's. Role-play a conversation about the issue of whether they should keep alcoholic drinks at home. Try it once with both stating your views in a way that becomes angry or irritated, with no agreed resolution of the issue. Try it again and see if, by conversing differently, a resolution might be possible. Carry on with the same role-play, but enlist the help of a third or fourth person to play other members of the family – Karen, David, Ken – who might join the conversation and put their own points of view. You could try it in the form of a consultation between Wendy, Bob and their doctor. Remember that the doctor thinks Wendy should be stricter with Bob. How does the consultation go? How does it leave Wendy feeling? Does the doctor think it was a useful meeting?

2

Long Day's Journey into Night
by Eugene O'Neill

Eugene O'Neill's play, *Long Day's Journey into Night*, must surely be one of the most powerful and heart-rending depictions of addiction and the family that exists in English language fiction. In fact it is scarcely fiction at all since O'Neill made no secret of it being closely based upon his own family and upbringing. He dedicated it to his wife Carlotta on their twelfth wedding anniversary, referring to it as a '. . . play of old sorrow, written in tears and blood . . . a tribute to your love and tenderness which gave me the faith in love that enabled me to face my dead at last and write this play – write it with deep pity and understanding and forgiveness for <u>all</u> the four haunted Tyrones'. Even some of the names of the characters are those of O'Neill himself and his own family: the brothers James (Jamie) and Edmund, and their dead infant brother Eugene. In their overview of twentieth-century theatre Richard Eyre and Nicholas Wright described this play as '. . . an excavation of his own life, his heart, his soul . . . [the] playwright is stating the central agony of his life . . . It's the saddest play ever written' (*Changing Stages*, pp. 150–1).

Mary, the wife and mother in the play, like O'Neill's own mother, has been addicted to morphine since it was prescribed for her after Edmund's difficult

Addiction Dilemmas: Family Experiences from Literature and Research and their Challenges for Practice,
First Edition. Jim Orford.

birth. The play occupies, in time, a single day from 8.30 in the morning
to around midnight. It all takes place in the Tyrones' summer home, and
revolves entirely around the discovery that Mary is again injecting morphine
after it had been thought that she had conquered the habit. During the
course of the day the family descends into argument and acrimony and
mutual accusations of blame, often relating to events that have occurred
years in the past. The excessive drinking of both James, the father, and
Jamie, one of the two sons, is also a theme.

What is illustrated so brilliantly in the play is the hesitancy and reluctance of this family, and probably any family facing a similar problem,
to accept and face up to the fact that Mary has relapsed. Mary denies it
for as long as she can, and it takes a long time for James senior's bubble
of optimism about her progress to be burst. Jamie is the most suspicious
but his father and brother round on him for being so heartless. This is
a family that finds it particularly difficult to pull together in the face of
a difficulty such as the mother's return to drug-taking. But the dilemma
that O'Neill described so well is a common one for families struggling to
cope with addiction. It is the early afternoon, and almost halfway through
the play, in Act 2, Scene 2, before it is openly stated (by Jamie) what it
is that they have been skirting around up until then. Up to that point it
had been a question of Mary 'not eating breakfast', 'going upstairs to fix
her hair', insinuations, and ambiguous references to feelings of suspicion
and alarm.

James Tyrone is 65 and has been an actor by profession. He is described
as, 'by nature and preference a simple, unpretentious man, whose in-
clinations are still close to his humble beginnings and his Irish farmer
forbears'.

Mary Cavan Tyrone, his wife, is 54. 'She still has a young, graceful figure
. . . Her face . . . is still striking. It does not match her healthy figure but is
thin and pale . . . What strikes one immediately is her extreme nervousness.
Her hands are never still . . .'.

James Tyrone, Jr (Jamie), their elder son, is 33. 'He has his father's broad-
shouldered, deep-chested physique . . . [but] . . . The signs of premature
disintegration are on him . . . His hair is thinning . . . [and he has an]
habitual expression of cynicism . . .'.

Edmund Tyrone, their younger son, is 10 years younger than Jamie and
is said to more resemble his mother. He appears sensitive and nervous and
looks as if he is in poor health.

From Act 2, Scene 2:

MARY . . . I'm going upstairs for a moment, if you'll excuse me. I have to fix my hair. (*She adds smilingly.*) That is if I can find my glasses. I'll be right down.

TYRONE (*as she starts through the doorway – pleading and rebuking*). Mary!

MARY (*turns to stare at him calmly*). Yes, dear? What is it?

TYRONE (*helplessly*). Nothing.

MARY (*with a strange derisive smile*). You're welcome to come up and watch if you're so suspicious.

TYRONE. As if that could do any good! You'd only postpone it. And I'm not your jailor. This isn't a prison.

MARY. No. I know you can't help thinking it's a home. (*She adds quickly with a detached contrition.*) I'm sorry, dear. I don't mean to be bitter. It's not your fault.

(*She turns and disappears through the back parlour. The three in the room remain silent. It is as if they were waiting until she got upstairs before speaking.*)

JAMIE (*cynically brutal*). Another shot in the arm!

EDMUND (*angrily*). Cut out that kind of talk!

TYRONE. Yes! Hold your foul tongue and your rotten Broadway loafer's lingo! Have you no pity or decency? (*Losing his temper.*) You ought to be kicked out in the gutter! But if I did it, you know damned well who'd weep and plead for you, and excuse you and complain till I let you come back.

JAMIE (*a spasm of pain crosses his face*). Christ, don't I know that? No pity? I have all the pity in the world for her. I understand what a hard game to beat she's up against – which is more than you ever have! My lingo didn't mean I had no feeling. I was merely putting bluntly what we all know, and have to live with now, again. (*Bitterly.*) The cures are no damned good except for a while. The truth is there is no cure and we've been saps to hope – (*Cynically.*) They never come back!

EDMUND (*scornfully parodying his brother's cynicism*). They never come back! Everything is in the bag! It's all a frame-up! We're all fall guys and suckers and we can't beat the game! (*Disdainfully.*) Christ, if I felt the way you do – !

Comments

That scene, with Mary leaving the others feeling worried, suspicious, uncertain, impotent to do anything, is one that must be played out thousands of times every day in families where an addiction has got hold of one of the members of the family. It makes everyone tense.

Tyrone is the one who takes responsibility for saying something to Mary as she leaves the room. But consider his dilemma. Despite the problems the family has had, he has been feeling that life was good. There were signs that Mary might be cured of her drug addiction and that the boys might be developing into men he could be proud of. They were there to enjoy a summer vacation. It would be so deflating if Mary had gone back to taking morphine. He could hardly bear it if that was happening. Perhaps Mary was only going upstairs to fix her hair after all. She doesn't make it easy for him: she makes out that all is well and accuses him of being suspicious. He knows he couldn't stop her anyway. As he says, it isn't a prison and he's not her jailor. When he does try to confront her, he ends up being ineffective and provokes Mary into making a remark that is very hurtful to him.

There are unresolved tensions in the family as the rest of the play makes clear, but this scene could be from almost any family struggling with an addiction problem. How should family members react in that position? Should they trust Mary and leave her to it, leaving it up to her to do what she wants and to tell them about it if she chooses? Should they assume that all is well until there is clearer evidence that it is not? Should they, drawing on their previous experience, acknowledge that in all likelihood Mary is taking morphine again, and should they try and prevent her doing so? Should they be honest, and tell her calmly that they are worried she might be using again?

All those are possible reactions, and each carries advantages and disadvantages. What is certain, and is so typical, is that families are torn about what to do. What generally happens in such a situation, unless family members have worked very hard at developing a united view, is that one family member takes one position and others then react, not just to the original dilemma, but to the positions that others have taken. In the process people tend to 'take sides'. That is exactly what happens here. Tyrone tries soft confrontation, which leaves him looking ineffective. Jamie is blunter, but expresses himself, not directly to Mary, but to the others. His brother and his father then round on him angrily, and Tyrone says things to Jamie that are irrelevant to the matter at hand and hardly helpful to Mary. Jamie reacts to their reaction, accusing the others of being less understanding of his mother than he is.

Note also the way in which the question of 'cure' comes into this short sequence of exchanges. Getting treatment for addiction is nearly always very important to family members. They often feel powerless to do anything themselves, and as a result put a great deal of faith in the possibility of successful treatment, and often work hard to encourage, persuade or cajole their relatives towards treatment. They know it does not always work, but at least then there is some hope. When Jamie bluntly says that in truth there is no cure for Mary's morphine addiction, and what is more that they have all been suckers to think there might be, he is making a statement that is bound to make the others feel wretched. Not surprisingly, Edmund reacts bitterly.

Questions

1. If a relative has an addiction problem, is it best to be realistic about the chances of relapse or is it better to err on the side of trusting that all is well unless there is clear evidence to the contrary? What are the advantages and disadvantages of each of those positions?
2. How apposite is Tyrone's analogy of the family member as a kind of jailor, if the family member tries to be too vigilant and controlling? Or, is there a danger in the use of that analogy of blaming a family member for simply trying to restore control over a family situation that is getting out of control?
3. To what extent, if at all, do you think the scene went the way it did because it involved three men reacting to a wife and mother's addiction? How might it have gone differently if one or more of the threesome had been a woman?
4. Are the three men ganging up on her? Is Mary and her use of morphine taking the role of a scapegoat for what is a more fundamental problem in the family, do you imagine?
5. If the scene with Tyrone, Jamie and Edmund, after Mary had gone upstairs, had been a therapy session, what would you try to do to help them help Mary?

Exercises

• Try re-writing the scene from the play starting from the point at which Mary goes upstairs, arousing the suspicions of the rest of the family. Try to re-write it so that the family avoids the acrimony that O'Neill depicted. See if you can get the others pulling together constructively. If you prefer, alter the characters – for example you might try it with a father and a son and daughter rather than a father and two sons.

- This is a role-play with four parts, one for James Sr, one for Jamie, one for Edmund and one for a professional – health worker, social worker, drug worker, counsellor – who has been consulted by the three of them. They are alarmed at Mary's relapse and don't know what to do. The professional's aim is to get the three men thinking more calmly and constructively about the issue and to formulate a plan of action together.

3

Tough Love

A Television Studio Discussion

Some years ago BBC television held a discussion programme, chaired by John Humphrys, in the Family Matters series, which examined a particular style of family responding known in the USA as 'Tough Love'. David York, the founder of the Tough Love movement, was a main guest on the programme, as were a number of families for whom excessive drinking or drug use had been a problem.

Some families were said to have tried Tough Love, others not. One family member, Tim's father (I have changed the names used in the programme) had reported his son to the police after several thousand pounds worth of goods had gone missing from the storeroom of the family firm for which Tim had been working. Asked how he had felt, Tim's father Peter said he had gone through the whole gamut of emotions any father would go through if he found a son or daughter had done something like that – he'd felt shattered, hurt, shocked. The audience was then told that Tim as a result had been sentenced to 15 months in prison and had served six months before being released. But his real problem was alcohol. He had been drinking heavily since he was a teenager, was drunk when he stole from his father's firm, and Tim himself blamed drinking for the theft.

Addiction Dilemmas: Family Experiences from Literature and Research and their Challenges for Practice, First Edition. Jim Orford.
© 2012 John Wiley & Sons, Ltd. Published 2012 by John Wiley & Sons, Ltd.

His father and mother had spent years trying to stop him drinking. Since coming out of prison a few months previously Tim had cut down his drinking and his relationship with his father had improved (several shots are seen of Tim and his father drinking calmly together in the local pub). Peter explained that he appreciated it had been a hard way to learn a lesson, but that the way Tim had been going it would probably have got harder still. Tim had been drinking and driving and had already had a couple of accidents and Peter and Tim's mother were afraid someone could get killed.

At that point Humphrys asked Tim whether he felt any resentment about what happened, to which Tim replied that the only type of resentment he felt was towards himself for what he had done. He denied feeling any resentment towards his father, but pressed to say if he was now glad that his father had told the police, there was a long pause and he seemed uncertain how to answer. Finally he admitted he was not glad he went to prison but did acknowledge that it had taught him a lesson.

The audience was told that for insurance reasons Peter couldn't give Tim back his old job in the firm. Tim was taking a positive attitude and looking for other work, although having a criminal record made that more difficult. For his part Peter said he believed he was now more of a loving father than he had been previously, a bit softer perhaps now he had done the hard thing. His greatest desire now was to help his son.

Several other families also told their stories, some of whom had used a tough approach with their young adult sons (all were sons) who had caused their families difficulties through their drinking or other drug-taking. Several had told their sons to leave home. One couple, however, had never taken such a step, and much of the subsequent studio discussion revolved around the contrast between that couple on the one hand and Peter and other 'tough' parents on the other. David York found himself in the hot seat. Humphrys asked David York what he would say to the couple who had not practised Tough Love; in fact what they practised seemed exactly the opposite of Tough Love.

York turned to them and told them he thought they had taken a very dangerous position. Taking drugs intravenously, he said, is a very serious thing and terrible things can happen to people who do it. The risk you took, he told them, was a big one for the whole family and they were lucky it had turned out alright for them.

Their son, now recovered from a drug problem, interjected quickly at this point to say that he thought the risk was no greater than that of throwing children out of the home or throwing them into prison because the risk then was that they were going to end up in an even worse situation. Addicts already feel lousy about themselves, he pointed out; they know they're failures.

Humphrys then challenged York by suggesting that parents are there to help their children, to give them that kind of support, not to shop their own son and send him off to prison. Wasn't that a much greater risk to take? York agreed that up to a certain age that was true but that a point is reached when children have to grow up, when they have to be responsible for their own behaviour.

Humphrys then introduced Dr Jerome Miller, another visiting expert from the USA, and asked him whether he accepted the position espoused by David York. Dr Miller took a very different line. In fact he said he thought it was bizarre to suggest that parents who protect and care for their children are taking a greater risk than others who throw them out. In the United States it had been suggested by people who run shelters for runaway youngsters that a third to a half of those who were thrown out by parents got into that situation. To suggest that Tough Love should be adopted as general social or national policy was a highly dangerous prescription in his view. Tough Love was, he thought, among the more useless things the US was trying to export.

York intervened here to accuse Dr Miller of failing to understand Tough Love if he talked only of throwing children out, because that was not what Tough Love was about. But it could be?, asked Humphrys. No, insisted York, that was not what Tough Love was about. They did not throw kids out.

A few minutes later, after other families had had a say, Humphrys challenged Peter directly. Surely the idea of parents informing on their own children was instinctively repugnant to many people. It might sound like the sort of thing you would associate with a totalitarian regime, with George Orwell's *1984*. To many people it just wouldn't seem right for a parent to do that. But why shouldn't parents respond in that way if they've tried all the nice things, Peter replied. At what stage do you draw the line? Humphrys didn't let this go, pointing out to Peter that he had gone one stage further and actually reported the fact that Tim had committed a theft. So Tim now had a criminal record that was going to stay with him. Peter argued that he thought there was no alternative. They had tried talking together and being nice with Tim. Tim would always admit what he had done was wrong, say sorry, and promise not to do it again. They had heard the word 'sorry' for 10 years.

Another father, who with his wife had asked their son to leave, offered his support for the Tough Love approach. The people who used Tough Love were very caring people he pointed out. They were not rejecting their families. The family is very much affected: it was like going through a very traumatic experience. Talking rationally to the person concerned had not got them anywhere. They didn't listen. They don't want to know.

So the emphasis is on the love just as much as on the tough?, Humphrys tried to clarify. York jumped in to express his irritation that Humphrys seemed to be so hung up on the word 'tough', which in the context of Tough Love should be interpreted as being firm and caring.

Miller then interrupted to say that he did know perfectly well about Tough Love. He had seen many youngsters who had been through Tough Love programmes and in his opinion it had been a disaster. It made good television, but where was the controlled research that showed that it works. He had not seen one shred of evidence. Humphrys pointed to the three families in the studio who said it did work, but Miller was having none of it. There was no research to support it, he said. Furthermore it played to a very harsh mood of rejection towards drug users, particularly prevalent in the United States.

Comments

Over the years British television has shown what I consider to be some first-class programmes about addiction and the family, and this was one of those programmes. Under the provocative facilitating of the expert John Humphrys, the key family dilemma of toughness versus caring is brought out in stark relief. The tough approach has its chief advocate in the Tough Love exponent David York. Faced with the challenge of Humphrys, Dr Miller and a recovered problem drug user, the Tough Love approach is made to look harsh, even totalitarian, and certainly not what might be expected of a caring parent.

But does the caring approach run the risk of slipping into accepting drug misuse, putting up with it, not examining it objectively or standing up to it resolutely if that is what is needed? Is it really the tougher approach that in the end is the more caring? Hence the catchy expression 'Tough Love'. The example of Tim and his father is a good one because it involved Tim's father doing something that most parents would find it very difficult to do: Humphrys refers to it at one point as 'shopping your own son and sending him off to prison'. Tim's father thinks he is now, having taken the tough action necessary to prevent outcomes that could have included the death of his son or of others, a softer more loving parent. Tim says he feels no resentment towards his father for doing what he did; but asked a straight question, whether he is glad that his father told the police about his stealing, he finds it difficult to give an unequivocal answer.

What the programme brought out so well was, not just the agonizing decisions that addiction sometimes requires of parents, but also the strength of emotions that accompany those decisions both for the parents who have to take them and for others who are in a position to witness them or comment upon them. The antagonism displayed between David York and Jerome Miller is simply a reflection of the strong feelings that everyone has about different ways of dealing with such dilemmas. This itself reflects the fact that there are potential advantages and disadvantages in each of the proposed courses of action. Each might work out well – taking hard but decisive action on the one hand or persevering in providing needed support on the other hand. Each, however, carries risks and these were nicely brought out by the antagonistic experts. Emphasizing support runs the risk of tolerating behaviour that would otherwise be seen as unacceptable, thereby contributing to maintaining the problem. Holding the addicted relative fully responsible for his or her actions and fully applying the appropriate sanctions runs other kinds of risk – a criminal record or homelessness, for example. These risks are so considerable, and people's views about appropriate parenting so strongly held, that parents themselves will carry a great deal of uncertainty, and often guilt, whatever they do, and others may criticize and blame them.

Although the programme was about parents and their young adult children, these are themes that we shall meet again and again throughout the examples given in the different chapters of this book. Although on the surface they may appear quite different, the dilemmas faced by parents in relation to their children, wives in relation to their husbands, sisters or brothers in relation to their siblings, children in relation to their parents, and even close friends in relation to those they are concerned about, are in essence very similar.

Questions

1. Could you have done what Tim's father did?
2. Could you recommend that course of action to other people in Tim's father's position?
3. What do you imagine Tim's mother's view was at the time, and is now?

4. Of the two experts, David York and Jerome Miller, to which did you warm most, and why?
5. Do you think David York was right when he said that Dr Miller was failing to understand Tough Love?
6. Which is the most dangerous in your opinion, to tell a drug-misusing son or daughter to leave home or to let them stay at home whilst the parents know that drug misuse is continuing?
7. Are there bigger questions here, to do with society's attitudes towards drug use and misuse?
8. Do you agree with me that this was an example of good broadcasting? Do you think John Humphrys was fair in his chairing?

Exercises

•   Imagine that you are a parent of a son or daughter who has stolen money from a friend's family in order to buy drugs to which he or she is addicted. The friend's family have reported the theft to the police but have approached you before deciding whether to press charges. Generate a list, either alone or with one or more other people in your group, of the advantages and disadvantages associated with allowing the law to take its own course in such a case.
•   Try a role-play, starting with three parts: Tim, his father and his mother. They have been concerned about his excessive drinking for some time, and Tim's theft from his father's firm has just come to light. Tim is 21 years old and lives at home. They are discussing the options. Make it into a counselling session, and introduce David York, advocate of Tough Love, as a fourth part. How do the family respond to his advice? Replace David York with Dr Jerome Miller, and run it again. What was the difference? How did it feel with the two different counsellors?

4

Wives of Gamblers

It is slowly being recognized that gambling, like alcohol and other substances, can be addictive. Organizations that have been in the business of helping people with drug or alcohol problems, and their families, are now starting to turn their attention to helping those affected by gambling problems as well. In Britain it is mainly organizations in the charitable, non-statutory sector that are doing this, and they are being helped by the national organization GamCare. The following are three cases of wives affected by their husbands' excessive gambling. Loosely based on interviews carried out in the course of one of our research projects, they are typical of such cases. We hear about these wives' experiences through the reports that their counsellors or therapists write after getting to know a client well. In the reports they are trying to convey, without too much interpretation or judgement, what their clients have said about their experiences. Each case description finishes with a question from the counsellor/therapist who is wondering how to proceed.

Addiction Dilemmas: Family Experiences from Literature and Research and their Challenges for Practice, First Edition. Jim Orford.
© 2012 John Wiley & Sons, Ltd. Published 2012 by John Wiley & Sons, Ltd.

First wife: Should I work on his communication or her coping?

They've been married for two years. When they got married she had no idea that he played on the fruit machines, apart from very occasionally. She's rather resentful that his family didn't tell her before they got married; she is sure they must have known. She's rather cross with herself too because she could see that his granddad would bet on a fly walking up a wall. She thinks she realized he was playing machines rather a lot soon after they got married. She used to give him money to pay bills and he always said he had paid them. It would only be later when she got a second bill that she would realize what had happened. Even then he would try and deny it. At the moment she thinks he owes her several thousand pounds but she isn't sure as he won't talk about his gambling. She knows he's borrowed money from her parents and on one occasion when she was pregnant and wanted a quiet life she lent him £100. His salary now goes straight into her bank account but they have two credit cards and he gets really abusive if she tries to take the cards from him. If he has any money at all it will go on gambling. He even went straight in the bookies and spent several hours there when she gave him a few pence to pay library fines. He denied it but she knows where he was and the library fine wasn't paid. The whole thing has affected her marriage badly. She threatened to leave on one occasion but now feels guilty about that, but still thinks she might be better away from him. She doesn't see how she can ever trust him again. Sometimes she feels just like beating him up and at other times she feels she's been taken for a fool.

She's tried many times to talk to him but he just won't talk or else he denies everything. She went to her doctor and told him about it, but when he went to see the doctor he said she was lying and the doctor told him to go away and to try to talk together. She did try but without any results and two weeks later he started to bully her again to get money.

They occasionally go out and she finds that difficult as she has to keep counting to know what change he has left out of money she's given him. If he looks as if he's going to go near a fruit machine she shames him out of it in front of his friends.

She's told her parents but they are now getting very fed up with the whole business and think he should grow up now that he has a family. She doesn't feel she can keep on talking to them about it. His parents have known about the problem for some time and she's talked to them as well but disagrees with their attitude, particularly his father's. The latter takes a very tough line and thinks that he should be beaten up for it or else put in a room and left there for a couple of weeks.

She feels she's had two years of this and particularly dislikes the feeling that he would cover up his gambling, which he has done in the past. She now tends to come straight out with it if she's at all worried. For example if he's half an hour late she'll ask him directly when he comes back what he's been doing and whether he's had a bet.

When I saw husband and wife together, he explained that he didn't like being questioned about whether he had been gambling. He thought that, if anything, it made him more likely to bet rather than less. If he had been gambling he would find it very difficult to say so, not so much because he'd think she'd go wild about it but because he'd feel badly that he'd let her and other people down. She said, 'I wouldn't go wild. I'd much rather know than not'.

We agreed it was better for him to reassure her, for example by phoning up to say he was going to be late, or by explaining what had happened, rather than her having to take the initiative and ask about it. They also agreed that it would be a good idea to have a set time each week (teatime on Friday) when he would take the initiative and start a discussion about how he had managed with the gambling that week. But the communication of personal things is not easy for him. My impression is that she is very supportive but she certainly comes across as the stronger partner with a tendency to talk to him in a way that seems very kind and understanding but perhaps a trifle patronizing and powerful. He tends to look to her for reassurance when answering questions.

Where do I go from here? Should I work on his communication or her way of coping?

Second wife: What support does she need and who will provide it?

She doesn't know very much about his gambling because he keeps it very much to himself and refuses to talk about it. She thinks he has a problem but believes it's really not all that bad. He goes through phases of gambling between which he gives the gambling up for a couple of months or so. Each time she thinks he's trying to give it up but he never quite succeeds. He does all his betting in betting shops. She doesn't really know how much he bets each time on a horse, but thinks he loses between £500 and £1000 a time. There's a big build-up for about a month beforehand, and then he seems to bet very heavily on horses for two or three months. His gambling hasn't really affected their home life (she was very contradictory and kept changing her mind on this point). The children don't really understand the situation; they think there's just a money problem generally. There really isn't a big problem (she kept assuring me) as they've always managed to keep their heads above water. The business cheque book is in her name and she signs all the cheques because of his gambling problem. Two years ago she first discovered he was forging her signature and this has happened on several occasions since then but she doesn't really know how much money he has taken out of the business. She gets angry now thinking about the amount of time he spends at work trying to make money for the family and then loses so much of it gambling. She knows a few years ago he took out a loan from the bank for £3000 and thinks that must have been to cover a gambling debt. He's not really a moody person but she can tell when he's lost money because he gets very irritable. It's only when he's gambling that he gets so edgy and very unpleasant to live with.

She can't speak to his mother because the latter is just a worrier about everything. His sisters don't really know and she doesn't think they would understand because they belong to his family, which is a gambling family. 'It's in the blood, not like my family at all', she says. She doesn't talk to anybody about the problem and tries to shoulder it all herself. It would be embarrassing and she would feel she was putting him down. 'Do you think he really has a problem?', she asks. 'He probably has because we're in a vicious circle of working extra hard to try and pay off gambling debts. Keeping up normal appearances is important to me.' She's resentful that as a family they are much more short of money than they ought to be with him working so hard and her working as well. He now thinks he can give up gambling completely and would be keen to get help.

I can refer him for treatment for his gambling. But what support does she need and who will provide it?

Third wife: Should I refer them for sexual health counselling and suggest she should let the gambling look after itself?

She's not sure that they have any real problems. She comes from a bookie's family and there was always a lot of poker-playing in the house. In fact it was she who introduced her husband to gambling and she thinks it was just unfortunate that he was the type to get hooked on it. She tells me, 'He's marvellous to live with, a super man, especially if you like an uncertain existence.' She'd hate to be married to a 9-to-5 man. She thinks the real trouble started a few years ago when she had just finished college and they were generally short of money. She got a hot tip for the Derby and told him about it. She expected him to put £5 on it but he withdrew £500 on a credit card and won several thousand. That was spent on themselves, not put back on other horses like he does with all his winnings now. His credit has run out and none of the bookies will let him bet on credit any more, and he owes massive bills. They've re-mortgaged the house several times. She's very happy for him to go to the races and enjoys it herself but over the last year or two since he's lost his job she's insisting on going with him to keep an eye on him. Since he lost his job she's kept a strict eye on the money and when they go to the races she makes sure they only take £30 each. That does *her* for about 10 bets but *he* usually puts it all on one horse and when he's lost it he then pesters her for more money. On holiday last year they went to the casino every night and had a great time with £20 a night. She played blackjack and he played roulette, which she disapproves of. Other people would spend that in an evening at the theatre or would drink, which they don't do.

He's bored with his present work and she thinks he couldn't really give up gambling unless he substituted something else that gave him the same buzz. She prefers him to gamble rather than drink. Every so often when he's been gambling without her knowledge she gives him 'a verbal ear bashing', but he rarely goes anywhere without her. They're going to the races this evening. Most of their friends gamble heavily and, 'some are going down the pan faster than we are'. At the moment he spends his time watching the share movements every two hours on Ceefax. He bought several thousand pounds worth of shares a few months ago without consulting her which annoyed her, but at least 'we're keeping up ok'. Her real complaint is that their sex life is a disaster. For several years it was active but it is now fairly non-existent. She would really prefer he got treatment for that rather than his gambling although she accepts the two are probably related.

I don't think this amounts to pathological gambling. Should I refer them for sexual health counselling and suggest she should let the gambling look after itself?

Comments

The three wives are in different positions in relation to their husbands' gambling, but they have much in common. One theme, common to the first two wives, as to so many family members affected by addiction problems, is lack of information. To a large extent both have been in the dark about the extent of their husbands' gambling. Wife number one is even cross with herself now for not realizing about his machine-playing until after they got married. The second wife does not even know the extent of her husband's betting nor even the degree to which it is really a problem. The therapist observed that she was being held back in acknowledging a problem by feelings of loyalty and fear of not being able to cope if she acknowledged the problem.

That uncertainty about the existence and extent of the problem, and the very understandable feelings that might stand in the way of acknowledging its full extent, are so common. The third of these three wives provides a very good illustration of another of the very common factors that make it difficult for us to acknowledge the seriousness of a relative's problem. Sometimes we have shared, and to some extent continue to share, with our relatives, the pleasure that drinking, drug use or gambling has provided. Since it is very difficult to get a clear and objective picture of what is really happening when a close relative has an addiction problem, the sharing of the pleasure is bound to make us ambivalent. This wife came from a family that enjoyed gambling, and she continued to enjoy going to the races and playing casino games such as blackjack herself. She knew that she had encouraged her husband's gambling. Although there are aspects of his gambling that she disapproved of, and she admitted that he had got hooked on it and now owed large amounts of money, she continued to compare his gambling favourably with drinking, and referred to their sex life as being her real complaint.

The third wife reported that she now insists on going to the races with her husband to keep an eye on him and a strict eye on the money. They have had to re-mortgage their house several times, although most of their friends gamble heavily, she says, and some were 'going down the pan' even faster than they were. In fact all three wives found themselves doing what most family members of addicted gamblers do at one time or another – and the same applies to many family members of relatives with other types of addiction problems as well – which is to try to take control of the money. The first wife had his salary paid straight into her bank account and tried to keep account of what change he might have left out of any money she had given him. But that is difficult, and there was mention of bullying and abusiveness over money matters. Because of her husband's gambling problem, wife number two signed all the business cheques. He had forged her signature on occasions, and she got angry to think of how much money might have gone out of the business to fund his gambling. Anger is a well-known feeling for affected family members, and all three of these wives have been made angry over financial matters. Wife number one admits that she sometimes feels like beating her husband up. But she has also felt guilty about threatening to leave him (although she thinks she might be better away from him), she experiences the feeling that she might never be able to trust him again, and at times feels as if she's been taken for a fool. All are feelings that will be recognized by many family members affected by addiction problems.

Because it is so easy to feel that you have been left out of the picture, that the wool has been pulled over your eyes, and that you have been made a fool of, one common dilemma for family members is whether to speak up and speak your mind when you see trouble coming. Wife one, for example, says she has shamed her husband in front of his friends if it looked as if he was going near a fruit machine. Similarly, the third wife had given her husband a 'verbal ear bashing' when she found out he had been gambling without her knowledge. Because her husband was inclined to cover up his gambling, the first of the wives said she now tended to come straight out with it if she was worried. Note, however, that when he joined in for a second interview, it was clear that he did not like being questioned about where he had been and what he was doing and thought it was counterproductive. She said she would much rather know if he had been gambling, as most family members would, but he said he would find it difficult to admit to it, would feel badly about it, and if anything would be likely to gamble more rather than less as a result.

Finally, there is the theme of the support that a family member gets, or sadly very often does not get, from other people. For all sorts of reasons, other family members and relations are often found not to be very helpful; which is a pity because united they could provide each other with a lot of support and perhaps more effectively help the addicted person. Wife number one's parents were fed up with the whole business and she did not feel that she could go on talking to them about it. Continuing to talk to his parents also does not seem to have been helpful because they did not have the same attitude towards it, his father in particular taking what she thought was an unhelpfully tough line. Similarly wife number two did not talk to her husband's family because, unlike her own family, they were very pro-gambling. In fact she did what so many family members do, which is not to talk to anybody and to try to cope with it on her own.

Family members often report that they find professionals unhelpful as well. Sometimes that is because the doctors, nurses or counsellors are un-informed or do not want to know. But as often as not it is because the professionals themselves do not know what to do. These three wives had been lucky in receiving some counselling for themselves in their own right which focused on their experiences coping with their husbands' gambling. But counselling family members of relatives who gambled excessively was new to each of these counsellors and none felt totally confident about what to do next. The first was torn between working on the wife's way of coping, which struck her as kind but possibly patronizing, or helping her husband to be more communicative about his gambling. The second was confident she could refer her client's husband for treatment but was not sure how a wife might best be supported. The third was inclined to accept that the couple's sex life was the problem that should be addressed and that the gambling was secondary and not serious enough to be deemed 'pathological'.

Questions

1. Do you think the problems faced by wives of problem gamblers are in all important respects just like those of wives or partners of men with drink or drug problems? Are there any particular differences do you think?
2. How would you respond faced with the kind of uncertainty that the first and second wives seem to have had about the extent of their

husbands' gambling problems? Is the concept of 'pathological gambling' (or the concept of 'alcoholism') a help or a hindrance for affected family members?

3. What other feelings, apart from the anger, guilt, lack of trust and feeling like a fool mentioned by these wives, do you think are commonly experienced by family members affected by the addiction problem of a close relative?

4. If you were counselling a couple like the first wife and her husband, how would you deal with the wife's wish to know more about how her husband was dealing with his gambling and his reluctance to talk about it?

5. It looks as if none of these three wives can call on helpful support from any other relations. Is that likely to be true? Is there no one they can call on to give them support?

6. What support can a counsellor or other helping professional provide?

7. What might the first wife's doctor have done differently faced with apparent direct contradiction between what she and her husband had told him? Could the doctor have been more active in some way?

8. What do you think of the remark made by the therapist about wife number one sounding a bit patronizing and powerful? Has she fallen right into the old trap of blaming a wife for doing what is expected of all wives, namely to protect her family and to safeguard the family's health and happiness? Is it the therapist here who is being patronizing?! Or do you think she might have a point?

Exercises

*   Assume that, like the first wife in this chapter, you are a woman whose partner is developing an addiction to gambling but who feels she can no longer talk to either her parents or her partner's parents about it. Your parents are fed up with the whole business and your partner's parents take a very different view of it than you do. Draw a hypothetical 'network diagram', with yourself in the centre, surrounded by all the people or groups of people who you can think of who might be able to offer you support. Think broadly in terms of relatives, friends, work people, neighbours, people connected with any leisure, religious

or sporting affiliations that you might have. Don't just think in terms of one kind of support, but think of who might offer useful information, material help of some kind, as well as emotional support or simply good company.

- A role-play with three parts – one a professional and the other two a wife and husband modelled on the first couple in this chapter. The issue here is one of communication. He finds it very difficult to talk about his gambling but she would like him to talk about it to her more openly. Can the professional find a way of helping them?

5

The Tenant of Wildfell Hall by Anne Brontë

The central characters in Anne Brontë's classic novel are Helen and her husband Arthur Huntingdon from whom Helen finally escapes with her child to live under an assumed name at Wildfell Hall. The central theme is Helen's struggle in coping with her husband's increasingly heavy drinking and unpleasant behaviour towards her. As a story of a woman facing a partner's problem drinking it has a ring of truth about it. Anne had herself witnessed her brother Branwell's excessive drinking. The preface to the book is dated 22nd July 1848. According to Stevie Davies (in the introduction to the 1996 Penguin classics edition), 'Branwell was at home, in advanced stages of addiction. Six days later, Charlotte wrote that his "constitution is shattered"; "he sleeps all day" and is "awake all night". Two months later, on 24 September, he was dead.' Anne herself died only eight months later.

The novel itself is divided into three parts, the largest, central part being in the form of a diary written in the first person by Helen as she wrestles with the problems caused by her husband's behaviour. That form lends the writing an immediacy and makes it more valuable as a text from which

Addiction Dilemmas: Family Experiences from Literature and Research and their Challenges for Practice, First Edition. Jim Orford.

we can learn something about family experiences in the face of excessive appetites.

Reviewers at the time, mostly men, disliked the way in which the novel portrayed Arthur and his friends as infantile or depraved, and Anne's sister Charlotte, according to Stevie Davies, '. . . recoiled with hot pangs of shock from the account of ugly facts which brought to mind the shattering disintegration of their brother: "Wildfell Hall it hardly seems to me desirable to preserve", she wrote betrayingly to her publisher. "The choice of subject in that work is a mistake" ' (introduction to the 1996 Penguin classics edition, p. viii).

The following quotations are from Helen's diary:

Feb. 18th, 1822 . . . I am married now, and settled down as Mrs Huntingdon of Grassdale Manor. I have had eight weeks experience of matrimony. And do I regret the step I have taken? – No – though I must confess, in my secret heart, that Arthur is not what I thought him at first, and if I had known him in the beginning, as thoroughly as I do now, I probably never should have loved him, and if I had loved him first, and then made the discovery, I fear I should have thought it my duty not to have married him. To be sure, I might have known him, for everyone was willing enough to tell me about him, and he himself was no accomplished hypocrite, but I was wilfully blind, and now, instead of regretting that I did not discern his full character before I was indissolubly bound to him, I am *glad*; for it has saved me a great deal of battling with my conscience, and a great deal of consequent trouble and pain; and, whatever I *ought* to have done, my duty, now, is plainly to love him and to cleave to him, and this just tallies with my inclination . . .

Dec. 25th, 1823 [By which time baby Arthur has been born, and husband Arthur is spending more and more time with his friends, most of whom Helen disapproves of.] . . . there was still one thing about him that I did not give up in despair, and one effort for his preservation that I would not remit. His appetite for the stimulus of wine had increased upon him, as I had too well foreseen. It was now something more to him than an accessory to social enjoyment: it was an important source of enjoyment in itself. In this time of weakness and depression he would have made it his medicine and support, his comforter, his recreation, and his friend, – and thereby sunk deeper and deeper – and bound himself down for ever in the bathos whereinto he had fallen. But I determined this should never be, as long as I had any influence left; and though I could not prevent him from taking more than was good for him, still, by incessant perseverance, by kindness, and firmness, and vigilance, by coaxing, and daring, and determination, – I succeeded in preserving him from absolute bondage to that detestable propensity, so insidious in its advances, so inexorable in its tyranny, so disastrous in its effects . . .

[Helen does confide in one of Arthur's friends, Mr Hargrave, because she feared that his friends might persuade him to join them for a night or two of pleasure which might have] ... ruined the labour of weeks, and overthrown with a touch the frail bulwark it had cost me such trouble and toil to construct. I was so fearful of this at first, that I humbled myself to intimate to him in private my apprehensions of Arthur's proneness to these excesses and to express a hope that he would not encourage it. He was pleased with this mark of confidence, and certainly did not betray it. On that and every subsequent occasion, his presence served rather as a check upon his host, than an incitement to further acts of intemperance; and he always succeeded in bringing him from the dining room in good time and in tolerably good condition ... It seemed wrong that there should exist a secret understanding between my husband's friend and me, unknown to him, of which he was the object. But my afterthought was, 'If it is wrong, surely Arthur's is the fault, not mine' ...

July 30th, 1824 [Arthur has been staying away in London and things have not been going well for Helen.] He returned about three weeks ago, rather better in health, certainly, than before, but still worse in temper. And yet, perhaps, I am wrong: it is *I* that am less patient and forbearing. I am tired out with his injustice, his selfishness and hopeless *depravity* – I wish a milder word would do –; I am no angel and my corruption rises against it.

August 20th, 1824 We are shaken down again to about our usual position. Arthur has returned to nearly his former condition and habits; and I have found it my wisest plan to shut my eyes against the past and future, as far as *he* at least is concerned, and live only for the present; to love him when I can; to smile (if possible) when he smiles, be cheerful when he is cheerful, and pleased when he is agreeable; and when he is not, to try to make him so – and if that won't answer, to bear with him, to excuse him, and forgive him, as well as I can, and restrain my own evil passions from aggravating his, and yet, while I thus yield and minister to his more harmless propensities to self-indulgence, to do all in my power to save him from the worse.

December 20th, 1824 ... Yet I do my part to save him still: I give him to understand that drinking makes his eyes dull, and his face red and bloated; and that it tends to render him imbecile in body and mind; and if Annabella [his mistress] were to see him as often as I do, she would speedily be disenchanted; and that she certainly will withdraw her favour from him, if he continues such courses. Such a mode of admonition wins only coarse abuse for me – and indeed I almost feel as if I deserved it, for I hate to use such arguments but they sink into his stupefied heart, and make him pause, and ponder, and abstain, more than anything else I could say.

At present, I am enjoying a temporary relief from his presence: he is gone with Hargrave to join a distant hunt, and will probably not be back before tomorrow evening. How differently I used to feel his absence!

December 20th, 1826 The fifth anniversary of my wedding day, and I trust, the last I shall spend under this roof. My resolution is formed, my plan [of escape] concocted, and already partly put in execution.

Comments

Although this is fiction it has the feeling of being a very personal statement by the author. Not only was she a close family member of someone, her brother, who drank excessively, but the fact that the largest part of the book is written in the first person in the form of a diary makes it appear almost as a document written by somebody who was going through the events described and who wished to preserve her thoughts, perhaps to aid her own reflection and perhaps to share with others. It is of course an early feminist novel and has probably been viewed over the years more as a story about the relative positions of women and men in marriage in the early nineteenth century and women's struggle for autonomy and emancipation, rather than as an account of a family member affected by a close relative's addiction problem. Indeed many would argue, including many who have fought for women's rights in the face of domestic violence, that the issue of excessive drinking is a diversion. What is at stake here, it might be argued, is patriarchy and the fight against it. To highlight the husband's drinking might serve to divert attention from the real issue. Indeed it might even, as has often been argued, provide husbands with some kind of excuse for their bad behaviour. But 'drink' is itself a gendered issued. Patriarchy may well be the bigger issue, but alcohol addiction is itself hardly a trivial one, and patriarchy and drink are closely related.

Fiction though it is, the fit between Helen's account and what women have been telling us, over a century and a half later, about their experiences of living with their excessively drinking husbands and partners, is remarkable. For one thing she reflects, as many do, on the circumstances of her marriage. She remembers that others had warned her about him, but love was blind and she was not then in possession of the fuller knowledge of him that she now possesses. That strikes one as perfectly understandable, but it is surprising how critical the supposed 'experts' have been in the past about women who married men who drank a lot. It has often been assumed that they must have had some pathological, fatal attraction for an addict. They would have been said to be 'neurotic', to be playing some sort of dark 'game' between two complementary dysfunctional personalities, or, in more recent times, to be 'co-dependent'.

One of the things that a new wife cannot be expected to know is the way in which the appetite for the object of an addiction, whether drink, drugs, gambling or something else, can grow from something that can be tolerated into something that governs family life and is unacceptable. Helen notices the increase in Arthur's appetite for wine. She can see how it was beginning to play a central part in his life, serving functions as medicine, comforter, friend.

Another theme in Helen's diary that resonates with much that family members tell us is that of the support, or lack of it, that Helen gets from other people. Like family members everywhere and at all times, Helen finds herself in an uncomfortable position in relation to Arthur's friends. Your partner's friends should be your friends, so social psychologists tell us. One's social world is out of balance if you get on badly with the friends of a friend or get on well with a friend's enemies. Just as parents in our times disapprove of those among their children's friends who they believe may infect their children with their drug-using habits, so Helen came to disapprove of many of Arthur's friends, but came to value the support that one of them, Hargrave, gave her by supporting her attempts to discourage his heavy drinking.

When it comes to describing the ways in which she responded to Arthur's drinking, Helen's diary in *The Tenant of Wildfell Hall* provides almost textbook examples of some of the main options that are open to family members in her circumstances. One option is to go into battle against the drinking, to pull out all the stops, to do everything one can think of to turn around the threat that the drink poses to the relationship and the family. Helen could hardly express better what so many families do when she described in the diary entry for Christmas Day 1823 her kindness, firmness, vigilance, coaxing, daring and determination. And for a while it seems that this strategy of engaging with the drinking problem was working.

By August of the following year her position has changed. Helen is disappointed that Arthur has returned to his former habits. Helen has responded, as is so common and natural, to live for the present, to be pleased when things are going well, and when they are not to excuse and forgive. One can well imagine that, in the face of what must seem like an intractable problem, that position, somewhat defeatist though it appears, must have the merit of bringing greater calmness and composure. Better to put up with it and get on as best one can rather than constantly engage in what seems like a hopeless battle. It is sad to notice another feature that persisted into the twentieth century and into the twenty-first, namely Helen's inclination to blame herself. She sees it as her duty, as Arthur's wife, to love him and cleave to him. She wonders if it is her that is insufficiently patient and forbearing. She writes about wanting to restrain her own evil passions from aggravating his. In the face of admonition from Arthur when she suggests that his mistress might go off him if he deteriorates further, she wonders if she has deserved his response for having used such arguments. She even feels guilty about the bit of social support that she gets from Hargrave. Like many family members she thinks it somehow wrong that she should have an understanding with a friend of Arthur's that Arthur does not know about.

Finally Helen's diary concludes with a way of responding that family members are very often forced to adopt, namely one of withdrawing from the person whose drinking has been causing so much concern. On her third wedding anniversary she expresses enjoyment that Arthur is away for a while. Two years later to the day her withdrawal has gone much further with her resolution and plans to leave.

Questions

1. Do you think we can learn anything from this nineteenth-century novel that is relevant to family members in the twenty-first century? Are wives better informed now than they were in Helen and Arthur's times? Do they know more about the dangers of addiction than they did then? Do they know more about each other nowadays before they settle down together?

2. Should Helen have found out more about Arthur before she married him, or at least listened more carefully to those who warned her about him?

3. Could Helen have done any more than she did to preserve Arthur from 'bondage' to the 'detestable propensity' of over-drinking? Could she have done anything differently?

4. Helen expressed the need to be a dutiful wife and often seemed to blame herself for her own reactions, for her own impatience, for aggravating Arthur, for gaining support from one of his friends behind his back. Are wives so dutiful today? Would they still blame themselves if put in a position like Helen's?

5. Was she right to leave Arthur eventually?

6. Do you know people like Helen and Arthur?

7. Can you imagine it having been Helen who drank excessively? Would Arthur have reacted any differently, do you think, than Helen did?

8. Do you think focusing on the issue of Arthur's drinking is a diversion from the bigger issue of patriarchy and the emancipation of women?

Exercises

- Imagine you are Helen. Write your own diary entries – two of them, let's say two years apart. The first one corresponds to a time when you are beginning to realize that your husband drinks excessively. You are worried but hopeful that you can influence him to reduce his drinking. Two years later you have tried various ways to do that but nothing is working. In both entries, describe how you feel, how you have been reacting, how you feel about how you have been reacting, and whether you have support from other people.
- Helen – or someone in a similar situation – has come to see you at a time when Arthur's excessive drinking has become quite clear to her and she is wondering if there is anything she can do to help him reduce his drinking and, if not, whether she should consider leaving him. You have already had one session together during which you gave her the opportunity to talk freely about what had been happening. On your own, or with others, formulate a plan for your next counselling meeting which you hope will be helpful to Helen in beginning to resolve her dilemmas.

6

British Sikh Wives and Daughters Stand Up to Men's Drinking

Imagine you are a 'fly on the wall' at a group meeting being held in a room in a *gurdwara* (Sikh temple) somewhere in Britain. The meeting has been called because of concern about alcohol problems in the local Sikh community, and the meeting is being run by a young Sikh woman psychologist who is writing a thesis on the subject at the local university. The following is part of the discussion that takes place at the meeting. The participants are all people with first-hand knowledge of alcohol problems in the family. Some of the participants are related to one another. Nearly all the wives and husbands are first-generation immigrants to Britain, and are in arranged marriages. Nearly all the daughters were born and brought up in Britain. It is imaginary but the things that are said are closely based on things that were said to Apninder Ahuja – herself a British Sikh woman – when she carried out individual interviews with Sikh men with alcohol problems, and with their wives and daughters, as part of her PhD thesis.

We join the discussion at a point where the participants are talking about how Sikh wives continue to maintain their wifely duties in the face of their husbands' excessive drinking.

Addiction Dilemmas: Family Experiences from Literature and Research and their Challenges for Practice, First Edition. Jim Orford.
© 2012 John Wiley & Sons, Ltd. Published 2012 by John Wiley & Sons, Ltd.

A husband/father. My wife gets me ready in the morning and always has my food ready.

A wife. I will always put him before anyone else, it is my duty as a wife to always care for him and place his needs before my own. I am never going to leave him and will always continue to look after him and stay with him. I always have his meals ready for him and constantly look after him when he comes home drunk. Although I always look after his needs he does not look after my needs and he still continues to drink.

A husband/father. They leave my dinner for me but I don't always eat it. My wife will sometimes refuse to cook my dinner for me but she always does. She will still leave me my food but there is not a lot of love left between us. Whether I eat or not my meal is always made for me.

A wife. I am always looking after him and cannot look after my needs because I am always concerned about him. I don't go out anywhere by myself because I don't want him to think that I am not involving him in family activities.

A wife. I too find it difficult to do the things I want to do because I am always thinking about him and how I can help him stop drinking. I find it hard to go out because I worry that he might get drunk.

A daughter. It's the same for us. I can't bring friends home because I always worry about the state that my father will be in. My father has changed and is no longer the father that I once used to know. I just feel that alcohol is killing my father.

A daughter. Initially I had thought about going to college but decided against the idea because it would just cause more trouble at home. Since I have started work I have been able to earn some money and financially help my mother.

A daughter. On one occasion my father threw us all out of the house and then asked us to return three days later. I was hoping that my mother would not go back to him but as always she did. I did not go home immediately but did eventually return two weeks later.

A daughter. My mother will not leave him because she thinks it is disrespectful. I think it is about time Asian women started to think about their needs and not what the culture expects of them. On one occasion my father got a broom and hit me over the head with it. I needed stitches but at least the police were called and my father was arrested. There was a case against him but unfortunately he was granted bail. My mother dropped the case against him by the time it was due in court because he had stopped drinking again. I was very unhappy about her decision but there was not a great deal that I could do.

A daughter. I know what you mean. My mother is less concerned about her own happiness and more concerned about what people will say if she left him. Occasionally she agrees to leave him but she never goes through with it. My mother believes that English people divorce their partners after an argument but Asian people always try and work things out. If I had a choice I would prefer not to get married. My family talk about my marriage as if I am not present in the room. In my culture if you are not married by a certain age people begin to think that there is something wrong with you. I am not going to follow the same pattern as my mother by getting married too young. I don't want to get married particularly if there is the possibility of my partner being like my father. I went out with a boy who had a drinking problem and I was left with no alternative but to end our relationship. I want a proper relationship and I want to marry for love. My mother does not envisage my marriage being successful because she believes that I cannot tolerate any unbearable behaviour.

A wife. But you must understand. It is my duty to look after my husband, not to start seeking help for myself. In our community this sort of behaviour brings disgrace to your family. In our community it is best to keep the problem in the family.

A wife. I agree. A marriage is for life, for better or for worse this is the person that you have to care for and spend the rest of your life with. We are not like the English where you can just leave your husband and marry someone else. In our culture you always have to stay with your husband and look after him.

A wife. My mother told me to leave my husband but I have told her that she chose him for me and now I am going to stay with him.

A wife. Yes. In our culture you always stay with your husband regardless of the circumstances. My father arranged my marriage and I promised to live with him always. I will always support my husband.

A wife. We have been brought up in a culture where a woman is not supposed to question her partner's actions.

A daughter. I always worry about my mother because she does not stand up to him in the way that I do. If I am not there to support her I really do not know how she would cope with the problem.

A wife. I often feel that my husband will stop drinking so I tolerate his drinking to avoid further arguments that will only upset the children.

A wife. I do try to stand up to my husband. I have often tried to stop him from drinking by spilling his drink down the sink or hiding it. I have also tried to forbid his friends from coming to drink in my house.

A wife. I started to lock the front door so that my husband couldn't leave the house but he started to leave through the back. I hid his shoes and his turban but he still left the house without them.

A daughter. I'd often refuse to lend my father money and I used to keep a constant eye on him. I even used to get him leaflets on problem drinking from the doctor's and chemist's to read. I hid and spilt his drink down the sink but nothing seemed to work. Initially he used to cry in front of me and this used to upset me a great deal and would always result in me crying. I have now realized that it is best to avoid him so I often just go away and do my homework.

A daughter. I have become a very private person and I just tend to keep to myself most of the time. I do not get involved with the family and avoid my father whenever possible. When he has been drinking I just leave the room because I know we will just end up arguing. There was a time when I used to worry about the problem but now I just get on with my own life.

A daughter. But I do feel my father is still my father and I do feel some love towards him. On one occasion this girl called my father an alcoholic and I was left with no choice but to beat her up.

A husband/father. Can I say something? When I drink my wife always moans but what she does not realize is that if I decide to stop drinking it will be because I want to and not because she wants me to. When she moans we argue and this results in me drinking even more excessively.

A husband/father. In my case my family do not stop me from drinking but if they do I just end up drinking more. When this happens no one in the family seems nice to me and I get very angry. If they say anything to me I drink and hit them. She tells me not to bring any drinking friends home and prefers it if I drink at home in her presence. She tries to make me understand that I should not drink but I never listen to her when I am drunk. She often pleads to me to stop drinking but I do not give in to her demands.

A husband/father. My daughter calls me a bastard and hits me. She should not use such language with me and when she hits me I feel that I am left with no alternative but to hit her. My wife should teach my children how to speak to me with respect but she refuses. I find myself drinking because I am so upset by the way my children speak to me. My daughter calls me a bastard yet my wife never tells her that this is wrong.

A *husband/father*. I slapped my wife on a couple of occasions but when you drink your mind is completely gone. Your brain cells disappear and you are completely unaware of what you are doing.

A *husband/father*. My wife keeps out of my way and has nothing to do with me. She has never felt frightened to say anything to me and no longer tolerates my drinking problem. She always puts her family before me and prefers to have nothing to do with me. She just acts as if I am not there.

A *husband/father*. My family also ignore me when I drink and just try and keep to themselves. But I prefer that because I like to be left alone when I drink.

A *husband/father*. All Indian women stop you from drinking whereas White women do not say anything to you. They go to pubs and drink with you but Indian women never want to drink anything.

A *husband/father*. My wife does not drink either and I think that's a very good thing. If women drank as well then life would be finished. If men and women drink a severe problem will be created. How can women prevent their partners from drinking if they also drink?

Comments

Although that imaginary discussion is based on research with British South Asian, Sikh, family members, it is unlikely that any of the themes that emerged are peculiar to Sikh families specifically or to South Asian families living in Britain more generally. Although they sometimes emerged in a stark form in that discussion, the ideas are ones we have met already and shall meet again.

One of the strong themes in these quotes is that of wifely duty. Wives felt it was their duty to stay with their husbands regardless, and to continue to prepare their meals and look after them. Their daughters, the next generation – nearly all, unlike their mothers, brought up in England – recognized the strength of their mothers' views about wifely duty without necessarily sharing those views. The subordination of the wives' own needs comes through strongly. Wives could not go out, had no time to look after themselves, and had little peace. Their concerns were more for their husbands and families and for what others might think, than for their own needs. Their daughters also made sacrifices, being worried about bringing friends home, deciding against going to college, having their social lives more restricted than they otherwise would be. Several daughters felt the need to support their mothers emotionally or financially.

But the theme of self-sacrifice in the face of addiction is one that is never far away when the impact of addiction in the family is being discussed and it is one that runs throughout the present book. We shall see later on, in Chapter 13, which takes the form of an imaginary conversation between four wives living in very different parts of the world, that struggles over the subordination of a family member's own needs are almost universal in the face of relatives' addiction problems. Very similar issues had to be faced by wives of men with drinking or drug problems in earlier historical periods (see Chapters 5 and 16) and by mothers and fathers in earlier and modern times with sons or daughters with addiction problems (see Chapters 3, 9 and 10). It is therefore difficult to determine to what extent cultural differences are operating in the lives of the Sikh family members who took part in this discussion. Clearly the wives themselves, and their daughters, were of the view that culture made a difference. Their culture, they thought, put limits on their freedom to respond in ways that they might have been inclined towards. Indeed, in the research programme of which Dr Ahuja's project was part, it was the case that we found Sikh wives to be putting up with their husbands' excessive drinking to a somewhat greater extent than White English wives. But there was a very large measure of overlap between wives in the two groups, and the differences were only a matter of degree.

It was certainly not the case that the Sikh wives were simply passive and unassertive. In fact they were remarkably resourceful and resilient within the confines of a life that placed limits on independence. There were accounts of trying to keep a husband in by locking the doors or hiding his outdoor clothes, hiding or spilling the husband's/father's drink, stopping his friends coming in to the home, and standing up to him in other ways. In our research family members have told us a lot about the advantages and disadvantages of these sorts of actions that combine to varying degrees elements of being vigilant about the relative's drinking, trying to control it, being confrontative about it, or being assertive in the face of it. Amongst the advantages are the feeling it may give a family member that the situation is not simply being accepted and that the family member is not going to be pushed around. It may help the family member feel that something positive is being done.

At the very least it may temporarily relieve built-up feelings of tension and anger. But there are potential disadvantages. Quite apart from the added stress, and often frustration, in standing up to excessive drinking (or gambling or drug use) in these ways, family members are only too well aware that the relative whose behaviour is upsetting them may feel resentful and may not respond in the way the family member hopes – as illustrated by the comments of a number of the Sikh husbands/fathers.

Questions

1. Is it possible to stand up against an addiction in the family whilst subscribing to a strong code of family duty?
2. Under what circumstances should a wife leave her husband if he is drinking excessively? Do you agree with the Sikh wives who thought that Western women (English in this case) turned to separation and divorce too readily?
3. How can a daughter support her mother in those circumstances?
4. One of the husbands said, 'My wife does not drink ... and I think that's a very good thing. If women drank as well then life would be finished.' What do you think about that? Abstinence from alcohol amongst South Asian women living in England, particularly first-generation immigrants to Britain, is very common. What would happen do you think if that started to change? Would it be different if the boot was on the other foot, and it was the wife who had developed a dependence on alcohol? What duty would her husband feel?
5. How would you advise a Sikh mother and daughter in these circumstances if they came to see you?
6. During the discussion there were several mentions of family violence. If you knew that violence of that kind had been occurring in a family, what difference would it make to the help the family should receive? Is there a danger that opening up discussion about ways of responding to a husband's drinking problem, as took place in this imaginary discussion for example, might be unsafe for the wives and daughters, perhaps making things worse rather than better?
7. If you were a daughter of a father with a drinking problem, would you be angry if another young woman referred to your father as an alcoholic?

Could you imagine reacting like one of these daughters did, by 'beating her up'?

Exercises

- In your group hold a debate on the nature of duty and sacrifice in the face of a close relative's alcohol, drug or gambling addiction. The motion to be debated might be something like, *If a relative with an addiction does not change in response to repeated requests and despite detrimental consequences for the rest of the family, then the best thing is for a family member to ask that relative to leave or to leave her/himself*. But find a form of words that is right for your group and which should lead to lively debate.
- A Sikh mother and her daughter have come to see you for advice about the husband's/father's excessive drinking. The daughter is very angry with her father and wants her mother to leave him. The mother, a first-generation immigrant to Britain, would not consider such a thing but has recently been trying to stand up to her husband in a number of ways. For example, she has been refusing to talk to him when he has been drinking and has banned alcohol and his drinking friends from the home. But nothing seems to be working and tension in the home has only risen. Try a role-play exercise with parts for the mother, the daughter and a counsellor. Try to establish what are their different coping options and the advantages and disadvantages of each.

7

Nil by Mouth

A Film by Gary Oldman

This powerful British film, written and directed by Gary Oldman and released in 1997, depicts an inner-London family of modest means in which the two main male characters are both shown as having substance problems, Ray's being drink and Billy's injecting drugs. The interactions quoted here involve Billy and his Mum, but the film also contains a lot of relevant material involving Billy's older sister and her husband Ray.

Mum, we are led to believe, is separated from her husband and lives with her own mother, Billy's Nan. In one scene, in their flat last thing at night, we see Billy being let out in order to spend the night in what looks like the garage.

> *Nan* (whispering to Mum). He's not stopping . . . doing drugs.
> *Mum.* Leave off Mum.

Mum lets him out. We see him disturbed by the milkman early the following morning and being let in by Mum, quietly so as not to disturb Nan. Billy asks to borrow the car. Mum suggests that he is in no fit state to drive, and voices get raised. He needs gear he says. Mum offers to drive him herself, but says:

> *Mum.* Make sure this is the last time.

Addiction Dilemmas: Family Experiences from Literature and Research and their Challenges for Practice, First Edition. Jim Orford.
© 2012 John Wiley & Sons, Ltd. Published 2012 by John Wiley & Sons, Ltd.

We see Mum waiting in the car while Billy buys drugs. He sits in the front seat and starts to prepare his injection. Mum insists that he goes into the back of the car to shoot up, but watches him over her shoulder with a very worried look on her face. 'You alright?', she enquires at one point.

Later we see Billy begging on the underground, apparently without success. Later still we see Billy waiting for Mum at her place of work. The interaction that ensues gets heated, and it attracts the attention of other people, presumably employees in the same firm where Mum works.

Mum. What are you doing here?

Billy. Have you got any money?

Mum. Don't be silly, I gave you money this morning. What have you done with it?

Billy. Well, you know, something came up, you know. I had to f. . . pay off a mate of mine . . .

Mum. Well I haven't got any money.

Billy (shouting). Oh Mum, don't f. . . about.

Mum. Don't raise your voice with me and show me up at f. . . work . . . (pause). How much do you want?

Billy. A score.

Mum. I haven't got a score. I don't go to f. . . work so you can spend it on your f. . . mates. What have you done with the money I gave you?

Billy. Done that haven't I.

Mum. What, on f. . . gear? Look, don't f. . . me about. Do you know how much money you've had out of me the last year? It adds up to f. . . thousands.

Billy. Don't be stupid. Thousands? How do you work that out?

Mum. Because you've got a £60 a day habit, and I've been supporting it like some c. . .

Billy. Right, just lend me a tenner then.

Mum. I haven't f. . . got any money.

Billy. You ain't got a tenner?

Mum (both are shouting now). I haven't got any.

Billy (raising his fist quite close to Mum's face before turning smartly to walk away). Bollocks you f. . . tight c. . . I can get the money. I'll go and steal it . . .

Mum. . . . go back to prison. Like your old man, you horrible, selfish bastard.

Further on, we see Billy sneaking into his sister and brother-in-law's flat and stealing what looks like money, pills, and apparently a picture of Ray's mother which we later hear he has sold. Needless to say it doesn't take much for the family to work out that Billy is the culprit. A bit later we see Billy turning up to see Mum at the home of a friend. Billy's mother and sister warn him to hide from Ray who is after Billy's blood, but they also see the funny side of the situation (a running theme in the film) and have a laugh together about the loss of Ray's picture of his mother.

Billy (handing Mum a wad of notes). Only come up to give you this.
Mum. What's this?
Billy. That's for you and Nan, alright, because she lends me fags when I go home, makes me cups of tea, and all that. Bit flush at the minute, so it's alright.
Mum. Billy, take it back, we don't want it . . .
Billy (walking away). Mum, are you still upset with me?
Mum (laughing, and then looking wistful). No, I love you.

Comments

Billy's Mum is in the kind of bind that mothers often get into with their wayward children. How can she hold things together? How can she go on being a good mother, loving and protecting her son, whilst at the same time protecting herself from abuse and exploitation? Billy's behaviour certainly doesn't make it easy for her. He demands to use the car although his mother thinks he is in no fit state to drive. He demands money, quite unreasonably from his mother's point of view, and turns nasty when she doesn't accede to his request. That kind of hassling, very often for money but frequently for help of other kinds, is extremely common in families where someone is experiencing an addiction problem. In some parts of the world they call it 'humbugging'. It sounds as if Billy has humbugged his mother for money on many previous occasions.

Mum has to find a way through all this unpleasantness. When confronted at her place of work – humbug often takes place in circumstances where it is most uncomfortable for the person who is being humbugged and where it is most difficult to adopt a thought-out, clear response – she stands up to Billy, assertively pointing out to him that he has had a great deal of money from her and that is because of his expensive drug habit. But notice that the price she pays for being assertive is a nasty escalation of her interaction with Billy. Billy uses language that a son should not use to his mother, and tries a bit of blackmail, suggesting that if she won't give him money he will have to go and get himself into trouble by stealing it. One could well imagine Mum's anxiety rising through the roof at that point. She sticks to her guns, but in the process says some things to Billy that she probably regrets. Family members nearly always say that they regret getting emotional in those circumstances, raising their voices, making threats or calling the person they are concerned about names. They say it makes matters worse rather than better, and in the process makes them feel terrible themselves.

Billy's mother's response to his request to borrow the car to get 'gear' is interesting. Again this is the kind of thing that family members very often say they do in an effort to 'cope' with a difficult dilemma. It represents a kind of uneasy compromise. It was rather like a family version of 'harm reduction'. It is not ideal, and puts the family member in the position of feeling that she is complicit in his drug dependence. But it may be better than Billy going into withdrawal, and much better than him injuring or killing himself or someone else driving the car. So she drives him herself and has to sit there while he gets his drug supply and while he injects himself. As a rather half-hearted attempt to maintain some control of the situation, she tells Billy to make sure this is the last time, and insists that he goes into the back of the car to inject.

These short extracts from the film also illustrate how difficult it is for families to maintain a consistent position, buffeted as they are by the ever-changing ups and downs associated with addiction, and the absence of any obvious answers to the question of how to best respond. In this case, following Billy's desperate theft from the family – something else that is very familiar to family members – Billy's mother and sister are protective of him in relation to Billy's brother-in-law, who after all is no angel himself. That may sound particularly counterproductive, but in fact it is not unusual and can be understood if one realizes that women family members often find themselves trying to protect a younger male member of the family (however badly they may have behaved) from the wrath, often violent, of an older or stronger male.

Note, also, what looks like a difference of opinion between Billy's Mum and Nan about how he should be handled. Because there is no obvious right way of acting as a concerned and affected family member, it is almost inevitable that different members of the family will think it right to take somewhat different stances. That can often mean that one family member feels unsupported by the others, or that the family as a whole finds it difficult to reach a consistent approach.

Note, too, the way that humour is used to lighten the atmosphere, and the way, at the end of this extract, Billy gets his mother to admit that she loves him.

Questions

1. What else could Billy's mother have done when he asked her if he could borrow the car?
2. How do you think she felt throughout that episode: when asked for the car, when driving Billy, when waiting for him, and while he was injecting?
3. In your opinion was the outcome of Billy and his mother's interaction at her place of work a satisfactory one? How might it have been different?
4. Do you identify with Mum, Nan or Billy here?
5. Can you see things from Billy's point of view? How do you think he views the ways his mother responds to him?
6. Do you think Billy's Mum is 'coping' well? What else could she do?
7. Suppose Billy's mother had come to see you on her own, what might be your aim in helping her?
8. If you were seeing Billy and his mother together, what do you think would happen, and what would you do?
9. Do you think it would be helpful to invite Billy's Nan along for a joint meeting with Billy and his Mum?

Exercises

• Plan what you might say to Billy's mother if she came to see you asking what she should do next time (1) Billy asks her for money, and (2) asks her if he can borrow the car in order to go and get drugs. Try role-playing it with someone who takes the part of Billy's mother. Then try a role-play between Billy's mother and Billy, with Billy making one or other of those requests and Billy's mother responding after she has had the chance to talk it over and think of alternative ways of responding.

- How should society respond to drug misuse problems like Billy's? Government has just produced a drug strategy document that places less emphasis than previously on understanding addiction as an illness and the need for treatment; there is now more emphasis on the need to recognize the harm that drug users' behaviour causes for others, and a shift towards punishment and control. In your group discuss where you think the balance should lie between care and control in cases such as Billy's.

8

Worrying for Drinkers
in Aboriginal Australia

Excessive alcohol consumption has been of great concern to a number of indigenous peoples around the world. Aboriginal and Torres Strait Islander people in Australia are amongst them. At the invitation of the Aboriginal Living with Alcohol Program of the Northern Territory Health Department, interviews were carried out with family members concerned about a relative's excessive drinking. Family members were living in locations that ranged from suburbs of the capital city to Aboriginal settlement communities in remote parts of central Australia several hours drive from the nearest town.

Those of us amongst the research team who were more familiar with the experiences of family members affected by addiction in industrialized, so-called 'developed', communities were struck by several things. One was the ubiquity of heavy drinkers in families and communities and the prominence of discussions about alcohol policies that affected Aboriginal people. Not only was the role of alcohol as a contributor to poor health and domestic violence a constant talking point, but so too was the heated debate about local policies. The latter included the idea of having 'grog-free days' in town to coincide with days when benefits were collected; and, more radically, whether a community should take advantage of Northern Territory law

Addiction Dilemmas: Family Experiences from Literature and Research and their Challenges for Practice, First Edition. Jim Orford.
© 2012 John Wiley & Sons, Ltd. Published 2012 by John Wiley & Sons, Ltd.

and declare itself completely 'dry', or alternatively should permit the setting up of a 'wet canteen'. The latter might stop people risking life and limb by driving, often intoxicated, to the nearest town and might encourage relatively restrained drinking in a regulated setting.

Another striking difference lay in the very concept of family. For Aboriginal people this invariably means an extended family that might include parents, children, aunts, uncles, cousins and grandparents. Aboriginal communities around Australia are highly diverse and classificatory kinship systems vary, but one common principle is the equivalence of same-sex siblings. Thus, two brothers are considered equivalent, and if one has a child, that child views both the biological father and the father's brother as 'father'. The same principle applies to two sisters and their offspring, who may refer to themselves as brothers and sisters rather than cousins. Moreover, family terms such as 'sister' or 'brother' are often used outside the genetic family group. The importance of this for how family members cope with addiction lies in the way relationships determine mutual rights, obligations and responsibilities. A 'mother' or 'father', for example, whether genetic or not, has an obligation to be concerned about a 'son's' or 'daughter's' excessive drinking (or petrol sniffing – another cause for great concern at one time).

Another notable, but often quite subtle difference was in the use of language. Although most of the interviews were carried out wholly or largely in English, in the reports of their interviews the interviewers on occasions needed to explain subtle differences in meaning. One word, much used by family members when describing their experiences of addiction, was 'worry'. Not only was this word used much more often than it would have been by non-Aboriginal family members in Sydney or London, but it was also believed to carry a much stronger meaning in Aboriginal usage. The interviewers explained that, whereas in non-Aboriginal usage 'worrying' might signify something private, passive, and perhaps in itself ineffective, to an Aboriginal person it had the sense of fulfilling a family and community obligation by engaging in a more active process of showing appropriate concern. It would be likely to embrace, not just one's own feelings of anxiety, but also actively expressing those feelings both to the relative whose behaviour was of concern but also to other members of the extended family and the community who might collectively 'worry' together.

Despite all those ways in which the Aboriginal context appeared highly distinctive, the thing that struck the researchers most forcibly was the similarities between what Aboriginal family members were saying about their experiences and the experiences of those affected by addiction problems elsewhere. It is a central tenet of the present book that those experiences are, in essence, the same wherever addiction is to be found in the world, and furthermore that they have remained essentially the same from one era to another. But a comparison of indigenous (particularly remote rural living) and industrialized peoples' ways of responding to addiction is about as severe a test of that thesis as it is possible to imagine. The reader can judge from the following three family case vignettes whether they agree with the thesis that the family experience of addiction is largely invariant from place to place and time to time. The three short case studies that follow are closely based on the research interviews that were carried out in the Northern Territory. Each is an amalgam of several actual interviews.

A son and his wife worry for his father

This household consists of husband and wife, their two young children, and the paternal grandfather who came to live with them a few years ago following the break-up of his own marriage. Father contributes something towards his rent and spends the rest on beer, spending much of each day drinking out on the veranda of the family's Housing Commission suburban home. He is about 50, unemployed and not in the best of health. His daughter-in-law says, 'I am frightened he might pass on. Because he's looking very tired, he's got diabetes and his diet is not good.'

One of their greatest concerns is the effects of the father's drinking on their children. His son remembers with fondness being taken by his father on hunting trips in the bush and he is saddened to think that his father is not setting his grandchildren a good example and is failing in his responsibilities to pass on information about traditional ceremonies. They particularly don't like the children to be around him when he is drunk. His daughter-in-law says, 'When he's really pissed sometimes he can come home and start getting angry and start growling and gets really scratchy. When he gets loud he growls at me too. That is OK, I can handle that. But not when it is our children.' Sometimes he is good with the children and she can leave him for a while with the children during the day. But not in the evening and not if he's drunk. Cousins are reluctant now to bring their children to see him. Her husband sums it up, sadly, by saying, 'I would really like him to get his life back in order. I used to be so proud of my father but now he is just a humbug.'

The son and his wife are a couple who pride themselves both on their roots in traditional Aboriginal culture and making their way successfully in mainstream White Australian society. They continue to be involved in indigenous ceremonial 'business' while pursuing higher educational qualifications and obtaining good jobs. They are sometimes frustrated by other family coming to see them about their own problems whilst contributing to the father's drinking problem by joining him on the veranda in drinking groups that can get large, noisy, messy and upsetting to the rest of the family. The children like to sleep in their parents' room when drinking parties are going on. They believe they have been successful in setting rules about such occasions that stop them becoming completely 'open house' and out of control (they think other members of their families, such as brothers and cousins, are much more encouraging of excessive drinking than they are). Even so they worry that neighbours may complain and even that their Housing Commission accommodation could be put at risk.

They have both tried to talk sense into him. His daughter-in-law says such things as, 'Relax, look after your diabetes, and your back problem – you know you feel it most when you've been drinking. Don't drink it all at once, just drink it at night, maybe try something else.' His son says, 'Look, you're a grandfather, now act like a grandfather!' His wife sees her husband as the softer of the two of them, because he feels sorry for his father. Her husband explains that his parents have been through a lot in their lives. Like many Aboriginal people of their generation they were separated from their families as children and brought up at a mission station, where they met. The son says, 'Even though I know it isn't right, I see my job as nursing him and his drinking habit, because he's still my father and I can see what he's been through. I can keep an eye on him and make sure he is OK. The bottom line is that he has a bed to sleep in and has food when he wants it.' Sometimes he feels he is successful in making rules and drawing boundaries but other times he feels he is giving into his father. For example, when the latter has no money his son may buy him a few cans of beer or get him to earn some beers by cleaning up the yard. Both he and his wife said independently that their relationship had been under a lot of strain as a result of the father's drinking and arguments over how to deal with it. They knew, though, that this was something that a lot of Aboriginal families like their own were going through.

One prospect for the father is to move to a rural 'outstation' where he can build his own house on land traditionally associated with his family. His son is in favour of this although he is concerned that his father does not seem to be planning very well to get together things such as fuel, materials and animal feed that he will need to live on an outstation in the bush. Although she would also like him to move out of their home, his daughter-in-law was worried that he would not survive in such an environment, and would rather he lived closer where she could keep any eye on him.

A sister worries for her brother

This woman also lives in the capital city where she came, she says, to escape the drunks and to concentrate on bringing up her children and protecting them from having a lot of drinkers in their lives. She returns often to the small provincial town where her mother and younger brother both live. She described many relations as being 'alcoholics', both blood relatives and relations by marriage, both in her own and the previous generations. Her younger brother was her main focus of concern but an older brother and his excessive drinking often came into the conversation as well.

She described her younger brother's pattern of drinking as concentrated at weekends, starting on Thursday, pay day, if he was employed at the time. On drinking days he could get through as many as 24 cans of beer, starting in the morning. He drank mainly beer but also whisky or 'anything that was around'. She was worried about his 'stupid' behaviour when intoxicated. For example he was often a target for theft and was regularly losing money. She knew he had been banned from several pubs and was now left with few friends, mostly heavy drinkers. He could be very demanding, going round to their mother's home insisting on being fed. He was like two different people, drunk and sober, and when drunk could be what she referred to as 'mentally violent' – unlike their father who had been physically violent as well. She said, 'Alcohol is a sickness, and it causes violence. I know the full extent of violence that alcohol causes, such as physical violence, mental violence.' He drove, and she was very worried about the possibility of an accident to him or others. Sometimes he would do 'wheeleys' outside their mother's house if she didn't give in to his demands.

A major worry was her brother's health. He had what she called a 'sick kidney' and had been hospitalized several times. In fact he had stopped drinking altogether for a while as a consequence, but had started again with encouragement from his 'brothers' – a genetic brother and a cousin. She knew the seriousness of his health problems: 'I don't want him to die. I'd like to see him old and grey. I'd like to see that we'd spend another Christmas together.'

When asked how she felt about her brother's drinking she said, 'Angry, afraid, frightened. When I go there and I see my brother come back really drunk saying, "Where's my mother? I want meat!", and I see my mother upset, poor thing, I tell her, "Sit down, I'll cook".' When she is there she tells her brother off for swearing at their mother and talks directly to both her brothers about the danger of accidents. She can try and quieten them down and do some cooking but she didn't feel she could be tougher on her brothers, for example by refusing them food, because they would simply go elsewhere and put themselves in greater danger. In any case she felt what she could do for her younger brother was limited because she had chosen to live away, coupled with the fact that in their culture adult brothers and sisters should avoid a close relationship. As a sister her influence on her brother was not thought to be an important one and she was clearly told by her brother that it was none of her business. She said, 'Yes, I'm just powerless. I just don't do anything. I can't go there and say: "... [brother], you're fucking drunk again, and you stink, you're really upsetting mum and look at what you've done to mum's life". I've never done anything like that because I know – it's not me I'm hurting. I'm hurting the family. Like, the family to me really is everything, and so I do everything to protect the family unit as well.'

Most of her energy for the family was going into supporting her mother whom she spoke to often and at length, on the telephone or during her regular visits. She said, 'I'm worried for my mother because she's old, she's been worrying about them for years. I feel sorry for her. I wish they would stop humbugging her and upsetting her. She feels that it's her fault. She carries the guilt. One of the things she says to me is that she feels responsible because she's the one who has caused it. She blames herself for her children's suffering. She's that type of mother. She doesn't blame him. If anything she's just supportive. She'll growl, get tense, sometimes lock him out, and say things like "I can't put up with this anymore" or "I can't put up with drunks anymore", but in the end she's very protective and says she's got to be there for him. I feel she has sacrificed her own life for her sons. I used to cry thinking about my mother's endurance and how she copes with my brother being sick. I see myself as a victim of alcohol because of my reactions to it. I can't face it. I prefer not to face it and so I deal with it with mum, through her. I'm a back-up for my mum. I'm committed to supporting her and I know I may have to go back to ... [small provincial town] if she gets ill.'

She compared the personal and professional support available in the capital to the situation in the town where her mother and brother lived. Not only were treatment services very minimal in their small town but a drinking problem was not something that she thought you could talk about publicly there: 'It's somewhere where I find you have to be *extremely* private with family affairs.' Families were often blamed for not looking after drinkers like her brothers, or for not stopping them drinking and behaving badly, and it could lead to a lot of bad feeling and anger between families.

A woman worries for her husband and her father worries for them both

This woman lives with her husband and their recently born infant and her two teenage children by a previous marriage, in a small tin dwelling in a camp on the outskirts of a remote provincial town. Also living with them are one of her brothers and his wife and two children. The dwelling is tiny, consisting of only two small rooms and a small veranda on which some of the household must sleep. Cooking is done outside where there is very little shade. In addition to members of the household, at any one time there may be up to a dozen or more different people visiting and camping around the house.

Little more than a hundred metres away lives this woman's father, now widowed and living alone except when family are visiting. In the past he and his wife worried about their daughter drinking. They were ashamed at her behaviour when she was drunk. She would hang around the pubs in the town, getting through a lot of money and not being able to remember what she had done with it, encouraging her sisters to join her in chatting up men, including other people's husbands, even stripping off and laying out in the park when she was dead drunk. She encouraged her brothers to drink as well, and her health had concerned them. At the time they had coped simply by discouraging her from such behaviour, settling her down when she got home and, 'just being there for her at the time. I would always tell myself that there will be a time when she's made up her mind that she doesn't want to drink any more and I'll be there to help her.' Although she had settled down since, she continued to drink and her health continued to be a source of worry for her father.

The main problem, however, for both him and his daughter, was now her husband's heavy drinking and the violence associated with it. According to her the problem was much worse when her husband was drinking 'moselle' (a general term used in the region at the time to refer to the popular cartons of wine) – he was better behaved when drinking only light beer, and was never rough when he had taken marijuana. She described two occasions when they had been drinking, he had beaten her, including using an iron bar, the police had been involved, and she had ended up in hospital. On more than one occasion she had sought sanctuary at the town's women's shelter.

Her father graphically described one of the several occasions on which he had become involved. 'That was really bad. He went out to the town and came back really really drunk. My daughter came and fetched me. It was about 4 in the morning, everyone else was sleeping. He was sitting outside saying all that rubbish talk. We opened a door and said to him, "You go to sleep now". "No, I don't want to sleep now, I want something to eat", he said, so my daughter got him some meat and some bread. "Sit down and eat it quietly", she said, but he kept on, drunk and talking rubbish. By then he was swearing at us. I got really angry with him and told him again he should go to his father's place. He turned around and punched me. He knocked me to the ground. I was bleeding badly from my nose and mouth. My daughter was trying to stop him from hitting me, but he got really angry and hit her, right here on the side of the head. She got a bad gash and was bleeding. I went next door and somebody went and got a police aide and he came round and my brother-in-law was with him too. By then everyone was coming in including the Baptist pastor who ran over from his house nearby. I asked him to come and pray for me and my daughter while we were still lying there outside the house.'

'My daughter was flown to hospital over 500 kilometres away where she spent about six weeks recovering. I gave statements to the police and so did the rest of the family. His father wanted to fight with me. He said, "You and your daughter are causing trouble". He didn't think his son had done anything at all. Nearly the whole community were saying to him that he should have been talking to his son to teach him the right way, that it was his son who was the one causing all the trouble. Everyone was supporting us. But he didn't take any notice. He just said to me, "You should be teaching your daughter". But I am teaching my daughter the right way.'

Quite apart from the effect of her injuries, this woman has a heart condition. She said, 'Last time I got really upset and angry with him, and I got really sick that time, I thought I was having problems with my heart. That's when I got really angry with him and said, "You've done this to me from all that drinking and arguing and stuff like that". Sometimes I get pains when I'm worrying.' Her father comments that his son-in-law won't give his unemployment benefit money to his daughter for food but just cashes it and goes straight off drinking. She said, 'If he had a job and wasn't drinking maybe we would have a nice house to stay in and live as one big happy family. I'm always thinking about having a good life and praying to God to look after me and the children, for him to change and live God's way.'

Praying is one part of how she tries to cope, along with giving him 'rough talk' and lecturing him, preferably when he is sober, and sometimes tipping his drink away. She and other members of the family have on occasions called the police and had him locked up for the night. Her teenage daughter has suggested to her that they run away together, and she herself has thought that '. . . maybe I will just take off with the children somewhere else where no one knows me, away from the family, sometimes I think like that'.

But there are positive aspects too. Because the problem can be such a public one, many people know about it and she receives a lot of positive support from family – notably her brother and his wife and an older couple who have shown a lot of concern for them – as well as the local Baptist minister and people at the women's shelter. In fact things have been noticeably better since the birth of their child a few months before. She says her husband has not been rough with her and has been much more careful. An ambition is to move to a country 'outstation' which the family might make a restricted place as far as alcohol is concerned. Meanwhile she thinks there should be greater restrictions on the selling of grog, or at least moselle, on pay days in the town.

Comments

The family members who were telling their stories here were all indigenous Australians, but living in different circumstances and facing apparently very different problems. The first couple were living in the territory capital city, in a suburban area mostly populated by whites. The second, concerned about her brother, was also living in the capital city but her concern was centred on the provincial family home town where her mother and brother lived. The third family were living in materially much poorer circumstances in a peripheral town camp for Aboriginal people.

All were concerned about close relatives with alcohol problems, but the nature of their concerns was quite different. In the first family the concern was the widowed father's excessive drinking and particularly the problems that caused for the family bringing up young children. In the second case the concern was a brother's drinking and particularly the problems that caused for their mother. In the third instance the focus of concern was the disruptive behaviour, including severe domestic violence, associated with the husband's drinking. The father in the third family described in some detail a very unpleasant incident that took place in the middle of the night and involved his son-in-law coming and creating a disturbance outside. A fight ensued that involved his son-in-law and several members of the family. It resulted in the police being called, other people including the local pastor coming in to try to help, and his daughter needing to be flown to hospital hundreds of kilometres away.

There are a number of common themes, however. One of these is concern about the health of drinkers, and sometimes about the health of family members affected by them. Although ill-health is a theme that constantly recurs in almost all depictions of addiction and the family, it is a central concern in all discussions of Australian Aboriginal drinking. Although there have been improvements in recent years, the state of health of indigenous Australians has continued to give great cause for concern, with high levels of acute and chronic illness in children and adults, and high mortality rates. As a poor minority in a rich country, Aboriginal people have been said to carry a double health burden, suffering both the typical 'diseases of poverty' as in poorer countries and the degenerative 'lifestyle' diseases more characteristic of 'developed' countries. Although excessive drinking is obviously not the only cause, it is almost certainly one of them.

Another theme is the desire on the part of family members to escape from, or at least avoid the harm associated with excessive drinking that is seen as holding others back and even as undermining the Aboriginal culture. The first family is particularly interesting in that regard. The son is worried about his father's health, his heavy drinking and drunkenness, and his ability to look after himself on the proposed outstation, but particularly about his role as a grandfather and his influence on his grandchildren. He thinks his father sets the grandchildren a bad example by his drinking, but also by his failure to pass on information about Aboriginal culture. It is probably important to appreciate the position that this man finds himself in as someone who is trying to make his way successfully in mainstream Australian society, whilst at the same time wanting to do what he can to preserve links with traditional indigenous ways and customs. His father's drinking is a threat to both parts of that identity. On the one hand it threatens to hold the family back from integrating with modern Australia. At the same time, as the senior male in the family his role is important if the link with traditional Aboriginal culture is to be maintained in the family.

Like the son in the first family, the woman in the second example was also conscious of there being a large number of 'alcoholics' or 'drunks' in her family and the community in which they lived. In fact that had been one of her reasons for moving to the city. The third family remained trapped in an environment characterized by a great deal of very unhealthy drinking. At the same time the extended family and closely knit community can result in a great deal of sharing of the worry occasioned by excessive drinking. The support the third couple received from a more senior husband and wife is a good case in point.

Some of those features of these three cases may give the impression that coping with a drinking problem in the family is distinctly different in indigenous Australian culture than elsewhere. But at the same time there is ample evidence here of familiar themes, notably the nexus of factors that constrain a family member from acting in a decisive, tough and dispassionate way. The son in the first case held back from being as tough as perhaps his wife would have liked him to be, partly on the grounds that he wished to make allowances for his father who he knew had experienced deprivations in his own life and had given his son some good family memories when he was young. The sister in the second family was equally held back, but in this case by her role as a mere sister and furthermore as one who had chosen city life over her family's provincial home. The wife in example number three had fantasies about leaving her husband but her circumstances and family obligations must have made that a very difficult course of action. Each, in their own ways, had opted for a kind of 'harm minimization': protecting the home and especially the children from the harmful effects of their grandfather's drinking; supporting her mother who bore the brunt of the problem; and protecting their newborn child, respectively.

Questions

1. From these three brief accounts of Australian Aboriginal families, are you persuaded that, in essence, the experience of having a drinking problem in the family is much the same throughout the world? Or do you think the differences are so great that the family problems need to be seen in a different way?
2. The sister in the second case thought that things were very different in a small town compared to a big city. Is that the important variable rather

than something to do with culture? Would you rather be coping with an addiction problem in your family in a big, relatively anonymous city, or in a small town or rural area where people are more likely to know each other?

3. There is a tendency in the industrialized world to see addiction problems in individual terms. To view them in the family context might be thought to be 'going one better'. But what about the social policy context that was so much more evident in discussions in the Northern Territory in Australia? Is that the same as is the case with illicit drug problems in industrialized countries and regions? Should families concern themselves with such things? Are families taking on all the blame by always looking inwards at how they have been coping themselves?

4. The last of these families, with its story of the very public fight in an indigenous community in an Australian outback town, may seem very foreign to those in many other parts of the world. But, can you think of a parallel scenario involving excessive drinking that might take place in a Western, urban setting? What would the similarities and differences be?

5. If someone was hospitalized in your country after alcohol-related domestic violence of that kind, would she get useful help and advice about her husband's drinking problem? What help or advice would be useful?

6. Do you think the son in the first case had found a good balance between being too harsh and rejecting his father and, on the other hand, letting his drinking spoil their family life? If he and his wife came to see you about coping with his father's drinking, how would you hope to be able to help them? What would your aims be for them?

7. The sister in the second family is clearly very upset about her brother's drinking and its effects on their mother. At the same time she feels helpless to do much more than she is doing already. How would you counsel her if she came to see you saying that she was not content with how she was personally dealing with the family situation?

Exercises

- Write the outline of a harm minimization strategy for the family members to follow in one or other of the three families described in this chapter. If you take the first family, the focus of the strategy should be on helping the son and his wife protect their children and the quality of the children's upbringing. In the second case the focus would be on aiding the sister in protecting her mother. In the third family the main aim of the wife and her father would be keeping her and her child safe. Whichever you choose, reserve some place in the strategy for drawing on the resources of social support that might be provided by other people outside the immediate family.

- Excessive drinking, drug-taking or gambling are often associated with some kind and degree of violence. The fight that the third family got into was a particularly nasty example. It involved several different people and the outcome was costly in all senses. Can you 'rewrite' the story to give it a different ending? How might it have turned out differently and why?

9

A Prodigal Son

The Mother's Story

Someone who was frequently in the news during the few years in which I was compiling material for this book was the popular musician Peter Doherty. He became known in those years as someone with a drug problem serious enough to make him enter drug rehabilitation on a number of occasions. He has been much written about not only in the press but also in a number of books. In 2006 there appeared one book that has a special place here because it is written by Peter's mother, specifically about her experiences as a mother of someone with a drug problem. As she says in her introductory note, 'So this is *my* story . . . This book is about how I have coped and how I am still coping – and, if it should help just one other person, then my efforts will not have been in vain' (p. xiv). The book therefore offers a rare extended description of the reality of life for a close family member, and is therefore very valuable to us. It is her reality, '. . . the truth as I see it' (p. xiv). In fact it is not unlike one of the long reports that one of my research colleagues would write, full of direct quotations from the interviewee, after a research interview with a family member that might have lasted for several hours. The difference is that Peter's mother's book is written entirely in the first person. The book is called, *Pete Doherty: My Prodigal Son*, and is written by Jacqueline Doherty.

Addiction Dilemmas: Family Experiences from Literature and Research and their Challenges for Practice, First Edition. Jim Orford.
© 2012 John Wiley & Sons, Ltd. Published 2012 by John Wiley & Sons, Ltd.

The first chapter talks of the early signs, the pointers to the fact that Pete might be misusing drugs – which with hindsight Jacqueline could see should have rung alarm bells but which at the time were missed. These were things like Pete coming home exhausted, unkempt, in an uncharacteristically belligerent mood, or at other times 'sloping off' (p. 30) without explanation. Like so many family members, even when the signs became unmissable, Pete's mother tried to convince herself that he was OK. Perhaps her fears had been exaggerated. Perhaps it was only cannabis. After she realized heroin was involved she found some relief in believing that he was only smoking it and not injecting. At one stage she was much reassured to hear that Pete was not suffering from withdrawal symptoms. Perhaps therefore he was not really addicted after all. The full reality dawned slowly. It turned out that Jacqueline's husband, Pete's father (also called Peter), had also been very concerned but had not disclosed his growing worries to Jacqueline, wanting, as family members do, to shield his wife from concern that might turn out to be unwarranted. Jacqueline had a very understandable reaction when fellow band members of Pete's made contact saying that Pete's behaviour was now out of control and that someone needed to take responsibility for him:

> What the hell were they talking about? Late for rehearsals . . . Mood swings . . . Bizarre behaviour . . . Why hadn't I heard this before? Why had they left it until now to say parental intervention was required? (p. 20).

Pete's mother was in for a number of shocks over the next few years. Like all severe shocks the feelings experienced are difficult to put into words. When it came out that he was smoking heroin and crack cocaine she describes being, '. . . mortified. I wanted to hit him. I wanted to be sick; to be deaf; to be struck down; to hold him; to cry out to God' (p. 24). When he went to prison, 'The day . . . [was] etched upon my memory forever. It's something I've never discussed' (p. 45). When she discovered that Pete had progressed from smoking heroin to injecting it, she says, 'I simply don't have the words to articulate how learning that Peter was injecting heroin affected me; perhaps only another parent in the same circumstances could fully understand' (pp. 123–4).

Much of the book is devoted to a description of Jacqueline's attempts to support her son and to encourage him to persevere with treatment for his drug addiction. Because theirs was an army family stationed in Germany and then in the Netherlands, her efforts involved a great deal of coming and going to and from England, sometimes accompanied by one or other or both of Pete's sisters and occasionally his grandmother. It often involved much effort in tracking down Pete's whereabouts, and it often resulted in only brief meetings with Pete. At one point in the book Jacqueline describes herself at those times as being, 'on a Peter chase' (p. 77). It was always exhausting and often highly frustrating. Sometimes the aim was to encourage Pete to enter or return to treatment (on one occasion he described this as blackmail when she told him she would not attend her breast biopsy after a lump had been found if he would not go back into rehab), on one occasion to influence him to have a Naltrexone implant, on other occasions to be there when he appeared in court, and sometimes simply to spend time with him or to see him perform. The latter occasions always elicited mixed feelings – admiration at his performance mixed with deep concern: 'This was most disconcerting for me; how could they shower all this adulation on someone who was, in my mind, so very, very sick?' (p. 42).

There are many places in this moving and excellent book where Jacqueline Doherty describes the feelings she has experienced. In one place she writes of having become in the process in many ways an 'emotional cripple' (p. 123). Elsewhere she describes it as a process of being worn down to the point of sometimes experiencing a desire to '. . . be able to get to sleep and never to wake up' (p. 222). The feelings were mixed and there was much crying, which Jacqueline describes as in a way therapeutic:

> Mixed with the sadness and the anger is the constant pain, the sorrow, the feeling of foreboding, the embarrassment, the guilt, the shame, the unhappiness, the helplessness, and the utter hopelessness of our situation (p. 166).
>
> I've coined my own personal phrase: 'If at first you don't succeed, cry and cry again.' Tears cover the desire to change things in those moments of awful hopelessness and complete helplessness . . . (p. 61).

She describes waiting as being a recurring pattern:

> For the loved one of an addict or an alcoholic, it is a double whammy. You lie there, night after night, unable to sleep because you're thinking of your loved one, or waiting for the phone to ring, or worrying about them, or praying long into the night for them. And each day can be very hard. You still have to get on with the normal routine of your day no matter how tired you are (p. 220).
>
> I'm always waiting, waiting, waiting. Even now. Never know what the next day will bring. Always waiting for the prodigal to return . . . Always waiting for the phone to ring and dreading it when it does . . . Always waiting for your neighbour to drop 'Peter' into the conversation. But all I'm ever really waiting to hear is that

he's recovered. And still I wait today. The news I dread to hear is that he's dead (pp. 50–1).

Meanwhile as a wife and mother she felt the need to cater to everyone's needs:

> So many problems to keep on top of, twenty-four-seven: the Peter Problem; trying to protect my daughters and letting them see that we will get through this awful time; trying and often failing to be a comfort to my husband; keeping my job going; maintaining any semblance of normal routine (p. 84).

Thoughts, familiar to almost all affected family members, ran through her mind. If only, 'I could just lock him up for a few months . . . ' (p. 35), or '. . . wrap him up and keep him safe where he'd come to no harm' (p. 81), or '. . . if I was stronger, I could push my way into Peter's apartment and keep some semblance of order; simply not allow the current state of play to continue' (p. 172). Other thoughts that ran through her head were inevitable, 'Why us?' (p. 48), and 'What had I done wrong?' (p. 50), and 'What had gone wrong?', 'Was there anything we could possibly have changed?' (p. 134). Jacqueline was hurt by some of the things that had been written about Peter having suffered because of the family's constant moving or reacting to a strict army upbringing. In fact all the indications, backed up by facts and photos in the book, are that Peter had a particularly happy childhood that enabled him to very fully express his considerable creative (poetry for example) and sporting talents. Like so many parents in this situation she feels that their own adequacy as parents is questioned by what has happened:

> Of course, I am sure we failed many times as parents and only the children can comment on this; but, hand on heart, I can say that we truly took our responsibilities seriously. We tried to nurture without stifling, love without spoiling, to be there for all of them and to uphold a united front (p. 167).

A sub-theme that runs throughout the book, and takes on greater prominence as the book goes along, is Jacqueline's perception of how her husband Peter has been feeling and coping. In fact, as is so often the case, their ways of coping have been rather different, to the point at which it seemed to Jacqueline that she and her husband might separate as a result. At several points Jacqueline describes Peter senior's feelings of hurt, anger, having

been let down, feeling 'out of his depth . . . [with] no control whatsoever . . .'
(p. 211). Indeed she says that, of everybody, she thinks he is the one who
has probably suffered most:

> . . . who could help Peter's father with this? Who does a once-proud man ask for
> help? I know of so many families who are ripped apart by lesser problems. My
> husband was a broken man. He still is. We are a broken family (p. 145).

She describes him as being unable to sleep, hearing him walking around
at night, knowing he was severely distressed, and at one point, when he
made it clear that he wanted to be alone at home for some days, fearing
that he might commit suicide. His way of coping as a father was different to
Jacqueline's. On one occasion he did his own bit of chasing Pete but it left
him feeling defeated and he didn't try it again. After a while he did not allow
his son home. Jacqueline described her husband's strategy as a distancing
one, which she did not share but recognized as his way of coping:

> . . . my husband needed to distance himself – emotionally, mentally, physically,
> professionally – from the whole thing. In one way, he adopted an approach
> that is often used with alcoholics and addicts and their families – an approach
> called 'tough love' which sends a message that says, 'This is no longer acceptable'
> (pp. 170–1).

It was just before Christmas one year that Jacqueline and her husband
spoke about their different ways of coping. Her husband explained to her
that he understood her wish to continue to keep in touch with their son but
that her continued involvement with him was making it intolerable for her
husband Peter. It was at that point that their marriage nearly ended. In a
brief Afterword from Peter senior, he wrote:

> I watched frustrated from afar as the public drama of his turbulent world heaved
> between drugs and brushes with the law; periods in Pentonville and rehab. His
> mother kept in contact with him. I dealt with it as only I could (p. 239).

Pete's mother acknowledges several times the support she has received
from her wider family and some special friends. But, as we have so often
heard from participants in our research, the advice that others give is often
wide of the mark or is insensitive or unsupportive in some way. Some friends
told her to take him to a remote location such as the Scottish highlands for
six to twelve months (she says the foolish thought that she might kidnap Pete

often came into her mind). A padre, well meaning, advised her that it was time to 'let go of Peter' (p. 75). Even worse was the perception that her son's world was full of people who did not care about her son's health or were even encouraging drug misuse or, in the case of the media, taking advantage of it. She recounts writing to one of Pete's associates, whom at one stage she blamed for encouraging Pete's drug use, subsequently becoming quite friends with this man. The media she finds it hard to forgive. She describes the media frenzy around her son's activities, the untruths that appeared in the press, the way in which she and her husband would sometimes learn where their son was and what he had been up to first in the papers. One of the worst things was the pictures of her son caught in a situation that reflected badly on him. She wondered who, besides members of an addict's immediate family, really cared, and where were the protestors:

> ... where are the protestors against the war in our streets and in our society? This is the drug war that is invading our youth and causing havoc in our neighbour-hoods – but this is a silent ravaging war that penetrates the very fabric of life, destroying lives, destroying families and destroying communities (p. 90).

At one point Jacqueline admits to an abhorrence of drug-taking, being unable to condone it, viewing it in fact as a sin (whilst not blaming the sinner). She makes an interesting statement when she says:

> We say that people take drugs but it's really the other way around: drugs take people. Drugs take everything a person has, from material possessions to their dignity, their hope, and, ultimately their life (p. 85).

Although reasons for drug misuse are complicated and should not be over-simplified, her belief is that, '... given the circumstances, it is possible that it could happen to any one of us' (p. 92).

In the end Jacqueline believes that, unlike her husband who has found it difficult to forgive him, she has come to the point of being able to forgive her son. In fact there is comparatively little anger or criticism expressed in the book towards Pete. It is understanding of him and the wish to support him and see him through difficult times that is much the dominant tone. There are points at which anger and frustration appear. For example she makes the observation that, 'He is oblivious to our pain while we struggle diligently to understand his' (p. 172), and later, 'He has no idea what each of us has had to endure...' (p. 225). She even acknowledges understanding how a parent might think of killing her son under these circumstances:

> That is the bottom line. I have even told Peter that was how I felt. I have said to him, and to my colleagues, how a dose of insulin would be just the ticket to stop the madness. It would put the Peter Problem to sleep for ever. It would kill him. What an awful thing to think and I'm not proud for thinking it, I'm ashamed. I say it out loud to act as a safety device – to express how low I'm feeling. To voice that sentiment, is, I think, very low indeed, but that's how I feel at times. And I think all mothers feel like this when they have addictive children (p. 144).

Comments

Because her son is so well known and commands such media attention there are aspects of Jackie Doherty's experience that are unlike that of most mothers of sons or daughters with drug problems. True though that obviously is, I also know from hearing stories of so many affected family members that almost everything she says in her book will ring true for many, many other parents and other family members. In fact Jacqueline herself says she has talked to other parents who, whilst not suffering the media abuse to which her family has been exposed, have had other experiences that Jacqueline has been spared – being beaten for money or having possessions stolen, for example.

It does not surprise me at all that she should have wanted to tell her story at book length. The experience of concerned family members, and of those who have come to know about the family experience at some depth through their helping roles or via research on the subject, is that the reality of family members' lives is not well known or appreciated. In our research family members have often told us that the lengthy interviews we have had with them have given them a rare, sometimes unique, opportunity to describe what life has been like for them. Many of the things that Jacqueline describes crop up repeatedly in such interviews. They include the looking back at the early signs that were missed, signs that something was going wrong; trying to convince oneself that nothing much was wrong and trying not to worry other members of the family; and then the series of shocks when the reality of what is going on is gradually revealed. There is a mix of feelings, the difficulty of putting these into words, the waiting and the worrying, the lying awake, the fear that he might die, doubts about one's own adequacy as parents, and sometimes a feeling that in the end one has become an 'emotional cripple' oneself.

So well described by Pete's mother is the desperate search for the best way of responding as a mother. The thought has passed through the mind of almost every family member desperately worried about a loved one with an addiction problem, that there must be some means of taking control. Surely, with enough determination and effort, one could rescue the person one is concerned about, force them to come away with you, be taken to a place of safety, preferably in a remote location, or at the very least to go into residential rehabilitation. Jacqueline's way has been to go 'on a Peter chase' as she puts it. Because there are no easy answers to the question of how to cope with a family member's addiction problem, it is something that inevitably tends to divide family member from family member or family member from well-meaning friend or adviser. In Jacqueline's case it is a padre who tells her that she should 'let go' of Pete, but there must have been others who thought the same. Conflict between the opposing stances of remaining fully engaged with an addicted family member – trying to maintain contact, attempting to continue to be of influence for good, picking up the pieces whenever you can – versus distancing oneself, is such a common one. Individual family members go through cycles of trying one thing and then the other. But very often the opposition is played out between two members of the family. Not infrequently, as in Pete's family, it is the mother who tries to remain engaged and the father who tends towards the distancing position. It is an additional strain on the family when that happens, and that seems to have been the case with Jacqueline and her husband. Jacqueline recognizes how much her husband has been affected and how his distancing has not brought him comfort, any more than her more engaged position has brought comfort for her. It is interesting to note that other women in the family – Pete's sisters and his grandmother – often seemed to have played a supportive role in Jacqueline's attempts to remain engaged. It looks as if gender roles are strongly at play here.

Despite all the pain that Pete's misuse of drugs has caused her and the family, note that Jacqueline has very little that is critical to say of Pete. All she does say is that he had little understanding of what they have had to put up with, which is something that family members very often feel. Like so many other family members, too, she blames the substances rather than the person – she says, 'drugs take people', not the other way round. Indeed she expresses abhorrence of drugs. Her criticism is also directed, on the other hand, towards all those who appear not to care about her son's state of health and well-being, those who cannot see how destructive drug use can be, and particularly towards those who might have encouraged his drug use and the media who appeared to take advantage of his circumstances for their own gain. Like so many other family members Jacqueline is angry at the conspiracy that appears to surround the use and misuse of drugs in society, and specifically around her son's own drug use. Where are those who should be protesting about the effects of drugs on families like her own? Why wasn't she told earlier what was happening to her son? And why do his admirers seem to care so little that he is so sick?

Questions

1. Do you agree with me that Jacqueline Doherty's experience is probably very similar in most important respects to that of any other mother worried about her son's dependence? Or do you think that Pete's fame and all the media attention he gets makes his mother's experience distinctly different?

2. Are you sympathetic to Jackie Doherty's wish to write a book about her experience of Pete's drug addiction? Can you see anything against it? What do you think might have been Pete's feelings if he read her book?

3. If you were a good friend of Jackie's would you think she was doing the right thing to 'chase' Pete in order to see what she could do for him? Supposing she asked you to help her in that quest in some way, perhaps by going with her or by acting as a go-between for taking messages or by helping her in trying to locate Pete. How would you react?

4. Some family members get very engaged in trying to keep in close contact with the person they are worried about, always trying to think of ways to influence them for good; others decide to keep their distance. In this case it looks as if Jacqueline was the engaged one and her husband the more distant. Is it a gender issue do you think?

5. Jacqueline Doherty makes an interesting remark when she writes that 'drugs take people', not the other way round. I know others who make very much the same point, putting it slightly differently, saying that it is not the case that 'people abuse drugs' but rather that 'drugs abuse people'. If you were in discussion with a family member like Jacqueline Doherty, what view on that subject would you express yourself, and why?

6. Jackie Doherty expressed anger at other people for encouraging her son's drug use. That is very common for family members to do, understandably. Family members often feel very alone, as if they are fighting a lone campaign against all the forces and pressures that have encouraged their loved ones' addictive behaviour, and which are not helping them give up. Do you think others do have a responsibility or do you think this is largely a matter for the individual addicted person and his or her immediate family?

7. When a young person develops a serious drug problem, what responsibility for that do you think his or her friends had?

8. Do you share Jacqueline's anger at the way in which the media depicts drug addiction?

Exercises

- Set up a discussion between two people, one playing a mother like Jacqueline Doherty, the other the padre who wishes to advise her to 'let go' a bit more. They each make a good case but their views seem irreconcilable. Join them as a neutral third party. Try to establish the advantages and disadvantages of each position. Can a compromise be reached or is a middle way impossible?

- You are a junior reporter for a national newspaper. A well-known figure in the music world, known to have a drug problem, has been photographed at a party behaving badly and looking as if he or she is under the influence. Your editor wants a sensational piece of a kind that you know would make his family angry and upset and which you think is prejudiced and unfair. Draft a piece – about 200 words – that you think your editor wants. Then re-draft the piece in a way that you think is more responsible, mentioning the family in the piece.

10

Parents of Problem Gamblers

Family members affected by addiction can feel very alone in their troubles. They may think theirs is the only family that is having the experiences they are having. They may be uncertain whether their suspicions about the addictive behaviour are reasonable or exaggerated. They are very likely to think that they themselves are to blame. They are certainly thrown into a state of indecision about how to cope. All of this is particularly true of parents who are affected by a son's excessive gambling – it is not always a son who is of concern, but it is more often a son than a daughter. The world has been slow to acknowledge that gambling can be as addictive as substances, and the problem has therefore been an even more hidden one than has been the case with illegal drugs or alcohol. The relief of finding out that you are not alone can therefore be particularly strong for mothers and fathers of young gamblers.

In what follows we listen in to part of a discussion that might have taken place at a meeting of Parents of Young Gamblers. There are some couples attending and some mothers on their own. They are all concerned about their sons' excessive playing of gambling machines (the meeting probably took place some time prior to the turn of the millennium; since then online gambling has become an added risk for young people).

Addiction Dilemmas: Family Experiences from Literature and Research and their Challenges for Practice, First Edition. Jim Orford.
© 2012 John Wiley & Sons, Ltd. Published 2012 by John Wiley & Sons, Ltd.

The group is imaginary, but what the parents say is closely based on the experiences of parents who have been interviewed as part of a programme of research on the effects of addiction in the family.

Mother A

Our son had been playing on fruit machines for many years before we realized what was going on. At the time we thought he was having a very difficult adolescence and we were trying to deal with this, not with his gambling which was the underlying problem. He was beginning to become troublesome at school and I was called in to see the teachers on a number of occasions. I discovered he'd spent all his lunch money and some bus fare money. Later I found out there was an arcade beside the bus stop. His school work went from bad to worse and he became extremely irritable and depressed and his relationships with his sister and brother and with us deteriorated. From being a rather extroverted boy he became very withdrawn from his family. He lost a lot of weight, and spent a lot of time in his room. When he was 16 he began to sell his bedroom furniture and belongings. Friends would come to the home saying he owed them money. That was the stage we discovered him in an arcade but we still didn't realize that was at the root of all his problems. But we don't approve of places like that anyway, so we confined him to home for a month, but nothing really seemed to change and his behaviour was still bad. He started work but he was found out pinching money and as a result spent some time in a police cell. It was while he was there that he finally admitted to us what was really happening.

Mother B

Ours started as young as 12 or 13 when he'd had a big win when he was on a school trip. By the time he was 17 we couldn't understand where all his money was going and there were many occasions when he didn't come home in the evenings but went straight out with his friends after work. His father bought him a bike which he was intending to pay back in regular instalments but after a while the payments stopped. He lost his job but we had no idea why, not knowing until later that he had had a lot of unexplained absences at work and college. We felt there was a chance he'd been sacked but we didn't know for sure. He had another job but lost that one as he felt he was being given all the menial jobs to do. Life at home has been hell, that's the only way I can describe it. His younger sister has been very affected but won't talk about it at all; she says she's sick of it. There are constant arguments and a bad atmosphere in the household. He will attend family celebrations, such as Christmas, under pressure but whenever possible he disappears at the first opportunity.

Father B

I find I can't think properly at work, I lose my temper easily and I have said things I shouldn't. I believe I've even lost friends due to being so moody and I know I've been laying into our daughter unfairly. I've had to apologize to her afterwards. I now have a serious sleeping problem that I've been to the doctor about. In fact at times I think I've come very close to having a nervous breakdown.

Father C

We know our son's real problem is his gambling but we have found it difficult to separate it from just his adolescence or him being a late developer or perhaps it's just his character. The amusement arcade seems to be a meeting place for 'low achievers' in life.

Mother D

We actually got to the point of being frightened to let our son out of our sight. He doesn't seem to care about his appearance, not properly washing and so on, and he has been verbally aggressive towards both of us on many occasions. We feel we have lost him really; he acts as if he doesn't care about us or anybody (she cries). There has been tension all the time at home, and our social life has been restricted because when we first found out we tried to take him everywhere and not to leave him alone. Our sleeping has been affected. We have spent many a night lying awake worrying about what would happen next. I must admit I have felt hatred and anger towards him, hating him for what he has done to his father. I have never seen you (turning to her husband) so upset in the way you have been about this. I feel ashamed at times for hating our son but I can't help it.

Father D

We concluded in the end that our son had taken money from us because there were times when we thought money had gone missing, although at the time we usually put it down to each other taking the money. There were two occasions when he stole larger amounts – several hundred pounds from his grandparents and over a thousand from us. At that stage we realized there was a problem but thought it was simply one of stealing. He had pocket money and a milk round but we never questioned him about where his money went, but we did wonder why he wasn't bringing records and clothes home like other boys of his age. His grandfather was too afraid at first to tell us his cash had gone missing because he thought we would be angry at *him* for having too much cash in the house. When it came out, we made him go back to his grandparents and admit he'd stolen it and he agreed to pay the money back a bit every week which he did. He then stayed off gambling for a few months. But he started again, all the time assuring us that he hadn't. Both of my parents knew about their money that went missing and they have been supportive in that they forgave and forgot about it and have continued to treat him normally.

Mother E

When our son was about 12 years old he started stealing from my purse. I used to try and remember to hide my purse and any money that I had, but I sometimes forgot and he was managing to steal money from me regularly. I tried punishing him in all sorts of ways but nothing seemed to work and he would never explain what he wanted the money for.

Mother A

I noticed a lot of my jewellery had gone missing. Since then I've realized that masses of stuff has gone from the house and attic. He'd obviously been selling things for a long time. He left home for a while but owed us a lot of money for rent and we had to pay out over £5000 to cover his debts and rent.

Mother B

Stealing of small amounts has occurred in our household as well. We now lock up drawers and cupboards and carry our wallets everywhere we go. He had a motor bike that he loved but he sold it to obtain some extra money, which he spent within a month. We had a call from the bank manager to say he was in debt and it seemed he was borrowing money. We have looked at his bank statements and found that at times he was withdrawing £80 or £90 a day in eight or nine different withdrawals. You can't trust a thing he says, he always lies. GA [Gamblers Anonymous] suggested keeping all his money and giving it back to him in controlled amounts. The main strategy has been to control his money and to always keep a track of our own so that we'd know if anything had gone missing. Nowadays we are not as wary but we do still keep our wallets with us.

Father E

Our son gives his mother some money out of his pay packet and then hands the rest over to me. He then asks me if he needs any money for anything, and I ask what he wants it for. If I think there is a good logical reason for it then I give him the money. For example, he asked for £20 for a pair of shoes which I thought was reasonable; he went and bought them and gave me the change back. After he runs out of money to play the machines he tries to borrow from his mother. You usually lend him some, don't you (turning to his wife), because you are scared he will start stealing and getting into big trouble if you don't. You say that if you don't give it to him he always has money somehow. He attends a social club where a raffle is drawn every week. Because he doesn't want anything to do with this, we give him a pound so that he is not putting his money towards it. He doesn't want to stop taking part altogether as he would then have to tell all the people at the social club about his problem. Since the majority of the people at the club are connected with his work he feels it would put his job at risk so he buys the ticket but with our money.

Mother F

This has been a problem for me because I've always said I wouldn't give my son money while he was gambling. He owed about £1000 and couldn't pay his rent and because of a previous dishonest act with the social security, he couldn't apply to have his rent paid for him. My husband pointed out that *he* hadn't made any decision not to give him money. In fact he paid a lot of his debts and generally sorted things out. I always contacted his father who paid money owing to Social Services so that he could get rent relief. I helped him by going to town and buying a basket of the cheapest groceries I could find. He was attending GA again and agreed that their insistence about not letting relatives give gamblers money was quite sensible. On the other hand it meant he would starve. So we made a contract. If he ran out of money a week before he got paid then he should have to go without, but if he had lost all his money in the first week of the month then I would buy him food. Of course he had trouble getting good jobs because of his lack of references and I eventually wrote him one on the grounds that he had wall-papered a room for me many years ago.

Father D

Personally I have decided that self-survival is necessary which means that I've dismissed him in a way. By that I mean not helping him out in ways I would have done in the past. For example helping him out financially.

Mother B

We differed in our approach for a long time but in the end I believe we've come out united. We reached a point where we won't offer him any more support. But we are attending GamAnon [for family members of compulsive gamblers] and encouraging him to go to GA, and we have decided on a final strategy of telling him to hand over his wages which we will give him back in controlled amounts. If that fails then we are going to tell him to leave and stand on his own two feet. If he doesn't go then the rest of the family will. I've felt so desperate and frustrated at times. But now we have decided on the final strategy we feel we know where we're going don't we?

Father E

Me too. My feelings have got so intense that I've wanted to throw things. It ruins your life. We are frightened what will happen if we do tell him to go. We feel guilty at times because we think we have gone wrong somewhere in bringing him up. We have felt angry towards him, and towards each other at times when we have disagreed about courses of action to take, so it has caused lots of upheaval in our marriage. We have adopted many different strategies but he is so devious he manages to get round all the rules we lay down. At times I admit our own emotions take over the way we react. My work takes me away from home most of the week. When I get home I always ask about whether the stealing is continuing. One particular weekend when I was told that £10 had disappeared. I took my belt off and nearly killed him.

Father G

I know how you must have felt. I was livid when I found that old coins I'd collected since being a boy were missing from the attic. I followed him down to the pub, manhandled him into the car and when we got home we talked for several hours, my son in tears some of the time and admitting that he had been silly on the machines. It was a hell of a fright for him, the first time I confronted him. Going quiet has always been his defence, he never speaks to us. Whether to confront him or not was the issue. Confronting was my preferred style, giving him a good lecturing, for example. But it wasn't effective. The only other approach I could think of was to let him stew in his own juice. If anything like the stealing of coins happens again I'm going to throw him out of the house. I've threatened to change the locks so that he can't get back in.

Mother G

I'm very worried indeed about this. At the moment I'm frightened to go out of the house in case he takes things while I'm gone. I try to talk him out of it and tell him it's wrong but he says it isn't. Sometimes I avoid him when he gets in such a mood and starts shouting. I've given up shouting back but his Dad shouts at him something terrible. We've become much more supportive towards each other recently. We're talking to each other more about the problems that we are facing now. Before I tended to support our son and be on his side rather than my husband's. I'm really worried at the moment thinking that things at home are reaching a crisis point. I am concerned about my husband. I don't know how he's going to cope if more stealing occurs. It is you (turning to her husband) I'm worried about.

Father H

I've tried to tell my son that the only winner is the machine. I had on a TV programme about gambling and I wanted him to see it and had kept him there for as long as I could. I think the nicking has now stopped. At one time I discovered he'd been taking money from the till over a period of several months. I had to sack him from working with me over it. I think he was upset about that. I am working very hard now to try and be with him as much as possible, to do things with him. We sat together quite a bit yesterday just talking. Often the three of us would joke around together. He is a smashing lad really. If he can just nip this problem in the bud he's going to turn out to be smashing (tearful at this point).

Mother A

I've always been open and honest with him if I can and I've never rejected him and always tried to be supportive towards him. My husband hasn't always agreed with the way I've dealt with the situation and that has caused problems in our marriage. It affects the whole family. I'm on my own most of the time as my husband is away a lot and his brothers are really rejecting him. He found his brother's cashpoint card and memorized the number and withdrew and gambled all his brother's money. When his brother found out he kicked him all the way down the high street, and he came home and tried to lodge a complaint of assault against his brother. The police came round but left it to the family to sort it out.

Mother B

Actually our most serious concern is that our daughter may have been affected without her or us realizing. She tries very hard to understand his problem but says she can't. She has bouts of temper about the issue and refuses to talk about it. She won't go to GA because she says she would find it too upsetting. We're concerned that she is bottling it up and that it may come out later.

Mother F

When our son was 18 he announced he was getting married. I thought he was far too young and debated whether to tell his wife about his problems but I decided not to. I did try to discourage them slightly from getting married but I knew it was going to go ahead. They had a baby and the marriage lasted two years. I feel very sorry for my daughter-in-law and I know she went through hell with him. He then went to stay with his sister.

All the brothers and sisters have been very supportive but I think that they've all possibly had enough by now.

Mother E

We got in touch with GamAnon through the Samaritans. We talked to someone who told us 'you are not alone' – I would describe those words as the most important few words of my life; knowing that there were other people with the same problem was a great comfort to me then.

Mother B

Our son went to GA and said he'd stopped gambling. He was much happier and brighter for a while but it didn't last. We don't think he's yet reached his rock bottom and we wonder what on earth we can do to help him reach it. Actually we were a little worried that the stories of other gamblers at GA might be more corrupting than therapeutic. We think he is going to GA just for our sake and not because he feels he has a problem and really wants to put it right.

Comments

In an earlier chapter we heard from three wives of men addicted to gambling. Many of the same issues have appeared here again in the present chapter. A regularly recurring theme is the difficulties that family members – parents this time – had in coming to a realization that gambling was a problem. Financial irregularities, including stealing from home, were amongst the signs of problem gambling – not always recognized to be such at the time – about which parents speak most often. One mother discovered her son had spent all his lunch money and some bus fare money on gambling, only later finding out that there was an arcade beside the bus stop – later he began to sell his bedroom furniture and belongings, and friends would come to the home saying he owed them money; another mother recalled how they had thought money had gone missing but usually put it down to each other taking the money. Parents described more general changes in behaviour and personality. From being a quiet child and no trouble at school, her son had become rude, was always out, and when in the house would hide away in his bedroom, one mother said. Another told how her son had stopped caring about his appearance, for example not washing, had been verbally aggressive to them, appeared not to care about them or anyone else, to the extent that they now felt they had 'lost' him. Crises had occurred. For example one son had spent time in a police cell after being found stealing money, and had admitted what had happened.

Like partners of addicted gamblers, feelings run high for parents as well. One mother admitted, with shame, to feeling hatred and anger towards her son. Another explained how she had felt desperate and frustrated, and her husband described his feelings as so intense that he had wanted to throw things. 'It ruins your life', he said. They felt guilty at times because they thought they had failed in the way they had brought their son up, angry towards him and sometimes towards each other when they disagreed about what action to take, and frightened about what would happen if they told their son to leave. Such feelings are well known to parents of addicted sons or daughters, whatever the nature of the addiction.

Parents' own health and relationships had been affected. Sleeping was often disturbed by worry and parents' social life had often been restricted. It is common for parents to feel that they cannot go away on holiday for fear that possessions might be taken and sold while they were away. Mothers had been tearful and depressed and fathers had been frightened by their own irritability and loss of temper. Couples had found themselves differing in their approaches to the problem but had sometimes moved towards a more united, mutually supportive position.

Other members of the family had become involved as well. In one case it had led to a violent confrontation between brothers after one brother had used his brother's cash-point number and spent all his brother's money on gambling. Another son had stolen several hundred pounds from his grandparents, but the grandfather had been too afraid at first to tell them about it, thinking that they would be angry at him for keeping too much cash in the house. One couple were particularly concerned that their daughter might have been affected. A daughter-in-law was also mentioned by one mother: the latter had debated whether to tell her son's wife about her son's problems but had decided not to. The marriage had not lasted long and the mother thought that the daughter-in-law had probably gone through 'hell' with him.

There were some examples of positive social support for parents, sometimes from family or friends and for one mother from GamAnon. She and her husband were told they were not alone, and she had remembered those words as being some of the most important she had ever heard: it had been a great comfort to her knowing that there were others facing the same problems.

When it came to deciding how to respond, it was ways of coping with the financial irregularities that were particularly prominent. Some talked in positive terms about strategies they had employed. For example, one son was said to give his mother some money from his pay packet each week, handing the rest to his father who would give him money for what were thought to be reasonable expenses such as buying a pair of shoes. It was very common for parents to talk about watching money carefully. In one case parents had simply stopped giving their son money, and they said he now knew better than to ask them for it. In other cases parents were not so firm. In one case it was said that the son tried to borrow from his mother and that she usually lent him some because she was worried that otherwise he would start stealing and getting into trouble. In another case parents had covered their son's debts and rent to the tune of over £5000. GA advised that relatives should not give gamblers money. But parents worry that their sons will suffer as a result, even starve. One couple made a contract that if their son lost all his money with most of the month still to go before he was paid again, his mother would buy him food. Such dilemmas over money figure large in the lives of family members struggling to find the best way to cope with gambling addiction.

Questions

1. Do you understand how these parents failed to realize earlier on that gambling was a problem for their sons? Is it possible that they were deliberately or unconsciously denying the problem?
2. Do you think with hindsight that these parents were exaggerating the role of gambling? Were these, in fact, just normal problems of adolescence?

3. What would you say to a mother who says that she hates her son, and feels ashamed for doing so?

4. What would you do if you found your son or daughter was regularly stealing from you, or was selling things from the home such as furniture or valued collections?

5. Is it crazy for a mother to keep on lending her son money when she knows he is gambling excessively? What about buying him food if he quickly runs through his monthly pay? What would you advise if mothers were to ask you whether you thought they should carry on doing that?

6. How can parents protect other members of the family, such as their other children, from feeling the effects of addictive gambling?

7. Was the mother right, do you think, to keep her son's gambling addiction secret from the woman her son was about to marry? Why do you think she didn't mention it?

Exercises

•   One of these mothers was very reassured to hear the simple message, 'You are not alone in this'. Brainstorm other simple messages that might be helpful to concerned and affected family members.

•   You have been counselling a mother and father who are so worried about their son's gambling that they are wondering whether to refuse an invitation to go away for the weekend to celebrate a very dear friend's fortieth birthday. You think they should go. How would you like the conversation to go? Try role-playing it.

11

The Tale of Caitlin Thomas

Caitlin Thomas, wife of the Welsh poet Dylan Thomas, has left us with one of the richest accounts of life with a partner with a drinking problem. That is partly because Caitlin herself had aspirations to be a successful writer. But it is also due to her natural fighting spirit, and the fury and bitterness that she felt before and after Dylan died at the age of 39. As a result she wrote several manuscripts of autobiography and collaborated with two other authors who wrote biographies of her.

Several of the autobiographical pieces were never published (Paul Ferris refers to these in his biography). One that was published in 1957, four years after Dylan's death, and which achieved some success at the time, was entitled *Leftover Life to Kill* (published by Putnam). Although it is an intriguing read for students of Caitlin's life, it is somewhat disappointing for our purposes because it says very little about Caitlin's life with Dylan. It concentrates, rather, on Caitlin's experiences during the months she spent on the Italian island of Elba where she went very shortly after Dylan's funeral. Later, in her other published piece of autobiography (*Double Drink Story* – see below) she would say of *Leftover*, unfairly in my view: 'As a literary work, its value was nil; it was no more than a splash in a puddle at a time when

Addiction Dilemmas: Family Experiences from Literature and Research and their Challenges for Practice, First Edition. Jim Orford.
© 2012 John Wiley & Sons, Ltd. Published 2012 by John Wiley & Sons, Ltd.

the whole world was smarting from Dylan's untimely death' (*Double Drink Story*, p. xiv).

Of more direct relevance to us here are three books that were published a quarter of a century or more later, by which time Caitlin had herself become a successful member of Alcoholics Anonymous. The first, and probably the most interesting of all, was co-authored with George Tremlett under the title, *Caitlin: Life with Dylan Thomas* (published by Secker and Warburg in 1986). Interestingly enough, the title page, inside the book, carries a slightly different title – *Caitlin: A Warring Absence*, that sub-title being taken from a poem that Dylan wrote for Caitlin shortly after their marriage, and which is also cited at the beginning of *Leftover Life to Kill*. One suspects that the latter title was Caitlin's preference. Perhaps this was another book where Caitlin felt upstaged by another writer, as she had by Dylan. George Tremlett, who was a fan of Dylan's and who got to know Caitlin through her and Dylan's daughter Aeron, was clearly the chief editor although the book is written in the first person. In the preface, Tremlett explains how the book was produced:

> I offered to work with her on a completely new book, which, I suggested, should be based on tape-recorded interviews which I would conduct, transcribe and then edit. It was my view then, and still is now, that this was the only way the book could be written because Caitlin remains much too emotionally involved . . . Our weeks together were highly traumatic. Many days she was crying, and on some days so was I . . . Caitlin was still in deep personal pain because of what had happened to her over thirty years ago . . . By the time we had finished our work together, Caitlin and I both realised that we had created a remarkable book. It is a love story but, as she says, a very sad one (*Caitlin: Life with Dylan Thomas*, pp. xiv–xvi).

The other biography of Caitlin, written in a more conventional biographical style, in the third person, was written by Paul Ferris. It appeared in 1993, the year before Caitlin died in Sicily. It was entitled simply, *Caitlin: The Life of Caitlin Thomas*. It was first published in hardback by Hutchinson, and Pimlico brought out a paperback edition in 1995 (quotations here are from the latter edition). Ferris had written a biography of Dylan Thomas that was published in 1977. In the Author's Note at the beginning of the 1995 edition of *Caitlin*, Ferris says that Caitlin had declined to co-operate with his biography of Dylan. He acknowledges, however, that *Caitlin* could not have been written without co-operation in the form of interviews and the right to quote from letters and other writings. Their agreement, which he says took several months of negotiating and 'haggling' (p. 4) to produce, included her right to read the typescript and to suggest changes. In the event by the time the book was written Caitlin was unwell and her Italian son Francesco, who read the manuscript, made only very minor suggestions. In those passages of Paul Ferris's book that concern Caitlin's relationship with Dylan, of which there are many, it comes across that the biographer's first loyalties lie with Dylan. Although the work is a rich and detailed account of a life, it is written as if that life were flawed and that Caitlin contributed to Dylan's downfall. It is thereby quite similar in many ways to some of the pathologizing accounts that health professionals have given of wives of men with drinking problems.

Finally, I shall refer to *Double Drink Story: My Life with Dylan Thomas*, authored by Caitlin and published posthumously in 1997 (quotations here are from the Virago 1998 edition). *Double Drink Story* is helpful to us in rounding out, here and there, the picture of Caitlin's relationship with Dylan provided by the book written with George Tremlett. One of its major themes is Caitlin's own excessive drinking, which appears to have worsened after Dylan's death, and in places *Double Drink Story* reads a bit like an AA tract.

Our protagonist was born Caitlin Macnamara. Her father's family had a grand but fading seat in the west of Ireland, but her father left the family when she was tiny and she was largely brought up by her mother, with sisters and a brother, in rural Sussex. By all accounts her upbringing was unconventional by present-day standards, with little emphasis on conventional education but with much opportunity for independence. The family had connections with writers and artists. Augustus John and family, for example, were close friends.

Caitlin and Dylan met in a pub, in an area of London then known as Fitzrovia where artists and writers tended to gather in the 1930s. In *Caitlin: Life with Dylan Thomas* Caitlin described to George Tremlett how Dylan, then aged 22, would spend every day in London going round the pubs, starting when they opened at 11 o'clock, setting up a line of light ales along the counter and downing them one by one, clearing his head from the night before with a recovery drink, telling stories, cracking jokes, playing pub games, meeting other writers and drinking endless pints of beer. She expressed her ambivalence about that life:

> It was the kind of world that I disapproved of and yet at the same time I was thrilled to be sharing it with him. These were the artists and writers that I admired, the people I wanted to be with . . . By the end of that first week, I felt I really had to

get back home . . . I felt I couldn't go on with all that pubbing which was so much a part of Dylan's life. I thought it extraordinary that someone could go on living like that. One side of me wanted to share it with him, but there was also another side of me to whom his whole way of life seemed very wrong. I was a person who believed in hard work, determination, and all that. And yet I wanted to be with Dylan, to have all the possible experiences that I could: it seemed to me – then – an advanced thing to do (Thomas and Tremlett, pp. 4, 6–7).

Years later, in *Double Drink Story*, her description of those early pub days has been simplified, but the ambivalence is still recalled:

> . . . pubs were our natural habitat. . . . [W]e became dedicated to pubs and to each other . . . it was the non-drinker who was disapproved of, looked down on, pitied. Dylan and I had invented a verbal system of denigrating them. The dedicated, sober, serious, hard daily workers were denigrated by us as smug, self-satisfied, complacent prigs . . . Miserable nonentities, cowardly dolts, insignificant lily-livered sags and softies, on the same abysmal level as conscientious objectors, vegetarians and, the most crawling scum of all, of course: teetotallers . . . But even then there was still a small stubborn block of resistance, a knot of opposition, a muffled cry of protest in me, that cried out in the dark, 'This not the way I would wish to be'. . . . [a] small desert island of detachment in me, from which I looked on and did not approve . . . (*Double Drink Story*, pp. 3, 5, 106–7).

Dylan was brought up in Swansea, south Wales, where his parents continued to live. Much of Dylan and Caitlin's married life was set in Laugharne, a small fishing village on the south Pembrokeshire coast about 20 miles west of Swansea. They were married in 1937, the year after they met, and after some time living with parents in Sussex and south Wales, settled in Laugharne, first staying with friends and then renting a house called Sea View. From 1941 to 1949 they mostly lived at a variety of addresses in London and elsewhere in the south of England, with occasional stays in south Wales. For the last four years of their life together they settled back in Laugharne, in the Boat House, bought for them by a longstanding friend.

There can be little doubting the fact that, although Caitlin was married to one of the great poets of the English language (the greatest since Shakespeare according to George Tremlett's English teacher at school), her life with Dylan was in many respects comparable to that of other women who have lived with men with serious drinking problems. As she put it in *Double Drink Story*:

> But ours was a drink story . . . just like millions of others . . . the only significant difference between our drink story and any of the other drink stories is that in the

middle of it was a genius poet. Otherwise nobody would have taken a fragment of notice of it (p. 169).

For one thing, 'Any money of his own went on drink . . .' (*Caitlin: Life with Dylan Thomas*, p. 56), and they were always short of money. The various accounts of their life are full of incidents such as having their bed taken away because they failed to keep up the instalment payment (p. 58) or selling all her girlhood riding cups for thirty shillings when they were broke (*Double Drink Story*, p. 58). Even when, towards the end of the war, Dylan was being commissioned to write film scripts, their financial position was much the same:

> This was the first time in our lives that we had ever had a regular income, and . . . we should have been able to manage quite comfortably, but we never did; whenever Dylan had money he drank it, and always wanted more. Dylan was still the generous friend whenever he had cash in his pocket, but he would now steal if he had to without the slightest qualm . . . Dylan used the pawn-shop quite a lot . . . When we went to a party, Dylan would often leave with a better coat than the one he was wearing when he arrived, and quite often he took people's shirts and left his own dirty ones behind . . . Though some people were furious with Dylan, no one ever called the police. On the whole people were very patient with him (Thomas and Tremlett, pp. 80–1).

For most of their married life they lived in accommodation loaned or bought by family or friends, or else, as at Sea View, they were living in rented accommodation but failing to keep up the rent. In the few years after moving out of Sea View and before moving back to the Boat House:

> . . . Caitlin . . . coped with life in a filthy studio in Chelsea, various flats in London, most of them belonging to other people, a primitive cottage, a flimsy bungalow and a damp summerhouse by a river (Ferris, p. 97).

Their husbands' unreliability is one of the things that wives of men with drinking problems talk about most, and Caitlin was no exception. She complained that he failed to turn up at the hospitals when she was having their three babies, and later on left her to face her two abortions alone (Thomas and Tremlett, p. 95), and if the children were difficult he wanted them kept out of his way at mealtimes or when they were travelling (Ferris, p. 103). According to Ferris she viewed herself as '. . . the real provider . . . the mature half of the partnership . . .' (p. 103), and Ferris himself notes the '. . . catalogue of appeasement' (p. 102) contained in letters that Dylan wrote to Caitlin when they were apart. Not that Caitlin was the only one to suffer in that way: a notable event was Dylan's failure to turn up as best man at the wedding of his old Swansea friend and fellow poet Vernon Watkins, and the elaborate excuses that he made afterwards.

In 1942 Caitlin wrote to her sister Brigit that Dylan was:

> Positive model bourgeois husband one day and the next suddenly disappears, and I may not hear of him till perhaps several nights later he strolls in a little battered and contrite but not one word of explanation (Ferris, p. 91).

In the last few years before Dylan died during a poetry reading trip to the USA, they were, according to Ferris, continually quarrelling and in debt and their life together was one of general disorder (pp. 115, 122). Caitlin was at the end of her tether by the time he died, and Ferris quotes from a letter that she wrote to him from south Wales but which she believed was never received by Dylan before he died:

> I don't care what you say after this, nothing will ever make me go near you again. I knew you were abysmally weak, drunken, unfaithful, and a congenital liar, but it has taken me longer to realise that on top of each one of these unpardonable vices, you are a plain, stingy, meany as well ... Will you please send me more money as soon as you can, as I can't bear being summonsed in all directions, and they are your bills as well as mine (Ferris, pp. 140–1).

They were both aware that he was also damaging himself personally. In *Caitlin: Life with Dylan Thomas*, Caitlin put it thus:

> I think he realised that he had made a mess of his life and that there was nothing to come back to; nothing to do next or to live on; no means of supporting his family. At the back of his mind he was always thinking about death and the possibility of suicide and not living beyond the age of forty, which he used to say quite often, sober or drunk, even when he was writing those serene poems. He always felt that he was doomed to die early ... he didn't want to get old and ugly, and he realised that he was getting that way, flabby and fat, with a beer belly. He had completely let himself go, physically (Thomas and Tremlett, p. 93).

In the last year of his life, Ferris tells us, he had deteriorated physically:

> He was asthmatic, prone to blackouts, almost certainly had potency problems, was racked with gout, and suffered continual gastric upsets and hangovers (Ferris, p. 139).

Dylan died in New York in November 1953 after, so Caitlin was told, drinking 18 whiskeys. Caitlin told George Tremlett that, had she been there, she '... would have made him vomit and then wrapped him up in bed and given him his bread and milk' (Thomas and Tremlett, p. 189). Bread and milk was a longstanding cure for Dylan's over-drinking, originally administered by his mother, and a tradition that Caitlin had maintained.

Caitlin told George Tremlett that in the last few years she had felt trapped and bitter (Thomas and Tremlett, pp. 105–6), and when they visited the Watkins three years before Dylan's death Gwen Watkins had found her 'permanently embittered' (cited by Ferris, p. 114). She later told Ferris that, 'Dylan's death was an enormous liberation for me' (p. 174).

Is there any evidence in this collection of biographical and autobiographical accounts of Caitlin's life with Dylan about how she coped with his behaviour? Much of the importance of this collection of works for us here lies exactly in the fact that they contain a great deal of such evidence.

A recurring theme is Caitlin's tolerance of Dylan's misbehaviour, putting up with it, even supporting it. There are several passages in *Caitlin: Life with Dylan Thomas* along those lines. For example when they first met:

> ... Dylan genuinely believed that the drinking life was the best way to live. I don't think he was ever totally honest, even with me. His way of impressing people was to invent things ... Because it was Dylan I was very tolerant. To me, he was so endearing, lovable and comforting that I could overlook this unreality ... (p. 56).

A year or so into their marriage:

> In those days I didn't worry when Dylan went away for a few days. I accepted that drinking with his buddies was an essential part of his life and it didn't upset me too much. Also I found myself pregnant, which ... gave me an enormous sense of calm (p. 61).

A decade further on:

> I had an enormous amount of pride and self-will – inner resources, I called it. I was strong, and anyway, I had to put up with it; I had no choice. I had no skills; I had never been taught anything ... (p. 106).

In *Double Drink Story* she says:

> In theory, as a good conventional little wife ... I should have been nagging Dylan about his ruinous drinking: ruinous to his finances, ruinous to his work and

ruinous to his health. I should have been wearing my head off at him night and day to desist, to moderate like his father, to go easy, to stop dragging himself and his family into degradation and ruin (p. 14).

More or less throughout their marriage Caitlin continued to accompany Dylan to the pub when they were together. Of the early years she was later to say, 'Not only did I make no attempt at controlling his drinking, I valiantly attempted to out-drink him' (*Double Drink Story*, p. 13). When she started a family she was in two minds whether to join Dylan in drinking:

> . . . but I couldn't let him down. So I joined him, so unalterable was the habit of obedience to the drinking virus, like a well-trained soldier briskly responding under military orders (*Double Drink Story*, p. 96).

Later:

> It was always the same routine: I'd be there with him, night after night, once the children were in their beds. All that drinking became frightfully boring after a time. I didn't mind it so much then because I was so involved with Dylan . . . (Thomas and Tremlett, p. 120).

Not being a conventional wife was a matter of some pride and importance to Caitlin. In *Double Drink Story* (p. 145) she said, '. . . the very term "housewife", as applied to me, made me squirm with disgust'. Caitlin accompanied Dylan on one of his tours of the USA and found it uncomfortable. One of the wives who entertained her found her, '. . . unresigned to being the background wife' (cited by Ferris, p. 129), and in *Leftover Life to Kill* (p. 59) Caitlin herself said of that visit:

> To the best, most patient, understanding wife, my position was not an easy one; but to me, stiff with rancour, my own teeming passions fermenting angrily inside me, it was a hanging execution of my all-important pride.

In *Leftover* she explained how, immediately following Dylan's death she was unable to play the part of the bereaved 'perfect Lady' (p. 17) and felt the need to escape. In one of her unpublished autobiographical pieces, written years later, she talked about never giving up on, 'the eternal problem of how to be a passive, submissive, yet fully fledged woman' (cited by Ferris, p. 192). Like countless wives of men with drinking problems, before and since, Caitlin thought of separation, but the factors against it weighed too heavily. Several passages in *Caitlin: Life with Dylan Thomas*, are relevant:

> I don't know how I put up with it, but what alternative did I have? To go home to
> my mother's? I could have done, but I was still very attached to Dylan, and when
> the man you are living with is the father of your child it gives him a much greater
> hold over you . . . I did think sometimes of going back home to my mother's but
> thought that would probably be even worse. It's not much fun going back to your
> parents when you've failed . . . There were times when I thought that if only I
> could manage to leave him, for a short while, he would soon see what life was
> like without me, and then perhaps he would come back chastened; but I didn't
> seem able to do that, somehow: I never had the money . . . I was captured, and it
> seemed so unfair (pp. 85, 106, 144, 153).

Drawing on another of her unpublished autobiographical pieces, Paul
Ferris quotes her as saying that if it had not been for the children, 'I would
have left Dylan a million times and a million years ago' (p. 171).

Besides the plentiful evidence of a tolerant Caitlin, drinking along with
Dylan, increasingly embittered and trapped in her relationship with an
unfaithful and excessively drinking husband, there is another recurring
theme. Caitlin could certainly not be said to have been passively accepting
of Dylan's behaviour. She describes herself as robust, well built, strong and
physically more than a match for Dylan. As their marriage progressed they
rowed more and their arguments were often physical. In *Leftover* (pp. 34,
60–1), she wrote:

> . . . the times, more frequent at night, when the house rattled, and banged, and
> thudded, and groaned with our murder of each other . . . these fights, which were
> an essential part of our everyday life, and became fiercer and more deadly at
> each onslaught . . . It seems extraordinary to me now that we did not kill each
> other outright, we certainly got dangerously near to it, on those bloodthirsty
> vengeances.

In several places in the various accounts of their life there are mentions
of the occasion when Caitlin hit Dylan over the head with a heavy torch and
other occasions when they literally fought physically in front of visitors. In
Double Drink Story (p. 12) Caitlin later wrote:

> I am confronted with the conflicting images of ritualistic fights to the death on
> the floor of our bedroom at night . . . banging each other's heads as hard as we
> could, with drink-enraged force.

It is no accident that this tougher, retaliatory side of Caitlin's behaviour
towards Dylan figures much more prominently in Paul Ferris's biography

than in the book written jointly with George Tremlett. At one point Ferris writes, 'Her mood had hardened as she grew less inclined to put up with an erratic husband' (p. 102), and a little further on, to '. . . a harsher, unforgiving Caitlin' (p. 116). He quotes Dylan writing to a friend at that time about, '. . . the vituperation of my golden, loathing wife!' (p. 117).

Like so many other family members who live with someone with an addiction problem, Caitlin was critical of her own way of behaving. On their joint trip to the USA, when asked by one of Dylan's agents about Dylan and the problem of his drinking, she said, according to Ferris (p. 128), 'Oh . . . that isn't the problem. I am the problem.' In *Double Drink Story* (p. 95) she said, 'I carped at Dylan like a fishwife, and if anything is guaranteed to kill love, carping will do it'. Ferris quotes from a poem of Caitlin's, almost certainly, he believed, written towards the end of their marriage. She had called it *Self Portrait*. It began:

Is this me,
This carping crock

and ends:

Can this tame nag
Be hagridden me? (Ferris, pp. 242–3).

How did other people respond to Dylan's misbehaviour, and how did others view Caitlin's predicament? It was Caitlin's opinion that Dylan was surrounded by tolerant admirers. In *Double Drink Story* she refers to his mother and a landlady 'coddling' him (p. 24) and he being '. . . everybody's lovable professional baby' (p. 129). She told George Tremlett that, 'He needed a good lesson from someone: he was getting so spoilt. He had been spoilt by his mother and spoilt by me, and later he was spoilt by America' (Thomas and Tremlett, p. 94). She had the following to say about the ways Dylan's parents tried to cope with his drinking:

When I first went to Bishopston, it was Granny Thomas [Dylan's mother] who kept lecturing Dylan about his drinking. Sometimes he used to come back on the bus from Swansea completely drunk, and she would tell him the obvious things – 'You are spending far too much', 'You are ruining your health', 'Spending all your money' – all the old clichés, which were true enough. Dylan didn't like that at all. When he married, she expected him to turn over a new leaf, she thought that I would save him, although she should have had more sense than that. Maybe she thought that I would start nagging him when we needed more money for the children, but I didn't want to become a nagging wife. We used to have huge rows, but never about drinking. I didn't want to row with him about little things, and anyway, I was hardly in a position to do so. The rows were always about his 'ladies' (p. 46).

His parents were the only ones who disapproved, and he never went near them till he was primed up well and good. The parents knew their lectures would have no effect whatsoever on Dylan, but they had to keep on going through the motions even when they were long past controlling Dylan's actions (*Double Drink Story,* p. 137).

According to Paul Ferris (pp. 100–1) there was 'a sizeable band' of other women who sympathized with Caitlin. For example he quotes Gwen Watkins, Vernon's wife, as saying:

... although she made me uneasy and often indignant because of her behaviour in public, I was firmly on her side and against Dylan's treatment of her. Her life seemed to be intolerable (p. 95).

Cordelia [Locke], a neighbour when they lived at South Leigh near Oxford, described how Caitlin slaved away while Dylan rolled a cigarette or read a book, waiting for her to help him bath in front of the fire. Elisabeth [Lutyens], a composer friend, wrote of Dylan's 'mischievous cruelty' and the way he expected Caitlin to, 'forego all independence or life of her own, staying at home as wife and mother' (Ferris, p. 121). In *Leftover* Caitlin had written of the '... goodness and kindness, as I have never been shown it before' (p. 69) that she received from some people when visiting the USA with Dylan. According to Ferris (p. 128), her most consistent apologist in the USA was Rose [Slivka] who later wrote, 'The world was killing her ... She was the artist's wife, and that can be a terrible place to be'. Another long-standing family friend, Wyn [Henderson] was staying at the Boat House around 1951 when Caitlin showed her some of her own poems, including one called 'On Being Married to a Drunk'. Wyn wrote:

When I thought of the happy, carefree young Irish colt that had married Dylan in Cornwall from our 'Lobster Pot' I felt the utmost compassion as she read these poems, aloud, and shrank from the thought of the damage that had been done to her by life (Ferris, p. 173).

But it is the attitude of Paul Ferris, Caitlin's biographer, which for us is the most interesting of all, since his perspective on Caitlin is so reminiscent, in places, of the psychopathological and other 'expert' views of women who live with men with drinking problems. For a start, Ferris had a theory about the 'fit' between Dylan's and Caitlin's personality needs:

> [Dylan's]... trick was to hide himself in a safe, childlike state where the world couldn't get at him, clinging and being clung to. It was this game that Caitlin, from the start, agreed to play; though the rules changed often before it was over, sixteen years later. At the deepest level, she suited him. He, in turn, a poet who needed looking after, fitted her requirements; she liked and needed men to depend on her ... [her] wish ... [was] to have a man who would be lost without her ... he fell easily into the role of dependant ... At the root of this may be Francis Macnamara, the lost hero of Caitlin's life, the dazzling would-be poet who deserted them all when she was an infant, and had to be replaced in her life ... [Dylan was] the poet she thought she could now control, as she could never control the cruel Francis ... The role of successor waited for Dylan Thomas like a man trap (pp. 71, 75, 83).

Like many professional commentators on the marriages of men with drinking problems, Ferris took the argument further, apportioning blame to the 'hardened' and 'harsher' side of Caitlin that came more to the fore in the later years of their marriage. In places he comes near to claiming that she killed him:

> ... if Thomas in the last three years of his life is to be seen as a man adrift, his powers faltering and his options closing one by one, it is hard not to see Caitlin as one of the reasons. He was, indeed, a dependent man; without the guarantee of her affection, he was in trouble ... his crisis of confidence had another element, the crumbling of Caitlin's affection ... if her strength and security had been important to him throughout their life together, and there can be no doubt that it was, then the anger she displayed increasingly after 1951 can't have left him unmoved ... her willingness to heap humiliation on him ... This was the other element in his psychological downfall, which in turn made him reckless with his life, and would lead to his death ... His despair had put him in the way of encouraging death; he had found the only possible way out of the trap ... He certainly depended on her; a fatal dependence, as it turned out (pp. 116, 133–5, 142, 242).

Throughout his biography Ferris shows less interest in Dylan's excessive drinking than in Caitlin's infidelities – her 'sexual proclivities' as he calls them (p. 121). Both Caitlin and Dylan were repeatedly unfaithful, it seems, and Ferris is at pains to argue that Caitlin's infidelities preceded Dylan's.

Interestingly enough, Ferris admits that Caitlin's one criticism to him on reading his earlier biography of Dylan was: 'not enough emphasis on the booze, not only at the last but from the first: it ate up all our money and all our lives' (Ferris, p. 235).

Ferris's wish to pin some blame on Caitlin is explicit in many places in his biography of her. At one point (p. 126) he accuses her of blaming Dylan himself, plus the influence on him of the USA: 'Never herself, never for an instant'. Elsewhere, referring to that final letter that Caitlin sent to Dylan when he was on his final visit to the USA, Ferris wrote:

> The letter carried no hint of an admission that her actions may have contributed to his, just as his contributed to hers. But attack, for Caitlin, was always the best form of defence (p. 141).

Comment

There are similarities between the kind of research interviews that colleagues and I have carried out in our research programme – interviews that sometimes take many hours – and the process that George Tremlett and Caitlin Thomas engaged in which resulted in their book together. That is one of the things that makes it so relevant here. There are a number of aspects of life with a husband with a drinking problem that are as well described in that book as almost anywhere. One is the way in which a relationship can deteriorate to the point at which the affected family member, Caitlin in this case, feels trapped and bitter. The dilemma about whether to leave him, and the rehearsal of all the factors for and against that course of action, are particularly well put.

What makes Caitlin's story particularly poignant is the self-criticism that even a strong personality like Caitlin can demonstrate as the relationship deteriorated and she became more and more involved in arguing and fighting with Dylan. She had never wanted to nag him, in the way she thought conventional wives nagged their husbands, and in the end she was accusing herself of 'carping', being a 'nag'. The comparison with Sara Coleridge (see Chapter 16), who lived more than a hundred years earlier, is a close one. There are also similarities with the fictional Helen in *Tenant of Wildfell Hall* (see Chapter 5).

But it is the juxtaposition of Caitlin's own writing about herself, on her own or with George Tremlett's help, on the one hand, and, on the other hand, Paul Ferris's biography of her, which makes this such an important example for those who are interested in addiction and the family. The fact that he is critical of Caitlin's increasingly 'hard' and 'harsh' way with Dylan, even to the point of seeming to accuse her of contributing to Dylan's early death, could be dismissed as vindictive or eccentric were it not for the fact that this is just the kind of criticism that family members have been exposed to down the years. Even the so-called experts have often perpetrated misogynist ideas about the contribution of wives and mothers to the development and maintenance of their husbands' and children's addictions.

Questions

1. Do you read Caitlin's story as that of a wife affected by the excessive drinking of her husband, or as that of a fellow heavy drinker who encouraged his drinking by drinking along with him? What evidence is there for reading one way or the other?
2. Did Caitlin knowingly marry a man with a drinking problem?
3. Stripped down to its essentials, was her experience just like that of so many other affected family members, or was it different, her being the wife of one of the greatest poets?
4. Could she have been accused of being over-tolerant of Dylan's drinking? What else might she have done in her position? Should she have left him for example?
5. What do you make of the suggestion that Dylan's death was a liberation for her?
6. It is not unknown for wives affected by their husbands' addictions to use physical violence towards their husbands. Why do you think Caitlin did?
7. In his biography Paul Ferris appears to blame Caitlin for what happened to Dylan in his last years. Do you think he may have been right to do so, or was it a typical case of 'blaming the victim'?
8. Paul Ferris referred to a 'sizeable band' of other women who sympathized with Caitlin. Are the issues raised by Caitlin's story, gender issues? What would be a feminist perspective on her life with Dylan?

Exercises

- Take the role of Caitlin and formulate a reply to Paul Ferris. You can do this in any way you like. You might write your reply or you could speak it as a monologue.
- Caitlin was aware that she was putting up with Dylan's drinking, even encouraging it. But, like many affected family members, she recoiled from the idea of nagging him. If, in a professional capacity, you had met Caitlin at a time when the harmful nature of Dylan's drinking had become obvious to her, how might you have gone about helping her see that there were other options for her besides putting up with Dylan's drinking and nagging him about it? With the help of one other person, role-play your encounter with Caitlin.

12

Dylan Thomas in America
by John Malcolm Brinnin

This is a book, published within three years of Dylan Thomas's death, written by the US poet and academic who arranged all Dylan Thomas's tours to the USA and managed all his arrangements while he was there. It details all that went on between the two men in the mere three to four years between their first meeting and Dylan's death. The book, which created quite a stir at the time, has long been out of print. I got hold of it only with the intention of finding out if it had anything to say about Caitlin and her relationship with Dylan, which was not already apparent in her own autobiographical books or books about her. There was a little of that, but not a great deal. What I was not prepared for was the richness of the description that John Brinnin provided about his own relationship with Dylan. There cannot be many such descriptions anywhere that provide such detail about the relationship between a man with a drinking problem and his good friend. Brinnin became, in the short time they knew each other, and then only for brief periods when they were in the same country, rather like a male 'wife' in relation to Dylan. Many of the things that Brinnin wrote about the effect of Dylan's behaviour on his own feelings, and what he said about the dilemmas that he was placed in and the ambivalence he felt, would be recognized by wives of men with drinking problems the world over.

Addiction Dilemmas: Family Experiences from Literature and Research and their Challenges for Practice, First Edition. Jim Orford.
© 2012 John Wiley & Sons, Ltd. Published 2012 by John Wiley & Sons, Ltd.

Brinnin's description of Dylan's time in the USA is full of references to the amounts of alcohol he consumed, his love of bars, the neglect of other aspects of his diet, his coughing fits, increasingly ill appearance, occasional falls, drunken and sexually provocative behaviour at parties, and one occasion, highly embarrassing to Brinnin, when Dylan failed to turn up for a speaking engagement. Added to the discomfort that Dylan's behaviour caused Brinnin, the latter got caught up in colluding with at least three affairs that Dylan had in the USA. That, in turn, got him into deep water with Caitlin whom he first met when he visited Britain and who accompanied Dylan on his second trip to the USA. John Brinnin described a number of very tense and uncomfortable social occasions when the three of them were present together.

Why, then, did John Brinnin continue to expose himself to the uncertainties and discomforts that Dylan's trips must have occasioned for him? One answer must lie in the brilliance of the performances that Brinnin arranged for him. Not only was Dylan Thomas at the time considered to be one of the greatest English language poets living, but many thought him to be the best public speaker of poetry of his era. There was often doubt whether he would be well or sober enough to perform, but until the very end he always recovered sufficiently to give a dazzlingly successful public performance. Not only that, but Brinnin clearly admired Thomas greatly, even it might be said loved him. Brinnin became attached to him straightaway:

> Since I handled all of his lecture engagements, and all of his finances, we were always in touch and always together in matters having to do with his career. His sensitivity to every nuance of human exchange, his hilarious self-deprecating wit, along with his great generosity of mind and soul – qualities that kept him above and apart from the damning, dubious, or scurrilous things that were already said about him – had within the mere space of a week made him the most exhausting, exasperating, and most completely endearing human being I had ever encountered (pp. 33–4).

Later he writes of his conviction that, '. . . behind the irresponsible facade of Dylan Thomas there lay a core of responsibility few people would ever see' (p. 44).

As someone who was so committed to Dylan, and yet at the same time so exposed to his troublesome behaviour (he refers for example to receiving, almost daily during Dylan's first trip, 'Surly letters and other distressed telegrams . . . some of them blaming me for having foisted Dylan upon them. . .', p. 44), like a close family member he found himself in continual dilemmas about how and how much to try and control Dylan's behaviour. He described, for example, his dilemma at a party at which Dylan was floundering around blind drunk:

> I asked him as firmly as I dared and as gently as I could to come along with me to the hotel. He said he would but, even after I had repeated my suggestion several times, made no move to join me. I debated with myself. Should I somehow force him to leave? By what right could I force him to do anything? I did not know it then, but I was in the dead centre of a dilemma that was to recur a hundred times. It had become impossible for me to carry on conversation with anyone. To turn my eyes from Dylan was but to encounter faces the spectacle of him made sad and uncomfortable, eyes that implored me to do something. Goaded by them and by my new ill-fitting sense of responsibility I still could do nothing but loathe my indecision and wish that I were miles away (pp. 18–19).

Another recurring dilemma concerned money. Although for much of the time that Brinnin knew him Dylan was earning two or three times as much as Brinnin himself, Dylan always seemed to be out of pocket and it was Brinnin who was helping Dylan out with expenses and trying to think of ways that Dylan could save some money and not go back to Wales having squandered all his earnings. He tried to persuade Dylan to put money straight into a Welsh bank for example. He even secreted $800 in a handbag that he gave Dylan to take back as a present for Caitlin. When Caitlin joined Dylan in the USA she and Brinnin agreed to keep secret from Dylan the extra expenses that Brinnin was giving her.

Brinnin's ambivalence towards Dylan Thomas was apparent early on:

> I tried first to comprehend and then to accept the quality (it was too early to know the dimensions) of my assignment, whether it be that of reluctant guardian angel, brother's keeper, nursemaid, amanuensis [literary assistant], or bar-companion; no one term would serve to define a relationship which had overwhelmed my expectations and already forced upon me a personal concern that was constantly puzzled, increasing solicitous, and, I knew well by now, impossible to escape . . . I knew that, above all now, I wanted to take care of him, against my will to impose my notions of sanity on his; even, inadmissibly, to protect him from himself. Just as certainly, I knew that I wanted to get rid of him, to save myself from having to be party to his self-devouring miseries and to forestall any further waiting upon his inevitable collapses. Yet I could do neither. This weakness, this ability neither to reject nor to accept, neither wholly to go nor to stay, troubled the air through which now I had to witness the phenomenon of Dylan Thomas (pp. 15–16, 17).

A recurring theme throughout *Dylan Thomas in America* is John Brinnin's struggle between wanting to spend time with the man he so admires and is so attached to and, on the other hand, his inclination to avoid Dylan in the interests of self-preservation. This was already clear during Dylan's first US visit:

> The hangers-on who seemed to make up his interminable retinue depressed me, and I refused to be counted among them. If I could not see him at leisure, I would not see him at all. I had accepted the alcoholic tenor of his life, but it still appalled and saddened me ... I had become ill-tempered, insomnious for the first time in my life, neglectful of my friends – some of whom, barely acquainted with Dylan, looked upon him as a monster – and unable to concentrate upon my work. When all of these factors led to a grating distress that became daily more acute and seemed continually farther away from any chance of relief, I resolved to stay out of Dylan's orbit except when professional matters forced us together. If I could do nothing to stop his largely self-inflicted agonies, at least I did not have to suffer the helpless anxiety of watching them. Curbing a hundred impulses to phone him, to drop by at his hotel, or to join him casually at one or another of his Village [Greenwich Village, New York] haunts, I succeeded in living by this resolution for about ten days. When I next saw him ... 'You've deserted me', he said, almost fiercely (pp. 57–8).

And during a later visit:

> As far I could see, my previous intimate attendance with all the affection it implied and the sometimes dredging effort that it demanded, had done nothing to help him or to make him happy; it had only reduced me to a kind of nervous despair. While my new attitude was self-protective, it was also dictated by a recognition I had never expected to make and never believed I could accept – the fact that Dylan's way of life was not merely wearisome and tiring but that, ultimately, it was just plainly boring (p. 144).

According to Brinnin the nature of their relationship was never openly addressed by the two men except in the form of jokes. For example on a trip to Europe Brinnin went first to Italy and then on to see Dylan in Wales:

> While he had long ago seen every evidence that I would choose to be with him over every other acquaintance I had made in the course of my travels, he still found satisfaction in teasing me into an explicit statement of preference for which I could never find the words (p. 168).
>
> ... I spoke again my decision not to be involved in its arrangements [concerning the possibility of a future tour]. In giving substance to this decision I made little of my reluctance to commit myself to another six months of onerous

correspondence, schedule-making, and vicarious financial anxiety, emphasizing only the harm I knew Dylan would be doing to himself. I had still never made clear to Dylan, except as a sort of conspiratorial joke between us, the devastation such responsibilities had brought to my general peace of mind and my attempts to get on with my own creative work (p. 173).

Brinnin strongly advised against another tour of the USA, not only because of the stress it caused Brinnin himself, but also because he had become convinced that the US tours were a factor in Dylan's fading creativity as a poet. But Dylan insisted on his last trip, a fateful one as it turned out.

Wives of men with drinking problems have so often been misunderstood, even blamed (as Caitlin was by Ferris – see Chapter 11), that it is fascinating to find that Brinnin had suffered the same fate at the hands of James Nashold (a doctor who made very thorough investigations of Dylan Thomas's health record and the circumstances of his death) and George Tremlett (the same author who helped Caitlin Thomas produce such an interesting autobiography) in their book, *The Death of Dylan Thomas,* published in 1997. They concluded that Dylan's heavy drinking had been exaggerated, that the major underlying cause of his ill health was undiagnosed diabetes, and that his death was caused by inappropriate medication that was given without proper tests being carried out. That is as may be, but what is so striking, knowing how readily family members – or, as in this case, a close friend and colleague – are criticized for the positions they take, is the vindictiveness with which Nashold and Tremlett deal with John Brinnin. Much as Paul Ferris appears to blame Caitlin Thomas for contributing to Dylan's downfall (see Chapter 11), so do Nashold and Tremlett accuse Brinnin of contributing to Dylan's posthumous reputation as a drunkard and, by failing to protect him on his last visit to the USA or making sure he had the best treatment, of playing a part in his premature and unnecessary death.

Comments

What so intrigued me about this book was the way it seemed to show how the experiences of close family members, affected by a relative's addictive behaviour, can be shared by someone who is not a member of the family at all, who has never even lived under the same roof, and who certainly does not have the long-term commitment of a mother, father, partner or child. This seems to suggest that the experiences of people who are closely touched by the drinking, drug-taking or gambling of another person are as much to do with the nature of addiction and what it does to relationships, as they are to do with the nature of particular types of relationship such as that of a woman to her problem drinking husband, or that of a mother and her problem drug-taking son or daughter.

But I wonder how many friends or work colleagues find themselves in the kind of special relationship with someone with a drinking problem as John Brinnin did with Dylan Thomas. As I was writing the first draft of this chapter we had recently had in the UK the funeral of Georgie Best, one of our greatest footballers of all time, who died prematurely of alcohol-related illness following many years of a highly publicized struggle with a drinking problem; and a minor political crisis over the revelation by the leader of one of our political parties that he had indeed been fighting a much rumoured but only now publicly disclosed, drinking problem. I cannot help thinking that in both cases there must have been fellow players and parliamentarians, and managers and party officers, and personal friends, as well as family members, who had been very concerned and who agonized over what to do. The extraordinary thing about John Brinnin's relationship with Dylan Thomas was that he only knew him for a period of a few years and was in direct contact with him only for a few short periods of weeks at the most, yet in that time he assumed a role that had certain features of a close family member and a close work colleague rolled into one. He even got bound up, as family members do, in matters financial. He was subject to the embarrassment, uncertainty, discomfort, criticism at second hand, that are all too familiar to family members. In fact while he was in contact with him, he shared many of the experiences known to Dylan's wife Caitlin.

Here again is that familiar ambivalence. Of course he wanted to be with Dylan. They were fellow poets, and it was a great opportunity for Brinnin to be the person responsible for bringing Dylan on tour to the USA. He admired him greatly, saw the good in him, thought of himself and Dylan as soul mates. Seeing Dylan ill and distressed, part of him was inclined to try and take care of him. But, like family members, Brinnin found himself playing a number of roles in relation to Dylan, not all of which were ones he had anticipated or found comfortable. Had he become, for example, a nursemaid, lowly assistant, or simply a bar-companion? Not surprisingly he experienced the same dilemmas over which family members agonize. To be with Dylan or to avoid him? To ignore his behaviour at a party or to try to force him to leave? To use devious tactics to conserve some of the money he was earning or to let him squander it all? To accept his behaviour whilst being appalled by it, or to stand up against it? These are some of the basic dilemmas that all family members face when there is an addiction problem, and Brinnin experienced them in acute form. He even describes the acute effects on his own health and well-being that are so familiar, very often in chronic form, in the accounts of family members. He wrote of becoming ill-tempered, losing sleep, being unable to concentrate on work, neglecting his friends, and generally suffering from a kind of nervous despair.

A final twist to this revealing story concerns John Brinnin's relationship with Caitlin. At the time they were probably the two people closest to Dylan, and they both had experiences with him of such intensity that they each wrote a book about it – more than one book in Caitlin's case. Many of their experiences were very similar, in essence one might say identical. They might have shared so much. Yet, the relationship between the two of them was a tense one, very occasionally involving joint actions – for example to make sure Caitlin got some of the money that Dylan was earning in the USA – but mostly not, because of Caitlin's distaste for Dylan's trips to the USA and, among other things, Brinnin's knowledge of Dylan's romantic liaisons.

Questions

1. Do you think it is possible for a friend or work colleague to have the same experiences in this situation as a wife, mother or other close family member? Was John Brinnin a special, untypical case? Were his experiences exaggerated in the telling, or perhaps only fleeting?
2. Is there something inherent in what addiction does to relationships?
3. What would you have done, had you been in John Brinnin's shoes, at the party where Dylan was drunk and causing everybody embarrassment?
4. What would you have done, in Brinnin's position, regarding the financial side of the tour that you were organizing for Dylan?
5. Brinnin expressed the fear that he had fallen into the role of being Dylan's guardian or nurse maid, or even the role of bar-companion. Can you think of other roles which affected family members might inadvertently find themselves taking on?
6. Have you personally known of a friend or work colleague who had a drinking, drug or gambling problem? If so, what action did you take

about it, if any, and how satisfied were you with any action that you took?

7.   John Brinnin and Caitlin Thomas were central figures in Dylan's social network at a crucial time in his life. Can you think of any way in which they might have got together to combine forces to help him?

Exercises

- You have been aware for some time that a senior person at work, whom you admire and who plays a vital role, has become dependent on alcohol and that it is affecting his or her work and the happiness and success of the organization. Hold a group discussion with two or three of your colleagues about what you should do. Consider the pros and cons of each suggested course of action.

- This time the person you are concerned about is a close friend and as far as you know no one else knows about his or her excessive drinking. List the possible courses of action that you might take and the pros and cons of each.

13

An Imaginary Conversation

Wives in Mexico, England, South Korea and Italy

Because in the course of our group's research, and reading reports of others' research, we have heard what wives in different parts of the world have said about living with husbands with drinking or drug problems, and because their stories contain so much that is similar, I have often imagined what it would be like if women from very different parts of the globe and from different cultures were to meet and to share their experiences. The conversation I picture is imaginary because, with very few exceptions, women in that position are trapped in their own worlds. If they were to meet there might be a language barrier to start with. But if that could be overcome I believe they would recognize the other women's circumstances as their own. Perhaps, in a more realistic but still quite unlikely scenario, they might meet as co-presenters at an international conference on addiction and the family, with simultaneous translation facilities.

Imaginary or not, I think they would have much to say to each other. Let's listen in to a part of their conversation where they are talking about the problems they have had, as wives of men with drinking and drug problems, including the difficulties they have experienced in getting a helpful response from other people such as other family members, friends or professionals.

Addiction Dilemmas: Family Experiences from Literature and Research and their Challenges for Practice, First Edition. Jim Orford.
© 2012 John Wiley & Sons, Ltd. Published 2012 by John Wiley & Sons, Ltd.

The imagined meeting is between Esther from Mexico, Reberta from Italy, Mrs Lim from South Korea (she prefers the more formal mode of address) and Sylvia from England. Esther lives with her husband of 20 years and one of their three older teenage children in their own home in an area on the edge of Mexico City. The area in which they live she describes as marginal and lacking in almost all the basic services. Reberta lives with her husband of 15 years and their two pre-adolescent children in a village in the south Italian countryside not far from Naples. Mrs Lim has also been married for 15 years and lives with her husband and their two children in a provincial South Korean town where her husband was brought up and where her in-laws still live. Sylvia has been married for 30 years and she and her husband live together – their children are grown up and have left home – in a comfortable suburb in the city of Bristol in south-west England.

What follows is closely based on what was said to research interviewers by four actual women in those countries. Each figured in either a book on the subject of addiction and the family (in the cases of the Italian and English women) or a university masters or doctorate thesis (in the Mexican and South Korean cases). This is how the imaginary conversation might go:

Esther

Shall I start? I knew my husband drank from an early age, from as young as 12 years old, but I thought he'd settled down when we married. He worked and supported us. But he started to drink again when the children were small and started to spend money going out on his own to nice hotels and restaurants without me. He was neglecting his duties as a husband and father to the point of the children going hungry. So then his mother started to look after the children and I went out to work. Since then his drinking has got worse. Eventually they got fed up with him at work and he lost his job, since when he started to drink every day and I support the family. My main concern has been to get him into hospital but I'm frightened of his reaction. He once said to me, 'If you do that I shall kill you'. I suppose in a way he's right; we ought to be able to resolve the problem at home.

Sylvia

My husband's had a problem for as long as I can remember. He always managed to work although he had lots of days off when he had a hangover and in the end he had to retire early on health grounds. He always drank a lot in the evenings and at weekends and it got worse as time went on and particularly after the children left home and then after he retired. He is a very strict, obsessive man and he gets worse when he's been drinking. He becomes a kind of tyrant when he's drunk. He lectures me and criticizes me for all manner of things. He even threatens me and makes me stand to attention while he tells me off. If I answer back he gets so angry and starts to shake me. It's been a big strain on me. It's an awful lot to carry, a lot to keep secret. I've dealt with the problem over the years by hiding it from everybody. It was a sort of conspiracy of silence. Nobody wanted to acknowledge the problem openly.

Mrs Lim

I have endured the same thing. After drinking my husband orders me to stand up and sit down repeatedly. I have to do as I'm told, otherwise he would beat me with a stick. My marriage was arranged by a match-maker when I was 23. The match-maker told my mother about my husband-to-be. After meeting him only once, my mother and brother told me I should marry him and I just followed their decision. When I got married I noticed he drank a lot. After a few years, he started to beat me, and life became very difficult. I contacted my mother-in-law for help but she said it was not serious. My children were afraid of him. He constantly hurled abuse at them. I told my children never to challenge his behaviour, no matter how bad, as he was still their father and they should respect him. I put up with it and just cried by myself. I feel really ashamed that my husband is an alcoholic. I do not want to tell anybody. Nobody knows I was beaten.

Reberta

My problem is a bit different because my husband takes drugs, heroin and cocaine, but otherwise I have the same problems. I have been fighting against this problem of my husband's for 10 years, but now I feel as if I'm going under (she cries). When he's not on drugs he's a very good and affectionate father and husband and we've had some good times. He was doing well on medication but then a few months ago something changed and he began on the cocaine again and now we're back where we started. If he doesn't resolve his drug problem it'll get worse and worse for me. Our financial situation goes from bad to worse when he's on drugs and I'm frightened of how aggressive he can get with cocaine. I am not getting any sleep at nights and I get palpitations. I'm always nervous and sad. I just can't take it anymore. I don't know what to do now and I'm not even sure what I feel for him anymore. I certainly don't feel any physical desire for him at the moment.

Esther

It's the unpredictability of his behaviour when he's drunk and the violence and aggression towards me and our 16-year-old daughter that is the most stressful thing. Until recently I've done nothing because I felt so frightened. I always just did what he wanted, including letting him insult me, and even having sexual relations with him when I didn't want to which made me particularly disgusted because when he came home after having been drinking he was often dirty and smelly.

Reberta

I feel a great sense of guilt about the children. My second, particularly, I think needs more attention from me. I feel guilty for not being a good enough mother. I get overwhelmed with anxiety and can't think straight sometimes; and then I think it's my children who are paying the price. I do try and hide the problem from my children. I think they know their father is ill and that's all.

Esther

My husband's drinking was a factor in my two older children leaving home. The daughter's at university now and has a grant and lives there, and my son is living with his aunt, my sister, whom he works with. My children have several times said to me things like, 'Why did you marry him?' Life with him has involved a lot of patience, a lot of sacrifice, perhaps it's because of love or because of the way I was brought up. My grandmother said that marriage is for always and one should always be faithful to your husband. I am not going to leave my home and I shall put up with it all, but the situation is very hard. I would only separate if he asked me to do so.

Mrs Lim

I had never thought of divorcing my husband, but life became so unbearable and one day I left him. I took the children but we had nowhere to live. I asked my sister-in-law to put us up for a few days, but when I was coming from work I discovered my sister-in-law had locked the door and my children were wandering in the street. I was very upset and I had no option but to return home. I wanted to be loved by my husband and I was hoping we might still have a chance of being happy again. I was influenced by my mother not to break up my family and, 'to put my children before myself' as she put it. She had seven of us and we lived in a hut but she never divorced and endured the hardship. If my family knew my troubles they would be very upset. I often felt like shooting him but in fact I would prefer to be beaten by him. My parents-in-law would also be very upset if I left my husband. I do not want to cause them pain. I have decided to accept my cross and get on with life. That is my life and my destiny. I told my parents I was going to leave him. But my parents and my parents-in-law objected. They said if I sought a divorce, it would damage both families', what do you call it?, '*chemyn*' (this causes the translator some hesitation, but she suggests 'face' or 'image' as the English equivalent). My parents-in-law persuaded me not to divorce and said if I remained and reared their grandchildren they would support me financially. I agreed but I did not expect anything from my husband. I just wish I did not have to see him again. I always thought if I left my husband I would never miss him, but I cannot leave my daughters behind me. If my children were males it would be different: my husband and his family would take care of them. But I am sure they would reject my daughters if I left. On many occasions I have packed my bag to leave my husband. I wanted to drown myself in the river. But my daughter followed me and begged me to come back, so I had to return to my house. Now I have to work in a public bath house during the day and delivering milk early each morning.

Reberta

I feel as if I've devoted my whole life to my husband and I've neglected myself in the process. I never go anywhere on my own. I go everywhere he goes. I can't simply ignore the situation. I couldn't cope with not knowing where he's going; he could spend all my money and things would get even worse. At least keeping tabs on him makes me feel less anxious. I'd feel guilty if I left him alone. Something bad could easily happen to him. Do you think it would be better if I sat back a bit? Perhaps he might realize that I just no longer have the strength to put up with things. He might be surprised and perhaps he might think that he could lose me after all. The only person I really have to turn to is my mother, but she is elderly and ill now and I have to protect her from knowing what is really happening to me. But it's more difficult to hide things from her than it is for the children because I often turn to her when I need money and I know I sometimes come up with excuses that don't stand up.

Sylvia

For a long time I didn't feel I could talk to other people about his drinking either, because it was unacceptable and other people wouldn't know how to deal with it. I once talked to my mother about it when she was staying with us and he had got very drunk, but she just thought it was because it was New Year and not an ongoing problem. I think she found it too hard to cope with then, although later my parents were very supportive when we were on holiday together and they were shocked about the way he behaved towards me. They didn't really get angry with him because they could see he had a problem of some kind. They wrote to him saying they wanted to help but that just turned him against them. I was close to both my parents but I haven't told either of them about his drinking. Later on I told my mother and she came to stay while he was in treatment and we both went to visit him together, but I never spoke to my father about my husband's drinking even though I spent a lot of time with both of them just before my father died, and I had very deep talks with him.

Esther

When I began to take over the responsibility of supporting the family, I stopped feeling submissive to him and started making my own decisions. Before that, I would only sit down and cry. Now, even though I don't know how to read, I feel I can do many things with the help of friends and neighbours. Sometimes I feel I hate him, but now I know I can make my own decisions and, yes, he is my husband and I owe him respect, but only to a certain point. I think you should detach your feelings from your husbands a bit as I have done. I'm proud of the fact that I work hard to support the family which he should be doing. I leave home at 4.30 every day to go to my morning job in a plastics factory and then on to my domestic job in a private house in the afternoon, getting back home every evening at 9 o'clock.

Sylvia

I eventually got help from Al-Anon [for family members of 'alcoholics']. I heard about them through a friend. I hadn't known about alcoholism until I started going to meetings and then it was quite an eye opener. I didn't like the first meeting I went to and felt disloyal talking about him, and I didn't like the horror stories the others told, it was too near the knuckle. But I continued going because I found support there. They were the only people who had been through it and could really understand, and it was through Al-Anon that I realized that the only person I had control over was myself. They taught me little things as well, for example when he was telling me off and making me stand to attention I could look beyond him or at his ear rather than into his eyes, and if I kept my coat near the door I could leave if I wanted to, which was a strategy I often used whether it was raining or cold or even if I had no money. I would just stand at a local shop or land on neighbours. I had thought that no one else knew what was going on but in fact I discovered that all my neighbours knew. Once I spoke about it they were sympathetic and said they'd seen him shaking me through the window. But until then I found doctors and others unhelpful. My husband's GP wanted him to go to the local alcohol treatment clinic but because he was reluctant to go the doctor said, 'Well I'm afraid you're not reduced to a low enough level yet. You've got a lot more drinking to do before you're going to be ready for this', and sent him away. I could see in a sense he was right but I thought it was really unhelpful. Having a lot more drinking to do was exactly what he wanted to hear. Later he saw a psychiatrist who said that his problem was only habitual and therefore not a major problem. I saw that reasoning as stupid. It really meant that the doctor was not willing to get him into a detoxification unit which my husband saw as the only possible solution because he didn't trust himself and thought he needed a doctor or nurses on the premises 24 hours a day while he dried out. I saw my own GP frequently and at first he wasn't that concerned. He was a Christian who believed in the sanctity of marriage and all he really said was that I must have a lot of grace to put up with the marriage. I found that a comfort but on reflection I think his attitude probably contributed to me staying with my husband. But I began going to church again and became very interested in reading books about Christian lives including someone who had suffered a lot of persecution and hardship in her life and I felt there were similarities with my own situation. Sometimes you can know the angels are around you keeping you safe and after it's over you thank God for keeping you safe. My religion kept me going, but because of all that had happened I was not actively religious. I felt that Him upstairs had forgotten I exist.

Reberta

I don't know who to turn to. I don't have friends and then when there's this tragedy in a family no one wants to know, you feel it in your bones because if you approach someone they stop talking. Still, it may also be perhaps that I'm prejudiced and to avoid their questions I'm the one who closes the conversation. I tell you this because I remember that when I noticed my husband's problem, I was so ashamed to go out of the house because I feared that people would come up to me and ask me about him. You know, I live in a little place and my husband's family is well known in the village. Just think, I didn't even go out to do the shopping. Now I go out, I take the children to school, but all my comings and goings are full of anxiety and fear, it's as if I was scared of other people. My husband works with his brother. I can't stand him and I think he takes advantage of my husband. He's treated me badly so many times. More than once, he has accused me of not being a good wife and of only getting on with housework without keeping an eye on my husband. More than once he has accused me of being the cause of his brother's drug addiction and, sometimes, he has even thought that I have been his accomplice because once I went with my husband to buy smuggled cigarettes and instead it was cocaine. His brother got to hear of this episode and you can imagine what he thought of me. Not only that but also I asked him to help me at a most distressing time in my life and he refused. Two years ago my husband was arrested. I had asked his brother to go with me to talk with my husband, but he refused and he and his family left me completely alone to manage a situation that was absolutely new to me.

Mrs Lim

I've also been accused of being the cause of my husband's problem, for example by my mother-in-law when I asked for her permission to send my husband to a psychiatric hospital. I had him admitted anyway and my in-laws were furious when they discovered it. When I asked for help from my neighbours, they said, 'How can a man survive without a drink in our society?' 'You should change your attitude towards your husband's drinking.' After this incident I never asked for help again. When I talked about my husband's drinking problem, people laughed at me, saying I should try harder to make my husband happier in bed. I have tried every way to make him happy so he would stop drinking. I do not want to socialize with my friends and neighbours because I feel they only are interested in gossip. I try to avoid them as much as possible. Now I do as I'm told and everybody praises me saying that I am a typical 'good Korean woman' because I am quiet and patient. They say I look after my husband very well and I am very patient with his drinking behaviour. I lost my self-confidence over my husband's drinking problem. When I meet someone I feel uncomfortable. I am conscious that they know the truth about him. I went to see the psychiatrist but he said I was too sensitive about my husband's drinking problem. He also said any man can drink like my husband. It's natural and he advised me to accept his drinking.

Comments

Perhaps such a meeting would seem forced and not be the success I antici- pated. The cultural and material differences between the four women might simply be too great for them to be able to identify with one another.

For example it would be very easy to attribute much of Mrs Lim's ex- perience to the very traditional, hierarchical family structure, which some would ascribe in part to the legacy of Confucianism, that she was living under. It placed wives like Mrs Lim in a subservient position in relation to her husband and to her mother-in-law in a way that might seem alien to women living in Europe in the early twenty-first century. Her marriage had been arranged, so there was no way that she could be accused, as in some older Western theories of alcohol problems and marriage, of having consciously or unconsciously 'chosen' a husband who drank excessively. Her in-laws were unsympathetic when she tried to distance herself from her husband or tried to arrange treatment for him. In fact at times they actively aided and abetted her husband's violence towards her. For her in-laws, and even for her own parents, the preservation of the marriage and avoidance of the shame that would fall on both their families if the marriage were to break up was more important than Mrs Lim's happiness, and sometimes that was made quite explicit to her. She preferred not to talk about the problem to other people such as neighbours for fear of gossip. When she did, they responded in a way that suggested that she was exaggerating, that her husband had a right to drink, and even that she might be to blame for not looking after his sexual needs better. Even a psychiatrist she spoke to implied that she was being over-sensitive. She had thought of both suicide and homicide, but had settled for putting up with it, enduring the pain, and being a good, patient Korean wife.

Might it also be difficult for the Europeans to identify with Esther, an illiterate woman working all hours to support her family in conditions of poverty on the periphery of one of the largest cities in Latin America? She has been in the position of having to give in to her husband's demands and he has even threatened to kill her if she tries to get him hospitalized. Perhaps she would find it difficult to identify with those like Sylvia, living in much more comfortable material circumstances.

But are those four women's circumstances actually very different? Esther would certainly understand how family pressures, like those Mrs Lim was subject to, can stifle any ambition to leave home and become independent, because she has been subject to and has absorbed the same family norms.

Mrs Lim would sympathize with Esther's long hours away from home working because she also does two jobs in order to make ends meet. But there are fundamental issues that link all these women's experiences. Reberta would well understand Esther's and Mrs Lim's sacrifices in the face of their husbands' drinking because she feels she has also been forced to neglect herself and devote her whole life to her husband because of concern about his drug-taking. She has taken on a sense of guilt herself because she thinks in the process she has neglected her children. She knows what it is to be accused by members of her husband's family for being part of the problem rather than the victim of it. Both Reberta and Sylvia could share with Mrs Lim and Esther the experience of fear in the face of aggression and violence or threats of it. Reberta is frightened of her husband's cocaine-related aggression and Sylvia can describe her husband's threatening tyrannical behaviour.

One of the things that unites these women is the common experience of feeling that they needed to hide the problem – in order to protect children or older relatives, to avoid malicious gossip in the local community, or simply because of the stigma, shame and misunderstanding that was thought to attach to husbands' drink or drug problems. Sylvia particularly acknowledged the strain of keeping such a problem secret. She referred to it as a kind of 'conspiracy of silence'. She later found out that neighbours had known much more about it than she had thought. She had a lot to say – much of which the others would have concurred with – about the unhelpful, often critical, response of some other family members, neighbours and even, sadly, doctors. Neighbours knew but said nothing. Sympathetic friends and relatives did not really understand or might give rather too strong, one-sided advice. Her GP was not very concerned at first, and being a Christian who believed in the sanctity of marriage said comforting words that may have contributed to her putting up with the problem. She was disappointed in the advice of a psychiatrist who told her husband that his drinking was only habitual and not a major problem. When she finally went to Al-Anon, where she did feel she got help and support, she initially felt disloyal talking about her husband.

Questions

1. If Esther, Reberta, Sylvia and Mrs Lim could be brought together, and language problems overcome, do you think they would see themselves as having shared the same experience? Or would the differences in their

circumstances make them feel that they did inhabit different worlds, despite all having husbands with drinking or drug problems?

2. Do conditions of poverty make the experience a qualitatively different one or does the experience of having a husband with a drinking or drug problem remain essentially the same whether the family is poor or well off?

3. Are these women in a sense their own worst enemies when it comes to covering up for their husbands and keeping the problems secret? What is to stop them being much more open about the problems? How could they be helped to do so?

4. Esther advises the others to detach their feelings a bit from their husbands, to be your own person and to make your own decisions even whilst remaining at home and putting up with things. What do you think the others would have made of that advice? Is it feasible? Is it a good idea?

5. Sylvia likens her situation to that of people who have been persecuted, for example for their religious beliefs. Does that analogy strike you as apt? What other sets of circumstances do you think are similar to those faced by these four women?

6. Neighbours, friends and other relations do not come out of these four stories very well. What can a good friend or neighbour say or do if someone hints that a close relative has an addiction problem?

7. Does religion always have to be a factor in favour of a family member putting up with this kind of adversity, or can it sometimes be a force for change?

8. Sylvia spoke highly of her experience attending Al-Anon. Closely related to Alcoholics Anonymous, Al-Anon is a mutual-help organization for those affected by someone else's 'alcoholism'. Whether you are familiar with the organization or not, what do you believe may be the special ways in which it might be helpful?

9. Can a case be made for saying that their husbands' drinking or drug use was incidental; what these women are describing is the common experience of patriarchy, domestic violence and women's oppression?

Exercises

- Concerned family members often regret remaining silent about their worries over relatives' drinking, drug or gambling problems. With one other person in your group generate some ideas about how a family member might be more open with other people about the problem in a way that could be helpful. Then share the ideas you have generated with the larger group.

- Write a 'protocol' for how a good neighbour should act if the neighbour suspects that a local family is being affected by one of its member's addiction problem.

14

Father Figure by Beverley Nichols

In the early 1970s, Beverley Nichols, a writer of fiction and non-fiction who was popular in the 1950s and 1960s, wrote a book called *Father Figure: An Uncensored Autobiography*. It recounts Beverley's story of having been brought up with a father who drank excessively. In many ways the experiences that are described are quite typical of the stories of sons and daughters of parents with drinking problems. But what is brought out so clearly in *Father Figure* is the divergence of stances taken by different family members towards the close relative whose drinking is excessive. In the case of the Nichols family, as is not uncommon, it was the son, Beverley, who developed what may appear to be a harsh and unforgiving attitude towards his father, and his mother who, at least from Beverley's perspective, took a more tolerant, self-sacrificing position.

The book begins with an illustration of an experience early on in Beverley's life, when he was aged six, witnessing his father drunk and injuring himself. There follows a description of a typical sequence of stages through which his father's drinking would repetitively pass. There would be a period of drinking round about a half bottle of whisky a day when his father would be foul to everyone, particularly his mother. That would be followed by a period of the heaviest drinking of all, at least a full bottle a day. That

Addiction Dilemmas: Family Experiences from Literature and Research and their Challenges for Practice, First Edition. Jim Orford.

would lead to a period in which his father was bedridden and the family therefore temporarily relieved, followed by some days of remorse and penitence, and finally a period of normality and sobriety for a few days before the next bout. So predictable was the pattern that Beverley and the rest of the family were acutely sensitive to the smallest of signs of his father's drinking. One such clue would be his father whistling softly to himself. His mother would go rigid if they came home to hear that noise because he never whistled when he was sober. There was the lavish use of cream to anoint the ends of his moustache, and the slight twitch of his right eyebrow, both of which were further signs that drinking had started. He believed he could gauge how much his father had been drinking by the way he carved a chicken.

In several places in his book Beverley tells of the foul, obscene language that his father would use to his mother. Mostly he did this when his sons could not hear but inevitably they overheard him on occasions. He describes the relationship between his father and mother as one of master and slave. He tells the reader also of some of the effects he felt his father's drinking had on himself as a child. One effect was a state of nervous tension, constantly listening and looking for the signs of his father having been drinking:

> When one's youth is lived at this perpetual state of nervous pressure, listening for the quality of the footstep outside a door – (is it firm or is it shaky?) – watching the grip of fingers round a carving knife – (if the thumb sticks out at a certain angle it means he is beginning again) – lying awake at night, trying to interpret the groans coming from the next room – (I learned to tell by their pitch and rhythm whether they betokened remorse, anger, or a simple attack of vomiting) – with all these signposts, the steps of youth (and the very echo of those steps) are remembered all too clearly (p. 12).

Another was the effect it had on making friendships, the inhibition Beverley remembered feeling about going to other people's homes and particularly about inviting people to his own. For example, describing one remembered occasion when he had not taken up another boy's invitation to go to his home for tea, he wrote:

> I was longing to go to tea with that boy, but 'home' to me was a place of guilty secrets. You must not ask people in to visit you casually; that would be courting disaster. They might come only after the most careful preparation and at certain very clearly defined periods, when 'he' was at the end of a bout, confined to bed – (but even then you had to be careful about the groans) – or a week later, when 'he' was up and about, shaky but sober, preparing to begin again (p. 13).

Beverley's distaste for the position his mother adopted is a main theme of the book and is introduced early on:

> . . . a conversation which I heard not once but a hundred times. It was my mother's theme throughout life. It is not *him* . . . it is a disease. I have heard that in Spring, Summer, in Autumn and in Winter – in the morning, in the noon and the night. I heard it as a child, as an adolescent, as a young man, and as a man on the threshold of middle age. Not *him* . . . the disease. In the face of insult, of humiliation, of peak disaster, my mother was faithful to this theme. She never changed her tune (p. 11).

Beverley described his mother's behaviour towards his father as very protective. One of the motives for this seems to have been that of avoiding a public scandal. It appeared to be very important to his mother that his father was not allowed to wander outside the house, perhaps looking for a drink, when he was in a bout. Hence it would be preferable to give him drink when he needed it rather than to let him go outside for it. They even had drink ready themselves in a special place to give him when he was at that stage. At one point there is even mention of the way that his mother would protect his father from the dustman knowing because of the mounting pile of empty whisky bottles. She spent much energy and ingenuity disposing of the bottles because it was so important that the dustman should not *know*. Her loyalty Beverley viewed as misplaced: 'When my mother spoke her wedding vows she was sealing her death warrant . . . There are situations in life when loyalty is akin to lunacy' (pp. 159–60).

By contrast Beverley himself came to adopt a different view:

> I did pity him. For many, many years, the long, long years of youth . . . There is an end to pity, and it is right that there should be an end for there comes the time when it is covering over the face of truth (p. 71).
>
> 'A soft answer turneth away rot'. I heard her say that a hundred times. I violently disagreed with this philosophy; and I believe it to be a fatal one with regards to my father. In his case there was only one effective form of treatment – physical violence. He had to be hurt, and hurt very hard. He had to be made to suffer great physical pain, and the day was to come when I was to be the instrument of his suffering. I have not the smallest regret about this, although I write as one who believes that cruelty is the worst of all sins . . . but . . . in such circumstances . . . it was a form of self-defence, and, in its way, a last desperate attempt to cure him where all other therapies had failed (pp. 36–7).

Halfway through the book he recounts his first two attempts to murder his father, or at least that is how he now interprets it. One was with drugs, the second attempt to run him down with the garden roller – neither was successful. It is not clear quite what age he was at the time but he must have been in the middle years of childhood. Later he recounts his third attempt to murder his father when he found him alone in Beverley's own country cottage and he left him outside in the garden to freeze to death. Again it didn't work. Immediately his father had recovered from this episode Beverley threatened that he would kill him if it ever happened again. This is probably the first time that he had actually spoken in such a way and directly to his father and he felt his father was outraged, astonished and genuinely frightened. He says there is a moral to this part of the story, because for six whole months his father continued to abstain. Beverley was constantly in and out of the 'haunted house' (the expression that he used to refer to the various homes that they had while he was a child and later after he had left home himself) and every time they met he gave him the same message although not necessarily spoken. It didn't last – Beverley was called away to the USA and his father began to drink again.

Beverley's older brother Paul is also mentioned. He went into the church and appears to have adopted a life-long attitude towards their father similar to their mother's. Beverley contrasts Paul's forgiveness with his own condemnation and hatred for his father. His father and mother, and then his father after his mother's death, lived with Paul, and Beverley clearly thinks that Paul's potential was severely wasted throughout his life by the influence of his father.

The book ends with a description of his mother making 'her only gesture of independence in 40 years of married life', by drawing up a new will leaving things to the boys – it looks as if Beverley was partly instrumental in at least helping her resolve to do this. He was then able to break the news of the change of the will to his father and obviously got a great deal of delight, in a way, from doing this and seeing his father's reaction.

Comments

It is very common for different members of the same family to adopt contrasting positions towards the addictive behaviour of a close relative. Beverley Nichols' family was a striking example. Beverley's own stance, as described in his autobiography, was bitter and tough, even to the point of recommending that physical violence is an appropriate response to make towards the addicted relative. He describes murderous feelings towards his father, and even occasions when Beverley was a boy and again as a man when he acted towards his father in a way that he interpreted as homicidal.

Certainly, the experiences he had as a child living with his father are very familiar to those who have lived with a parent with a serious addiction problem and to those who have talked at any length to people who have done so. Witnessing arguments between parents and seeing one parent subject the other to verbal and sometimes physical abuse, are common elements of that experience, and are ones that are particularly salient in the memories of people who have lived through experiences like Beverley's. The sensitivity to signs of the parent's addictive behaviour, in this case drinking, is also very typical, and is well described in the autobiography. No wonder he felt himself in a state of nervous tension much of the time. There is overwhelming evidence from studies that have been carried out in a number of different countries, involving both children living with parents with drinking problems, and adults who recall what it was like as children in such circumstances, that in these circumstances children are more likely than others of their age to experience a whole range of psychological difficulties including signs of anxiety and nervousness such as nightmares or fits of crying, problems at school such as truancy or difficulty concentrating, and anti-social behaviour problems such as signs of aggressiveness. The autobiography also expresses very well the dilemma, which the children of problem drinking parents so frequently describe, about making friends with other children. It is often not just a matter of reluctance to invite others to your own home, but also uncertainty about accepting invitations to others' homes because it would be difficult to reciprocate, and even reluctance to talk openly about one's home life because of a feeling of shame associated with it.

Nor is Beverley Nichols' criticism of his mother's way of coping unusual. Children often, as they get older, find it difficult to understand why their mothers have remained so loyal and protective towards their fathers whose excessive drinking, drug-taking or gambling seems to them to have been so destructive of family life and so undermining of their mothers. His mother took her marriage vows seriously, and made efforts to protect Beverley's father from harm, including the harm of other people knowing about his drinking. Beverley strongly disagreed with her view that his father was suffering from a disease and that a kindly, soft approach was the right one. Interestingly, a minor character in the book is Beverley's older brother who went into the church, and apparently took a similar line to that of their mother.

Questions

1. Do you understand the sensitivity that Beverley as a child, and his mother, displayed about what they thought were tell-tale signs of Beverley's father's drinking? It sounds as if they were watching and listening all the time, even noticing the way he whistled or carved a joint. Is there any way family members can avoid doing that?
2. If you were a teacher and discovered that a pupil was having difficulty concentrating on his or her school work, and appeared to be lonely at school, and you discovered that this could be traced to worry about a parent with an addiction problem, what would you do?
3. Beverley Nichols had little sympathy for his mother's position towards his father. Do you feel any sympathy towards the position she took? If you had to defend her position, what arguments would you use?
4. What else might Beverley's mother have done? If she came to you as a counsellor, what would you be trying to achieve for her, and how?
5. Beverley was critical of his mother's use of the disease concept of a drinking problem. Are there any advantages of the disease idea do you think? What is the balance of advantages or disadvantages of that way of understanding Beverley's father's behaviour?
6. Do you have sympathy for the rather harsh and unforgiving position that Beverley Nichols expressed in his book? Do you think that position is justified? Do you think it is helpful for the adult son or daughter of a parent who drank excessively in that way?
7. Beverley advocated physical violence. He is certainly not alone in that. In some social and cultural groups it is widely considered a very appropriate response to someone who is behaving so badly, particularly towards a female member of the family. Do you think it could ever be justified?
8. Do you think Beverley's mother was right to cut her husband out of her will?

Exercises

- This is a role-play exercise with three parts: an 11-year-old boy who is showing problems of concentration and difficult behaviour at school, his mother, and the professional adviser. The boy is very angry with his father who has an alcohol dependence problem and with his mother for putting up with it. His mother acknowledges her husband's problem but prefers to take a more loving and supportive position towards him. How does the professional find a way to reconcile those apparently irreconcilable stances?

- Debate the advantages and disadvantages for affected family members of the disease concept of 'alcoholism', 'drug addiction' or 'pathological gambling'.

15

Growing Up with My Mother by Virginia Ironside

The heading for this chapter is taken from the title of a book written by Virginia Ironside, the journalist and author who for many years has been an agony aunt for periodicals and newspapers. The book was published in 2003, over 20 years after the death of her mother Janey, a very well-known fashion guru of the 1950s and 1960s, and who was for a number of years Professor of Fashion at the Royal College of Art.

In common with Beverley Nichols, writing about his relationship with his father, this is the story of a child of a parent who developed a serious alcohol problem, although in this case it is the story of the relationship between a daughter and her mother. It shares many features with Beverley Nichols' account and with countless other stories that have only been told in confidence to researchers, therapists or other confidantes, or which have never been told in detail to anyone. Like Beverley, Virginia writes of the emotional struggles over how to feel and act towards her excessively drinking parent. Like Beverley, she at times also wished her mother dead. In the end her relationship with her mother is different to Beverley Nichols' relationship with his father. Part of the difference may be due to her being a woman relating to a mother, but that is unlikely to be the whole explanation.

Addiction Dilemmas: Family Experiences from Literature and Research and their Challenges for Practice, First Edition. Jim Orford.

Like many daughters and sons of parents with drinking problems Virginia was more aware, during her childhood and early adolescence, of an increasingly tense and unhappy relationship between her parents than about her mother's excessive drinking. It is not clear to what extent the latter was itself a problem at that time or whether it came later, but what is made clear in the book is the deterioration of the relationship between her parents, their lack of affectionate demonstrativeness and their increasing arguments. Although there are references to her mother's lack of keenness about family holidays with her own parents on account of there being so little to drink, and later reference to the Bohemian way of life and drunkenness amongst the coterie of artists at the Royal College, drinking itself was not the major theme of Virginia's account of those years. However, like many offspring of parents who have alcohol problems, Virginia is able to recognize the problem with hindsight. For example:

> I wasn't aware at the time that she was drunk. But there was something about the sight of her two big moist eyes staring at me, her full, almost seductive mouth, her dead-white skin and her jet-black hair, perhaps a bit awry, which, when I recall it, fills me with terror and revulsion (p. 153).

What she was aware of was that all was not right and that her mother's attentions were distracted by other interests:

> . . . at ten, I was starting to realize that I had been brought up by a charming, sweet, talented but totally self-centred and wayward child (p. 147).

In her teens Virginia's mother and father separated. Far from being upset, she says, she settled down to a happy life having her father all to herself. From there on her mother's drinking becomes more and more the focus, and the story of her relationship with her mother, as someone with a drinking problem, is one that is played out between a mother and her older adolescent and young – and then not so young – adult daughter. Virginia developed that acute sensitivity about her parent's drinking that Beverley Nichols also wrote about, and which most close family members of relatives with such problems develop. She writes of visiting her mother in her flat, pressing the buzzer to let her know she was on her way, and knowing even from, 'The way the receiver was lifted off the hook, the pause before her voice came . . .' (p. 170), whether she was drunk or not. Later her mother had a teetotal period of 18 months when work and a new relationship were going well. But she started to drink again, apparently after an unpleasant conflict at work in which she felt her own contribution to the college had not been recognized. Again Virginia's sensitivities were acutely at work:

> I watched her progression back into her old drinking patterns with terror. Every time she telephoned, I listened, my ears pricked like a dog's, for any tiny sign of a slur. When I kissed her hello, I sniffed her breath. When she went out of the room, I tasted her Slimline tonic to see if it was spiked. I made mental notes when I looked at the bottles of drink in the kitchen – could John [her mother's partner] really have drunk all that whisky by himself since I was last there? (p. 206).

She said she began to dread her mother's telephone calls and invitations. She and her mother's partner tried to get her to take some treatment but nothing came of it. From some doctors Virginia had a reaction which, sadly, has been all too commonly the experience of family members:

> One doctor told me privately: 'There is no hope for her. She will just continue drinking until she dies.' 'Your mother's an alcoholic and there's nothing I can do for her', and another, 'She'll never stop being one' (pp. 208–9).

Like so many other family members of people with drinking problems she tried the tactic of emptying all her mother's bottles of drink down the sink, only to find that her mother simply bought more to replace them. Her mother lied about her drinking. People at her work covered up for her. Virginia describes the all too common toll this takes on a close family member, even one who is not actually living under the same roof:

> ... there was never a moment when I wasn't anxiously worrying about my mother's drinking ... I always managed to remain the sensible adult in charge when it came to my mother. I was now having to look after her, to tick her off, to encourage her through her various College crises. But the situation was becoming too much for me (pp. 21, 215).

There came a point when Janey resigned from her prestigious job that had once seen her at the forefront of fashion design and often in the media spotlight, and from then on the story is an increasingly sad one. Virginia's mother became depressed and made two attempts to commit suicide, although finally she died from cancer. What is of particular interest to us here is the ambivalence of Virginia's feelings about whether her mother lives or dies. Although the often caring tone of her description of her mother stands in contrast to Beverley Nichol's bitter tone when writing about his father, they share with each other and with so many other family members an awareness that part of them would be relieved to see the relative dead. In Virginia's case, she was acutely aware towards the end of her mother's life that her mother herself wanted to die. At one point, Virginia describes her feelings when her mother asked her to promise not to let doctors keep her alive:

> I didn't really care whether she was in pain or not. My feelings about her were blank, as if a wind had blown a great dust-storm through my mind and left all the spikes and bumps covered with an endlessly flat, even sand (pp. 228–9).

And after visiting the hospital to be told that her mother was still alive after one of her suicide attempts:

> I had become exhausted with listening to how unhappy she was. I found the stress of never knowing whether she was drunk or not too much to take. I had my own enormous emotional problems to deal with, and just hearing my mother's voice on the phone sent my adrenalin soaring into a panic attack. I felt faint and numb, like a blinded elephant, barely knowing my own name, crashing around in a maelstrom of anxiety (p. 230).

In the later stages of the book Virginia is honest about her feelings when it is discovered that her mother had developed cancer:

> I don't know who was more relieved, my mother or myself, when it turned out that she had developed breast cancer ... I remember the mixture of relief that rushed over me. I imagined life without her. I saw myself running out to greet a new life, tumbling into the open fields, arms spread wide to catch the sky. This feeling was naturally swiftly obliterated by a huge black dollop of guilt (pp. 258, 261).

One agonizing dilemma was what to do with her mother's supply of pills on which they both knew she could overdose. At one point Virginia decided to leave them with her mother, only later to change her mind. Having taken them out of her mother's access, she then felt guilty for depriving her mother of the opportunity to take her own life if she wished.

Comments

Although both their books are principally about the experiences of having a parent with a drinking problem, there are a number of obvious differences between what Virginia Ironside has to say compared to Beverley Nichols' earlier account. The major difference is the tone that they adopt towards their respective drinking parents. Virginia is critical looking back, exasperated, later driven to distraction with worry, and finally exhausted, but mostly she maintains a caring stance towards her mother. Another apparent difference is that Virginia only became clear about her mother's excessive drinking in late adolescence. In fact that is not at all uncommon. It is very frequently the case that children of parents with drinking problems can see with hindsight that such a problem probably existed for a number of years before they realized it for what it was. A complicating factor for Virginia, as for many other young people, was that her contact with her mother during part of her childhood and adolescence was disrupted by separation; even though later her life became closely entwined with her mother's. It is more often the case than not that children of problem drinking parents are able to piece things together in retrospect. That is probably attributable to the often shadowy, secretive, guilt-ridden nature of addiction problems. What children are usually very conscious of at the time is the tense and unhappy atmosphere in the family and arguments between their parents, and Virginia Ironside was no exception.

A similarity in Virginia's and Beverley's accounts is the sensitivity they developed to signs of the parent's drinking and their fearfulness about discovering that their parent was drinking again. In Virginia's case this went beyond listening, watching and using her sense of smell, and involved some of the kinds of vigilant activity that family members very often get involved in: tasting the relative's drink and emptying booze down the sink are actions that countless family members will recognize, often with a sense of guilt, knowing that such actions were born of despair and met with little success in the long run.

There are hints in Virginia Ironside's book of the unhelpful reactions that family members very often experience from other people from whom they might have expected some constructive support. For example, there appears to have been a culture of heavy drinking in the artistic circles in which her mother worked, and some of her colleagues covered up for her drinking. Not that a particularly heavy drinking culture is necessary for that to happen. Most family members affected by a loved one's addictive be-haviour have stories to tell about other people unhelpfully covering up. Nor are professionals always very helpful from a family member's perspective. Virginia mentions two doctors who conveyed to her their view that it was hopeless to think that her mother would stop drinking.

Despite the more caring stance that Virginia Ironside takes towards her mother in her book, compared to that adopted by Beverley Nichols in his, the ambivalence towards the addicted relative that is such a feature of the stories that family members tell, comes through strongly in the end. After all the experiences that she had gone through with her mother, Virginia describes graphically her state of mind in which she is ambivalent about whether her mother lives or dies – even the sense of relief at the diagnosis of cancer, and, poignantly, her vacillation over whether to leave with her mother the pills that would enable her to overdose.

Questions

1. Virginia Ironside's attitude towards her mother seems very different from that of Beverley Nichols towards his father. To what extent do you think that can be explained by the fact that in one case it is a daughter talking about her relationship with her mother, and in the other case a son talking about his father?

2. Given that the role of excessive drinking may not have been clear to Virginia when she was a child, to what extent do you think it is possible for someone in her position to exaggerate with hindsight the role of drinking? Or, alternatively, is it more likely that the role of an addictive behaviour will be minimized, remaining obscure or hidden?

3. Why do you think family members do things like sniffing a relative's breath, tasting their drink, emptying booze down the sink? Can such actions have advantages? What would you say to someone who described doing such things and asked for your opinion?

4. It is quite common for affected family members to admit to the thought that the addicted relative's death would bring some relief. Professionals have often misunderstood this, failing to appreciate the ambivalence towards the relative and the relative's excessive behaviour that addiction entails. Do you feel sympathetic towards Virginia when she expresses some feeling of relief at her mother's likely death? Would

you understand, on the other hand, if a professional was shocked at that?

5.   Family members are often enraged at the social or work cultures that seem to be encouraging their relatives in their addictive behaviour. What can affected family members do with that rage, if anything?

6.   What should a doctor say if consulted by an adult daughter worried about her mother's drinking?

7.   Is there any way in which we could provide a service for people in the position that Virginia Ironside found herself in the later years of her mother's life? Could we have helped her feel less agonized, exhausted, more effective? What would need to be in place for that to happen?

Exercises

- Role-play a discussion between a brother and sister, both in their mid to late teens. They are swapping notes about all the ways in which they have learned to be vigilant about their mother's drinking – sniffing, watching, listening for the change in her voice, when she is whistling – and the things they have secretly done like tasting her drink to see if it has been diluted, even pouring some of it away. They admit to one another that it makes them very tense and doesn't work. They wonder if they are doing the right thing. They are joined by a professional alcohol and drug worker who tries to help them find a different way of responding.

- You have had several meetings with a woman whose mother has a serious and longstanding alcohol problem and you understand well what the daughter has been going through and how she feels. You are now meeting with their general medical practitioner. The latter has formed a negative opinion about the daughter's influence, saying, 'She even told me that she wished her mother were dead!' Formulate an explanation for the GP about the circumstances facing an affected family member like this daughter and the ambivalent feelings which these circumstances provoke.

16

Mrs Sara Coleridge and Friends

One of the rich sources of insights about addiction has been writing by and about the romantic poets of the late eighteenth and early nineteenth centuries. They lived at a time when opium-taking was tolerated in Britain and quite unrestricted. Opium-containing preparations were used to treat all manner of discomforts and disorders for infants, children and adults. The most famous description of addiction to laudanum – a mixture of opium and alcohol – is Thomas De Quincey's *The Confessions of an English Opium Eater*, first published in the London Magazine in 1821 and thought to have been influential in the growing awareness of the addictive properties of opium. But it is the wife and friends of Samuel Taylor Coleridge (STC) who are the focus of our attention here. That is because of a book that I stumbled across when visiting Coleridge Cottage, preserved as a museum by the National Trust, in Nether Stowey in the Quantock Hills in Somerset. The book is a rare treasure for someone with an interest in addiction and the family. Entitled *The Bondage of Love: A Life of Mrs Samuel Taylor Coleridge*, it was published in 1986. Not only is this a biography of the wife of a famous person who was addicted to opium but it takes as its central theme the effects of STC's opium addiction on Sara Coleridge, their marriage, their family and their friends. Along the way there is much of interest about

Addiction Dilemmas: Family Experiences from Literature and Research and their Challenges for Practice, First Edition. Jim Orford.
© 2012 John Wiley & Sons, Ltd. Published 2012 by John Wiley & Sons, Ltd.

how some famous friends, including fellow poets William Wordsworth and Robert Southey, became involved in responding to STC's addiction.

The book was written by Molly Lefebure. She had earlier written a biography of STC himself, also focused on his addiction, entitled *Samuel Taylor Coleridge: A Bondage of Opium*. In the preface to that book Molly Lefebure explained how her work as private secretary to the then Home Office pathologist, and later her work with young people, many with drug problems, enabled her to appreciate the significance of STC's addiction when later, as a writer, she had carried out research for work on the Lake District and the Lake poets. From her studies, particularly of the poet's letters and notebooks, which had not been available to his earliest biographers, she concluded that his opium addiction, unlike the accusations of his plagiarism which had been so fully worked over, had been consistently under-estimated and misunderstood. In her view the evidence was incontrovertible that STC was not only 'one of the select handful of history's poet-philosophers of genius' (*A Bondage of Opium*, p. 53) but also a classic case of opium addiction.

But it is Sara Coleridge's posthumous reputation that concerns us here and which Lefebure was at pains to put right in *Bondage of Love*. In the preface to that book she wrote, 'Mrs Samuel Taylor Coleridge must surely rank among the most maligned of great men's wives ... Mud-encoated, she has become a symbol of the unloved, unloving and unlovable wife ...' (pp. 15, 18 – all quotations are from *Bondage of Love* unless otherwise stated). For that she blames: primarily Coleridge himself who put it about that his wife's lack of sympathy towards him was a major cause of his distress and recourse to opium; Dorothy Wordsworth (William's sister) who was close to STC and repeated his view of things in her own writings, which had become more and more popular over the years; and De Quincey who, in *Confessions* and other essays published after STC's death exposed the latter's addiction, accused him of plagiarism and, '... by repeating all the malicious things said by him about his wife, gravely misrepresented her' (p. 16).

It is not known for certain when STC's laudanum-taking began but it has been suggested that it was prescribed for him during a bout of rheumatic fever, which later developed into a chronic condition, in his last year at school. It seems that his friendship circle while he was a student at Cambridge may have contained a number of friends who were using opium for the pleasures it gave and not merely for the physical pains it might be relieving. He did not achieve as much at university as had been hoped and he was acquiring a reputation for 'sloth' (his word) and 'indolence' (an interestingly ambiguous word, often used at the time as a euphemism for laudanum addiction, but one that served to mask the truth). He and his new friend Robert Southey – who became STC's brother-in-law through marrying Sara's sister, and was later to become Poet Laureate – also acquired a reputation for having Jacobin, anti-government sympathies, and had wild ideas, that never materialized, of emigrating to the North American back-woods to set up a community pursuing liberty, equality and fraternity under the banner of 'Pantisocracy'. Sara was warned by her family not to marry such a man but she was enchanted by him and took no notice. In later years she was known to make wry comments about those who were lucky in what she called the 'marriage lottery'. She was determined that her own daughter Sara should be well educated: she hoped she would remain single and certainly warned her against impetuously marrying a penniless youth as she herself had done.

Between their marriage in 1795 and finally settling at Greta Hall just outside Keswick in the Lake District in 1800 the couple had moved a number of times between Bristol, Nether Stowey and London; STC had been away on a lengthy trip to Germany; and two sons had been born – Hartley and Berkeley, the latter dying in infancy. The couple had already started to quarrel, alarming their Nether Stowey friend Thomas Poole, but the seriousness of STC's indolence and ill-health seems not to have been clear until after the move to the Lakes. According to Lefebure it was shortly after that move that Sara '. . . began to remonstrate with her husband, declaring that the opium, far from alleviating his sufferings, was clearly contributing to his languors and dejections, while the brandy was equally bad for him' (p. 135). She complained that he was bringing no money into the home, that she and her children deserved a better, more comfortable life. He responded that living innocently and joyously was more important than money. He saw her increasingly frenzied outbursts of recrimination as evidence of her lack of sympathy and affection for him. Years later their daughter was to observe that her mother's 'honesty stood in the way' of living in harmony with her father and lacked the 'meekness and forbearance which softens everything'. STC, too, expressed views, both before and after his marriage, about the desirability of a wife being 'a compassionate Comforter', someone who shared her husband's opinions on all important subjects, who was docile and could be replied upon to promote 'domestic peace'. His wife clearly failed on those counts: 'She continued to pursue what she saw as the correct course of criticism, rebuke and warning, despite her husband's riposte that "blunt advice" invariably did him more harm than good. Sara, ignoring this, persevered with her blunt outspokenness. Somebody had to tell him the truth!' (p. 140). STC would often escape over the hill to the Wordsworths – who never gave him 'blunt advice' – where he would speak contemptuously of Sara, complaining that she was ruining his 'moral character' and 'incapacitating him for serious creative work'.

STC's health deteriorated rapidly. On one occasion, after an argument in which the possibility of separation had been talked of, he declared he was on the point of dying. Sara, shocked and frightened, begged his forgiveness for her behaviour and promised to fight against her tendencies towards 'Thwarting and Dispathy' as STC called it. Sara, Lefebure says, was now drawing the conclusion that her husband required delicate handling, like a small child: 'Nothing but tranquillity keeps him tolerable, care and anxiety destroy him' (p. 155).

Sara was anxious that the true extent of the problem should not be known outside the family, and Lefebure believed that no one besides she and STC knew the full extent of the problem at this time:

> Sara knew that, on many counts, she was pitied by her family and friends. This she
> spiritedly resented, she would not have anyone pitying her; above all she would
> not listen to a word against her husband. She, as his wife, maintained the right to
> speak to him bluntly in private (yet with discretion, now that she understood the
> effect that blunt speech had upon him) but to hear him harshly judged by others
> was a thing she would not tolerate (p. 160).

The couple agreed that he should go abroad for at least a year in the hope that recovering his health and fighting his opium habit might be aided with a change of climate and undisturbed by domestic worries. He was away in all for two years, in Malta but also for several months in London waiting for a ship and in Italy on the way back. Sara appears to have found this time very restorative and blossomed during his absence. STC on the other hand had not been cured by the trip. His notebooks suggest he had come close to suicide while in Malta, and the Wordsworths were shocked by his appearance and manner when they met him on his return. He stayed in London for some time, reluctant to return home, and when he did it was to announce that he wanted a separation. Although Lefebure explains that Mary Wollstonecraft's *A Vindication of the Rights of Woman* had been published 14 years earlier and the position of women had become a fashionable subject for debate, it was still the case that legal dissolution of marriage was virtually unobtainable and separation inevitably cast stigma upon a wife who must have failed as a spouse, and, since women enjoyed no property rights, it often meant financial and material disaster for her. Not surprisingly Sara put up a great fight against the injustice of separation, but it seems that she finally accepted the idea of 'a friendly separation, with visits' which in any case might not constitute a great change from the status quo.

The friends

There followed a period of a year or so during which STC stayed with the Wordsworths, first over one winter at a home they had been lent in Leicestershire, and later, off and on, at the Wordsworths' new home in the Lakes (they had moved from the small Dove Cottage to the roomier Allan Bank). In this drama of addiction and the family and friends, the Wordsworths take major parts. Their lives and those of the Coleridges were intertwined over a period of many years. The early bond between STC and the Wordsworths was evidently a very strong one and it increasingly excluded Sara as time went on, particularly after her children were born and she was taken up with domestic responsibilities. STC found Dorothy and Sara to be very different characters. He was impressed by Dorothy's support of William which contrasted so much with Sara's thwarting of STC. Dorothy was 'wild' and Rousseauesque, while Sara was 'deficient in organic sensibility'. Lefebure described some of the things that Dorothy wrote about Sara as bordering on the spiteful. Sara's and the Coleridges' longstanding friend Thomas Poole believed the Wordsworths to be a bad influence on STC. The Wordsworths thought Sara was an unsuitable wife for such a genius as Coleridge and encouraged their separation.

When STC returned from Malta the Wordsworths were determined that they could save him by firm but sympathetic handling. They would show him sensibility of a kind that Sara had not. He would no longer need opium. As Dorothy put it at the time, 'If he is not inclined to manage himself, we can manage him' (p. 175). According to Lefebure this was 'the voice of blissful ignorance' (p.175). They soon discovered what it meant to live with a man who was addicted to opium. They were unable to manage him any more successfully than Sara had done. Dorothy had to conclude that he might never be able to leave off laudanum entirely. In the end Dorothy was completely disillusioned. As she wrote to a friend, ' "We have no hope of him . . . His whole time and thoughts . . . are employed in deceiving himself, and seeking to deceive others . . . This Habit pervades all his words and actions, and you feel perpetual new hollowness, and emptiness". She concluded: "It has been misery, God knows, to me to see the truths which I now see" ' (p. 196).

STC had developed feelings of jealousy towards William, partly to do with rivalry between fellow poets and partly over their relationship with Sarah Hutchinson – who takes a small but important part in the drama – to whom STC had been openly attracted and affectionate for several years. But William and STC's famous falling out was, according to Lefebure, provoked by an incident involving another friend, Basil Montagu, who had offered to take STC back to London to stay with him and his wife. William had warned Montagu about the seriousness of STC's condition, and Montagu had withdrawn his offer, explaining to STC what William had told him. STC felt wounded and insulted as a result, Sara reacted with furious indignation towards William for having betrayed STC's failings, and Dorothy was in turn indignant that William should be charged with responsibility for having upset STC. For a long time William and STC did not communicate and STC refused to visit the Wordsworths when he came to the Lakes.

Another very important part was played by Robert Southey. Youthful friends, fellow pantisocrats and then brothers-in-law, his and STC's lives were also closely joined. Lefebure argues that Southey never understood drug addiction, the hold it could have on a person and the need for treatment, and that when he did understand the seriousness of STC's condition he was inclined towards a moralistic attitude. In fact, very early on before they were both married Lefebure believes Southey began to realize that STC's 'indolence' was related to opium and lost his enthusiasm for the joint North American venture, pulling out of it and causing a rift that lasted for some time. Some years later we find Southey and his wife (Sara's sister) and family sharing Greta Hall with Sara, her children and, when he visited, STC. His attitude towards STC now seems to be one of tolerant resignation. When STC was resident with the Wordsworths, but regularly visiting Greta Hall, he commented, 'We never know when Coleridge may come, nor if he comes when he may go' (p.194). Some time later, after the Montagu incident, with STC now staying in London with other friends, Southey wrote:

When he is tired of his London and Hammersmith friends he will come back again as if he had done nothing amiss or absurd, and we whose resentment has long since given place to regret and compassion, shall receive him as kindly as we took leave of him, but more cheerfully, or rather with less inward sorrow, for if he will destroy himself with self-indulgence, it is better he should do it here than among strangers (p. 200).

Three to four years later his attitude appears to have hardened into angry indignation. He had himself taken on paying the rent for Sara's part of their house and the support of herself and her daughter. When another mutual friend, Joseph Cottle, offered to raise money for STC to receive treatment in a 'private madhouse', Southey had reacted by saying that any such subscription should go towards his children who had been left dependent 'upon chance and charity'. In any case STC's was a form of insanity, 'which none but the Soul's physician can cure' (p. 212).

Although Southey was clearly of immense material and emotional support to Sara, on at least one occasion he took pains, according to Lefebure, to hold back from her information about the seriousness of STC's circumstances. In London, en route to Malta, it was widely reported to Southey that STC was behaving in a quarrelsome and embarrassing way wherever he went. Southey kept this from Sara as much as he could.

Amongst the many friends caught up in one way or another in the dilemmas of how to respond to STC's troubles, Thomas Poole is one who amply deserves mention. It was he who encouraged STC and Sara, in the early days of their marriage, to move to be his close neighbours in Nether Stowey in Somerset. He was a great admirer of STC and shared with Sara – after the Nether Stowey period, through many years of correspondence and the occasional meeting – concern about the damaging influence on STC of his friendship with the Wordsworths and growing concern about STC's health. He was conscious from early on of STC's sensitivity and according to Lefebure his consistent advice was that STC should not be upset, should be kept on an even keel. He should be protected from 'disagreeable subjects' (p. 112) such as the serious illness of his infant son Berkeley while he was away in Germany. Lefebure refers to Poole, years later, 'falling back into his old habit of encouraging and rallying STC' (p. 225).

Unlike De Quincey in his *Confessions*, Coleridge left no such work describing his opium addiction and many of the references to it in his writing and that of his friends are indirect and euphemistic. But, having read STC's collected letters and notebooks and other material, Lefebure was in no doubt about the increasing evidence of the dark side of his opium use, the worsening of his health, his morose and discouraged state, and finally his complete incapacitation, as evidenced for example by his failure to deliver scheduled lectures. STC himself, in letters to friends, referred directly to his 'crime of opium', the 'dirty business of Laudanum . . . this free-agency-annihilating Poison', and 'a Slavery more dreadful than any man who has not felt its iron fetters eating into his very soul, can possibly imagine' (*A Bondage of Opium*, pp. 40, 51, 57). His friend Joseph Cottle wrote to him:

> And now let me conjure you, alike by the voice of friendship, and the duty you owe yourself and family: above all . . . by the fear of God, and the awfulness of eternity, to renounce from this moment opium and spirits, as your bane! . . . My dear Coleridge, be wise before it is too late ! I do hope to see you a renovated man! And that you will still burst your inglorious fetters, and justify the best hopes of your friends . . . (*A Bondage of Opium*, p. 37).

To which STC famously replied:

> You bid me rouse myself – go, bid a man paralytic in both arms rub them briskly together, & that will cure him. Alas! (he would reply) that I cannot move my arms is my Complaint & my misery (*A Bondage of Opium* p. 37).

The later years

Sara's years in the Lakes were ones of increasing realization of the seriousness of STC's 'poor health' and 'indolence', the role of opium, and the difficulty of effecting change. Lefebure comments that early on in those years Sara clung to the now reduced expectation that if STC could free himself from opium and recover his health they might still enjoy modest success and simple comforts, enabling them to bring up their children creditably. A few years later and Lefebure comments that Sara, 'had long since learned the uselessness of reprimanding and upbraiding; or attempting, with coaxing or cajoling, to persuade him to cut down on his consumption of his drug' (p. 197). In his notebook STC referred to Sara asking him whether he had taken too much or too little opium, and notes, 'Too much? Or too little? Alas! alas! needs must it always be the one or the other: for of a poison there is no "Enough" ' (p. 197).

Sara's written confidences to Thomas Poole are revealing. Following the period during which STC stayed with the Wordsworths, she wrote:

> . . . it has taught C one useful lesson; that even his dearest & most indulgent friends, even those very persons who have been the great means of his self-indulgence,

when he comes to live wholly with them, are as clear-sighted to his failings, & much less delicate in speaking of them, than his Wife, who being the Mother of his children, even if she had not the slightest regard for himself, would naturally feel a reluctance to the exposing of his faults (p. 205).

Later, in response to Poole's cheerful encouragement about STC's writing, she replied, 'What you say about STC is likely enough to happen; Alas, I dare not look forward' (p. 225). After STC's departure from the Lakes and the failure of his promises that they would be reunited, Sara wrote to Poole, 'His promises, poor fellow, are like Castles, – airy nothings!' (p. 209). It seems that Sara and Robert Southey – himself made unhappy by his wife's illness, described by Lefebure as chronic depression – attempted to maintain a light-hearted and happy atmosphere in their joint home, full of jokes and pranks, or what Lefebure calls a 'charade of merriment' (p. 220). Sara, Lefebure comments, 'knew what it was to maintain a show of light, frisking high spirits while privately deeply miserable and consumed with anxiety; she had been doing this for years . . .' (p. 219). Lefebure writes that, 13 years after their move to the Lakes and 18 years after their marriage, Sara 'was obliged to see herself, starkly, for what she was: a wife who had been deserted by her husband' (p. 214). In a letter to Thomas Poole four years later she wrote, 'It seems to me impossible we ever should live together under a roof of our own, for we have not the means . . . Our separation has, on the whole, been for the best . . .' (p. 225).

As well as offers by friends such as the Wordsworths and Basil Montagu to provide care and cure for STC, there had also been the suggestion that he should go to a 'retreat' in Edinburgh for treatment, but both Sara and Robert Southey had been strongly against it, believing that encouragement in the family home at Greta Hall would be far better than being sent away. Finally, at the age of 44 he was taken in by James Gillman, described by Lefebure as an apothecary and surgeon of Highgate, who undertook to cure him of his opium addiction. Remarkably, he stayed there for the remaining 18 years of his life. In *Bondage of Opium* Lefebure expresses great regard for Gillman's professional attitude towards STC's addiction – 'free of moral prejudice or prejudgement' (p. 42) – in contrast to the attitude of friends such as Cottle or Southey (Gillman later wrote his own sympathetic biography of Coleridge). Combined with a tranquil routine, STC's treatment in Gillman's hands consisted of 'above all, loving, skilled and unremitting medical attention . . . his addiction was brought under control and he only received carefully supervised quantities of the drug in a degree necessary to maintain him on an even keel' (*A Bondage of Opium*, p. 48).

In the last five years of STC's life there came about what their son Hartley was to call 'the great reconcilement' (p. 248), as a result of Sara and STC's daughter, Sara, marrying her cousin Henry and moving to Hampstead where her mother came to live with them (the possible impact of STC's troubles on their children, and especially on Hartley, is yet another main theme of *Bondage of Love*). Henry acted as a carrier of messages between the two north London homes and STC and Sara finally met again for the first time in eight years and were reconciled in the last 18 months of STC's life.

Comments

Bondage of Love is a goldmine for anyone with an interest in addiction and the family. In the detail it provides about the struggle of a family member faced with the dilemma of how to cope with a close relative with an addiction it ranks alongside Caitlin Thomas's *Life with Dylan Thomas* and Anne Brontë's *Tenant of Wildfell Hall*. But it offers a second rich vein, namely the fullness of the picture it gives us of the social network of friends and relations, their reactions to Coleridge's addiction and the way those reactions interacted with those of the chief protagonist – Sara Taylor Coleridge herself. The ways in which other relatives and friends can be helpful and supportive, or not as the case may be, towards a wife, mother, father or other person who is in the direct line of fire emanating from an addiction problem, is something about which family members often talk. Coleridge and his wife seem to have had a dense network of family, friends and acquaintances. Coleridge was the subject of enormous admiration, but also worry on his behalf, and being literary, many committed their thoughts to paper. Molly Lefebure did us a great service by bringing them together. As is generally the case with addiction, reactions to Coleridge's troubles were very mixed and not all were well received by Sara.

Regarding Sara's ways of coping with STC, the remarkable thing to the present author is how modern it all sounds despite the two hundred years that have elapsed since then. Like nearly all the family members who have taken part in research on the subject in modern times, Sara came gradually to the realization that all was not well with her husband and that his laudanum-taking had something to do with it. As many wives do (and other family members also) she started to remonstrate with him. This was met by accusations that she was giving him 'blunt advice' and that all he got from her was 'thwarting' – a word that well expresses how those with an addiction problem view the advice they may get from concerned others – and 'dispathy' – not a word now in use but neatly expressive of STC's view that Sara's attitude lacked the sympathy that he expected from a wife. What is then so telling, and so typical, is the way the victim comes to be blamed and often comes to blame herself. Not only did STC put it about that he was misunderstood at home, but their daughter in later life wrote that her mother lacked the 'meekness and forbearance which softens everything', and Lefebure found some evidence that Sara herself saw her tendencies to 'thwarting' as something she had to fight against.

We saw in the chapter on Caitlin Thomas how a spirited wife of a husband with an addiction can acquire an undeserved reputation in some quarters because of her quite understandable reactions to her husband's excessive appetite. As if that were not enough, some professional views of addiction and the family have been unsympathetic. The author of *Bondage of Love* referred to Sara as 'among the most maligned of great men's wives'. Her book was an attempt to restore Mrs Coleridge's good name. In that respect Sara Coleridge can stand for all the wives and other family members down the years who have found themselves in her position or one very like it.

In *Tenant of Wildfell Hall* the way of coping of the central character Helen undergoes a significant transmutation over time in a way that many family members will recognize (see Chapter 5). The same was true for Sara Coleridge. At first we see her remonstrating and trying to give advice. Later her expectations have been lowered, realism has set in and she has concluded that her husband needs delicate handling. Like so many family members she learnt that reprimanding, and attempting to get STC to reduce his drug consumption by 'coaxing or cajoling', had little effect.

Another aspect of Sara's experience with which many family members can identify (the four wives who figured in Chapter 13 for example) is the attempt to hide the full extent of the problem from other people. Sara and STC were living at a time when addiction to opium was little understood and references to it were often euphemistic – use of the term 'indolence' is a good example. But family members of any era have good reasons for keeping the wraps on the problem. A strong motivation for Sara, as for so many family members, is to protect the person they are centrally concerned about and his or her good name. What Lefebure says about Sara reserving the right to speak bluntly to STC in private but not liking others to say a bad word about him, is very much what modern parents of drug-dependent sons or daughters say about their children. At the same time we know that family members run risks for themselves by exposing their dirty washing in public. To the criticisms and accusations to which family members have so often been exposed can be added the even greater stigma and material disaster that attended the breakdown of a marriage in Sara Coleridge's day. A further facet is the sheer covering up of feelings of hopelessness and misery, not only in the interests of trying to keep cheerful for one's own peace of mind but also for the sake of others, children especially. Indeed a lot of protecting of others' feelings surrounds addiction: even Robert Southey on occasion tried to hide the truth from Sara.

Turning to their rich network of friends and relations, it has to be said that the Coleridges' network, although it is full of famous names, can serve as a very instructive example of the diversity of ways of reacting to the addiction problem of a friend or relation. We have Robert Southey, very close friend, close relative by marriage, co-resident with Sara and children, and finally partial material provider for the family. From Lefebure's account his attitude to STC's addiction seems to have swung from concerned support to resignation and thence to indignation. Like many people two hundred years later he seems to have had limited understanding of addiction and his view was more or less a moralistic one. Thomas Poole appears to have been more consistent in his line that STC was a highly strung genius who should be gently encouraged and not upset. Lefebure has only good things to say about James Gillman who provided such extraordinary, and seemingly successful, personal medical and residential care for Sara's husband for so many years.

But it is of course the triangular relationship between Sara, STC and the Wordsworths that is most intriguing and instructive. For most family members worried by close relatives' addiction there is part of the social sphere that represents those external influences that have led the loved one astray. This may be represented by other drug users or suppliers, individual older relations or friends who encouraged drinking or drug use at an early stage, or the local pub or gambling arcade. For Jacqueline Doherty (see Chapter 9) it was one of her son Pete's musical associates in particular who she thought had encouraged his drug use. For Sara Coleridge, and Thomas Poole agreed with her, it was the Wordsworths. Addiction has the capacity to drive wedges between people and Sara and the Wordsworths are a perfect case in point. William and Dorothy took STC's side (taking sides is almost certainly an unhelpful thing to do) and believed that Sara was not good for STC. What makes this triangle so additionally interesting is the fact that the Wordsworths thought that they could do a better job of caring for STC than she could and actually took him in under their roof (many people criticize family members affected by addiction but they rarely test out their beliefs in such a practical way). Lefebure's analysis, and Sara's subsequent wry comment, suggest that in the role of carers the Wordsworths had been forced to see the reality of Coleridge's addiction and had consequently changed their tune.

Questions

1. Coleridge used the expression 'free-agency-annihilating' to describe his addiction to laudanum. Thomas De Quincey in his *Confessions* wrote of becoming 'enslaved' to opium, and of 'the accursed chain which fettered me'. Do you think such language is apt or is over-blown? Do you think Molly Lefebure might have been in danger, in her enthusiasm for putting right the neglect of Coleridge's addiction, of exaggerating the role of addiction in his life and their marriage? Or is it the other way round: are family members like Sara Coleridge stigmatized by others' failure to recognize the stress they are under?

2. Do you agree that in all important respects Sara Coleridge's circumstances were the same as those of the wife of any drug-addicted husband at the beginning of the twenty-first century? Or, have the substances available and the nature of drug dependence, or the role of women in society, changed to such an extent that we should be careful about how much we can learn from this historical example?

3. In the Coleridges' day the word 'indolence' was often used as a cover for opium addiction. Is drug addiction in the family still covered up today, and if so are there any expressions you can think of that are in common usage to help conceal it?

4. Molly Lefebure is clearly sympathetic to Sara. Do you think she is guilty of taking sides? Is her approach too coloured by a feminist viewpoint?

5. Coleridge accused Sara of 'thwarting and dispathy', and her daughter later remarked that her mother lacked the 'appropriate meekness

and forbearance'. Are women still criticized today for trying to stand up to their menfolk's excessive consumptions? What are some of the equivalent terms that might be used in modern parlance?

6. It seems that the Wordsworths sympathized with Coleridge and not with Sara, that Southey became resigned, that Poole was consistently accepting and Gillman outstandingly caring. If you had been a friend of Coleridge, in what direction do you think your reaction to his addiction would have leaned?

7. Like a number of others I am critical of the use of the word 'carers' to describe family members who are affected by and worried about close relatives' addiction. The word doesn't seem to fit the bill. Surely it is not like caring for someone with a chronic illness or disability? Or is it? When thinking about the Wordsworths taking Coleridge into their home or the remarkable Doctor Gillman looking after Coleridge in the later years of his life I find the word 'carer' seems not inappropriate. Perhaps this is because Coleridge himself often seemed to be in poor health and seemed to invite caring from his friends and relations. What do you think?

Exercises

• This lends itself to an extended role-play exercise with several parts. You will need someone to play Sara, and others to play Dorothy and William Wordsworth and Robert Southey, and another to play Thomas Poole. The five people who take those parts need to re-read this chapter again carefully in order to understand the parts they are playing. They have got together at a time when Coleridge's opium addiction and associated ill-health cannot be denied. They disagree about what should be done. If your group is a largish one, other people should observe and have an opportunity to comment. You may, in addition, assign someone the role of STC himself. If you do, you might give him the option of interrupting from the wings at any stage to make a comment, either addressed to the audience or to one or all of the players. You could then wind the clock on and assume now that STC had been living with the Wordsworths for some time. They are disillusioned about being able to help him and he is now living elsewhere and giving his friends and family more concern than ever. Assign to someone the role of Dr James Gillman who explains what his plan for STC is.

- The government is about to produce a new 10-year drug strategy and at last has agreed to highlight the needs of affected family members. They are receiving conflicting advice about how to refer to family members collectively – some favour 'carers', others not. In group discussion produce what you think is the best collective expression for the family members that we have met in this chapter and in the book as a whole.

17

Five Husbands of Wives with Drinking Problems

A Focus Group

One of the things that has interested my colleagues and myself while under-taking our research programme has been the question of gender differences in coping with an addiction problem in the family. For example, if in a marriage or partnership one partner or spouse has an addiction problem and the other is affected by it, does gender matter? Does it make a difference whether the one who is trying to cope with the other's addiction is male or female? Does it make any difference if the marriage or partnership is a same sex one? Broadly speaking there are two possibilities. Either the experience of having a close relative with an addiction problem is such a particular ex-perience that it overrides gender differences so that gender itself is relatively unimportant; or gender differences are themselves so important that they trump anything else, so that coping with a relative's drink, drug or gambling problem is itself a gendered activity. In that case we should find that the experience is very different for men and women coping with an opposite sex partner's addiction, and probably different again if the partner with the addiction problem is of the same sex.

In this chapter we hear from five men, all in heterosexual marriages – I shall call them John, Jack, Tom, Gordon and Eric – who are taking part in a focus group about the experiences of husbands who are living with wives

Addiction Dilemmas: Family Experiences from Literature and Research and their Challenges for Practice, First Edition. Jim Orford.
© 2012 John Wiley & Sons, Ltd. Published 2012 by John Wiley & Sons, Ltd.

with alcohol problems. The group is fictitious but the things these men have to say are all based upon things that individual men said in the course of research interviews. All five would most probably have been recruited at alcohol problems treatment services which they would have attended in order to support their wives' treatment. One thing is for certain, and that is that it would not have been easy to set up this focus group. To the always half-hidden problem of having to cope with a close relative's addiction would have been added the fact that men in that position are even more difficult to find and to persuade to talk about their experiences than are women. Despite the evidence that the gender gap in the prevalence of addiction problems has been narrowing for some time, we have always found it more difficult to recruit men.

Assume that one of my colleagues was leading this group and that I was sitting at the back taking detailed notes. My colleague and the five participants would be seated in comfortable chairs around a small table which holds cups of tea and coffee and a tape recorder to make a recording to supplement my notes later on. What follows is part of the report that we might have constructed after the event, leaving out some of the detailed interactions and concentrating on the answers to a number of key questions. We pick up the discussion after people have introduced themselves and my colleague has explained the purpose of the group. She puts the first question.

The first topic I want to ask you about is the impact on you as husbands. What has it been like for you? How has it affected you personally?

John

I've got a job that keeps me very busy and when I'm working I don't think about my wife's problem. As long as I can keep my brain occupied, that is the way I've coped. But I never know what I am going to come back to when I get back from work. The place may be in a mess and a meal half prepared and then forgotten while she is sleeping it off. I used to get terribly worked up about it but I've learned that doesn't help. I used to feel very bitter and frustrated and angry but now I shut off my feelings about the drinking and accept it as just part of life. I've learned to be the eternal optimist. One of the bigger stresses is the drain on our finances. She has been running through a couple of hundred pounds a month on the booze and this year she's actually started to steal from our relations just to get money for it.

Jack

We are really powerless to do anything about it, aren't we? It means there are things that you can't do, you can't plan for things in life. For example, you can't plan that you're going to have friends in because you don't know whether the drinking is going to spoil it. I feel I'm in control of my life really now but when things were bad, especially before I went to Al-Anon, it was different. The thing takes you over. It's the last thing you think of before you go into a fitful sleep and the first thing you think of when you wake up. You just come to the end of your tether, you don't know which way to turn. But I feel I've come out the other end and learned a lot since going to Al-Anon.

Tom

I know what you mean about it being constantly on your mind, and I can't plan ahead either. I'm often thinking that maybe now she is coming round to admitting the problem, but then maybe not. You feel hopeful one week and then let down the next. I felt depressed, hopeless about it, certainly very run down and exhausted with it all. I've cried about it, in fact she and I have cried together over it.

Eric

What's it been like? I would say lonely. Perhaps I've always been a bit of a loner but when my wife is drinking I have no one to talk to because sensible communication becomes impossible. We've lost friends and interests through it and we rarely have visitors now. You never know where you stand. I've felt angry inside, as much as anything anger directed at myself for allowing myself to have got in this situation. I resent all the wasted time.

I've felt hopeless at times, bordering on the suicidal in fact. Now I would say I'm fatalist, defeatist, I've given up, I'm resigned to it. I've been on the point of giving up, but I won't. But if I had a heart attack and popped off that would be great.

I know it is a sensitive subject, but I wonder about the children. I think all of you have children, mostly grown up or nearly so now. How have they come into the picture? Have they been a support to you? Have they been stressed by the problem themselves?

Eric

I think it may have affected my son. He dropped out of his studies and got paid work instead, I think in order to get enough money together to leave home. He and his partner have got a baby now but I know for a fact that his partner doesn't like to visit because she worries about how my wife will be with the baby.

Gordon

I have exactly the same. I think my son was almost pushed out of the house by my wife's behaviour. The birth of a granddaughter helps but my son has to be careful trusting her with the baby. He and his sister had to put up with a lot, the shouting and screaming and throwing glasses around, their mother being sick upstairs, having to look after her and do more housework than they should. I felt it wasn't fair on them. In fact I would have left if it hadn't been for the children. I ended up putting up with it and trying to keep things on an even keel for their sake. I remember my son came home from school once after having a class about drinking and drug problems, being cross and saying 'don't they know I've got it all at home'.

How does one cope with a problem like this? Is it always a case of having to put up with it? Are there things you can do? What have you found yourself doing to try and cope with it all?

Jack

Al-Anon say you should leave the alcoholic to his or her own devices, let them take the responsibility. But I can't do that, it affects me. Some things are useless like pouring the drink down the sink. It's the natural thing to do when you don't realize what you're dealing with. In the early days I was convinced I could stop her drinking. But what was essential was getting control of the money. Money was pouring out like water and it would have been a disaster if I hadn't taken complete control of the finances. It was a matter of survival. I wouldn't be sitting here now if I hadn't done that. It's essential for me to take control of things. It's brought stability to our lives.

Gordon

Yes, I took over complete control of the family finances at one point. We used to go shopping together. I didn't think she needed to feel I was checking up on her but she did actually feel very resentful about it. It just didn't work out – the hatred directed towards you was just unbearable. Anyway she always had the family allowance book and would be off to the post office and then down to the off licence. And there was always something that I had to hand money over for. In the end we decided together that it wasn't a good idea and we went back to having a joint account.

Eric

I forced arrangements so that my wife went into a residential drying out clinic for a couple of weeks. The result was good for about six months but then she started drinking again so I felt trying to take control like that had been a waste of time.

I'm going to ask you a question that I know is difficult. I know several of you, perhaps all of you, have felt very angry from time to time and it must have been difficult to know what to do with those angry feelings. You must at least have felt like expressing your anger in an aggressive way. Is that something that we can talk about?

John

Before I went to Al-Anon I would do all the wrong things. For example I would rile her up and criticize her and sometimes lose my rag completely. I even kicked her sometimes when she was lying on the floor drunk. My behaviour at that time was completely wrong. I was handling the situation completely wrongly. I now let her rant and rave on until she falls asleep, without giving anything back at all.

Tom

For me it's the beginning of one of her drinking bouts that is the worst. She can get very abusive and she denies that she's been drinking although it's obvious that she has. Sometimes I get really angry at that point. I know it's not a helpful reaction but it is a natural reaction. There was once we got into a big argument about it and I did hit her, the only time I have. She called the police who called social services but by then she was at the unconscious stage and things were under control.

Eric

There's been no actual violence in our case but I certainly get tetchy when she has drunk and have ended up saying things I shouldn't say, or perhaps I do mean them. Getting blatantly angry is the least useful way to react. If I do that she denies the problem and my blood pressure just goes right up making me feel really unwell. I don't bother to say anything anymore. I couldn't care less now.

Gordon

I admit I have actually hit my wife on occasions but only after being punished hour after hour. It's hard to explain well enough how the shouting, screaming and foaming at the mouth can affect you after hours. She's been very angry with me, pointing out my failings, things in the past. She was particularly angry about me taking over financial control. I found it difficult to understand all the anger towards me.

Would I be right in thinking that the thought of leaving had at least crossed your minds?

Jack

I did leave once but in the end it was only for a few days. I went to stay with my parents but when I came back to the house it was obvious that all she'd been doing was drinking. She wasn't eating, the place was a shambles and she hadn't washed. She went downhill. Really she was next to death's door. There were no other relatives to look after her and I made the decision to come back home. It had got to the stage where she was completely reliant on me and I would never have forgiven myself if she had died. I came back to my marriage vows – I decided that I'd take them seriously and live up to them.

Gordon

In the early stages I tried leaving the house for long periods due to all the arguments. She would ring round her friends who didn't really realize about the drinking and thought I was behaving unreasonably and told me not to go off like that. What has been decided in the therapy now is that if any of us feel that she's drunk and we can't cope and what we want to do is go out and leave her, instead we're to say to her 'you're drunk and I'm going out or I'm going to my room' and her side of the bargain is to leave us to do that. Mostly that has worked.

Eric

I've never left her although my doctor actually once advised me to do so. But I wouldn't, I felt obligated. Perhaps if I was 10 or 20 years younger I would. Marriage is not all it's cracked up to be. It would be nice to be able to build another life outside. I do have an open invitation from my son to go and stay if I wanted to.

Tom

It's certainly affected our relationship. The closeness and love are disappearing. I'm not sure whether to stay or not. The fact is I don't have the money to move out. If the house were in my name I'd throw her out. I've taken legal advice about making sure the children are mine. What I hope for is that this problem of her drinking will go away and that we can get married and be happy.

Another question I would like to ask is about support from other people. Do you find other people understand or misunderstand your situation? Are there friends or relations who have been particularly supportive? Or doctors or other professionals or groups? Where do you get your support from?

John

I've not found everybody helpful. Some of my wife's relatives have tended to blame me for her drinking problem. One of them is quite a feminist in her outlook and she thought it was despicable that I hit my wife, quite rightly, but she couldn't accept that she was drinking and she still can't accept it. She tried to get my wife to start divorce proceedings and I don't think that helped her, it just confused her. Perhaps I have had a part to play in her problem. Some of her relatives certainly see it that way. But then one or two of them turned round later and said they didn't want to see her again until she was cured, and I had to explain to them that saying that was unhelpful.

Tom

My partner's family are certainly no use, in fact they're part of the root cause in my opinion. They're all heavy drinkers and if they ever visit they drink all the time and encourage her to drink.

Gordon

I found you can't trust anyone else. Everyone else is wrapped up in their own problems and confiding in them doesn't help. That's why I came here on my own at first, before my wife joined in. Because here you can safely confide. It enables you to reflect on things and get a better perspective. And you discover you're not the only one.

Jack

I agree. People don't understand. I have one relative who thinks it's just a weakness and is very intolerant about the drinking. She's a health worker and I think she should know better.

A couple of you mentioned Al-Anon earlier. What have people's experiences been of Al-Anon? Is it helpful, and if so how?

John

It's been good for me. It teaches you that you've got to look after number one and stop blaming yourself for the alcoholic's problem. It's taught me that I've got to let go. It's been a wonderful relief to hear about other people's problems that aren't dissimilar from one's own. For example when I used to hit and bruise her everyone else has been through similar frustrations and now I don't feel so guilty, although men are stronger than women and therefore can inflict more damage. If I'd handled it better in the first two or three years we wouldn't be where we are today. Everyone at Al-Anon says if only they'd known about it before. One problem with Al-Anon though is that it is nearly all women. It is a problem that there are so few men there.

Jack

Yes, I have found it positive as well. It's the only place where I can really understand what I've gone through. And still go through. If you do feel over the top you can always pick up the phone and speak to another member. I know people from all around the area now; it does widen your social contacts. All the people in the fellowship are there for the same reason. They understand about living with the problem – I thought I was the only man in the world that had this problem. It's the biggest help in my life. Everyone does their utmost to help if they can. I would feel very isolated if I didn't have the fellowship because I would have no one to discuss it with who would understand the problems I was going through.

Eric

I must say I found Al-Anon completely unhelpful. I did attend a couple of meetings, but the religious component crept in and I have no sympathy for people who use religion in that way. As half the people there seem to be separated, or are about to be, perhaps that is the right way to go. I know some people get help or comfort from seeing that others are in the same boat but I don't. They weren't able to suggest any approaches to the problem that I hadn't already tried without success.

What about the statutory services, health and social services and so on? Have they been any help to you in your position? Do services exist for people facing the problems you have been facing?

Gordon

In my case it was a new family doctor who got things going. When he took us on as new patients he wanted to know all the details about smoking and drinking and so on and took urine samples. He knew all about the programmes here and he encouraged me to come. It was when the psychologist made a visit to our house that was really a turning point. She said she wanted to see how we all related and what the children were like and how they might react. It was a difficult visit but she got the lot. She asked the children in front of us how things were. Things didn't improve immediately but it was a turning point.

Tom

Well, our GP has been useless. I don't blame the GP because I think they're powerless to do anything unless she wants it. Social services are the same. There is no practical help they can give. It's just an hour's disruption; nothing will change. It's the same with all the professionals – they come and talk to you and then they clear off to their normal situation and leave you in the same muddle that you were in. When you're in the situation the one thing you need is practical help and that's the one thing that never seems to be forthcoming.

Eric

I've spoken to my wife's community psychiatric nurse a few times and she's very good, but as a professional you would expect that she'd come up with suggestions for things you hadn't done. But this hasn't happened. I have visited the local community alcohol team and found the person I saw very helpful; he came out with some good ideas. But there's a limit to what I am prepared to do. It's my wife who needs the help and I don't want to become a professional carer. If there was someone to take the problem off my hands that would be great. That kind of support should come from the social services because caring for someone in this situation requires innate patience or professional ability, and payment for doing it.

John

None of the doctors I've seen have ever offered any help to me as the patient's partner. The help has always been for the patient and there's been no guidance for the partner. It's a major fault of the health service in my opinion.

I've got a last question here and it's this. After all the experiences you have had, how do you view the kind of drinking problems that your wives have? Are we right to think of it as an illness? Is anyone to blame for it? I know those are big questions but I wondered if you had any reflections on them.

Eric

I don't believe that problem drinking is a disease. My son thinks the same way and doesn't understand why his mother can't stop drinking. We have a similar attitude to her drinking, in fact I'm worse because I don't make allowances for other people's weaknesses. I suppose I am intolerant. I would be sympathetic if it wasn't something that she had brought on herself. Self-inflicted wounds annoy me. I can't understand why people can't do something about their weaknesses as I would. I see the drink as an evil poison in the house and I throw it away whenever I find it. Cause and effect is a difficult question. I wouldn't rule out me being at least part of the cause. I know I'm not the romantic kind or responsive type. It's made me feel guilty, as if I was neglecting her, as if I was some sort of ogre figure. As a carer I am expected to be totally devoted. Society says you're selfish if you want to do anything for yourself.

John

I certainly thought that I was part of the cause of my wife's drinking. Al-Anon says you shouldn't do that, blame yourself, but in the midst of things your mind is in such turmoil. You have to ask yourself why she has turned to alcohol. Perhaps I've had a part to play; I know some of the relations see it like that.

Tom

One of the reasons I don't find some of her relatives supportive is because they don't regard the drink as an illness. They feel she could stop it if she wanted to whereas she and I firmly believe that it's beyond her control. My attitude's changed in that respect. I'd never come across this before and I didn't understand it, but now I regard it as an illness. So once she's had one drink she has a genuine need for more. That's one of the reasons I've changed in my behaviour so that I'll now buy drink for her knowing what it would do to her if she didn't have it, because regardless of what state she's in she'd go out and get it somehow.

Comments

Because we have been interested in our research group in the extent to which coping with an addiction problem in the family is a gender matter, I am on the lookout here for ways in which these men might have responded to their wives' drinking problems in a fashion very different to the much better documented ways in which women have coped with their male partners' excessive drinking. I must say that on the whole I am struck, not by the difference, but rather by how familiar much of it sounds. When these men talk about their feelings of bitterness, frustration, anger, being wound up and at the end of their tether, thinking about the problem all the time, feeling depressed, hopeless, exhausted and resentful, sometimes hopeful but then let down, and perhaps now resigned to the problem, it doesn't sound as if there is anything particularly male about that. It sounds like what spouses and partners nearly always say when their loved one has a serious addiction problem, irrespective of the sex of the person they are concerned about and irrespective of their own sex. The deterioration in the relationship and the spin-off effects on their other relationships and friendships is also familiar. Several of these men were as concerned about the effects on their children, and visiting grandchildren, as wives of men with addiction problems are. When Gordon says that he tried to keep things on an even keel for the children's sake, what he says could be taken straight out of a description of the experiences of wives of men with drinking problems based on a whole series of studies.

Several things that these husbands say about the support they either get or fail to get from other people could also be out of an informed description of the experiences of partners whatever their sex. They describe other people as often being unable to help, even being outright intolerant. The spouse's or partner's relations can come in for particular criticism for being unhelpful, sometimes blaming, sometimes for being heavy drinkers themselves. The health services are portrayed in mixed terms. Some find their GPs of little help, others were luckier. This group of men were mostly recruited for the focus group via specialist treatment services being attended by their spouses or partners. Some had found the specialists very helpful, others less so. John could be expressing the view of many wives of addicted husbands, as well as husbands of addicted wives, when he says that in his experience there has been no guidance for the partner and that that is a major fault of the health service.

Particularly interesting were the very positive comments about Al-Anon made by two of these husbands, although Eric's view on Al-Anon was a dissenting one. Most members of Al-Anon are women so it was heartening to hear both John and Jack talk about the ways the fellowship had helped them in terms very similar to those used by women members. Jack's sentiment – I thought I was the only man in the world who had this problem (until I met others at Al-Anon) – is a familiar one amongst both women and men who have struggled alone to cope with family addiction problems and then come across a group, a self-help book, or a knowledgeable professional, and are surprised to discover that after all they are not alone in their troubles.

But are there any signs here of the gender differences that might have been expected? Is there a hint of a difference when the men say that they never knew what they were coming home to? The uncertainty associated with a family addiction problem is a common experience, the not knowing where one stands from one day to the next, the difficulty of planning, the hopes raised and then dashed. But the coming home to an untidy home with the evening meal unprepared, and husband and children having to set to and do more of the housework than they expected, has more of a gendered colouring to it. What about the taking control of the family finances that several of these men mentioned? This might be a peculiarly male way of coping. But then again this is something that women partners of men with alcohol, drug or gambling problems very frequently describe. Perhaps it is a case of financial control being something that is often more easily accessible to men as a way of coping than it is to many women, for whom financial control would represent more of a struggle.

Several of the men admit to physical violence. Perhaps this is the strongest candidate for a gender difference. As John says, men can inflict more damage. The men described their violence as having been extremely provoked, but each also described it as wrong, and unhelpful, and they felt guilty about it. It is not, of course, only men who are provoked to the point of physical violence. Caitlin Thomas is one famous example of a wife of a man with a drinking problem who was provoked to violence herself (see Chapter 11). But it does seem that men are more likely than women to have included some violence in the repertoire of ways in which they have responded to an addiction problem in the family.

What about separation? It has often been said that men require less provocation before they consider leaving a wife with a drinking problem than is the case if the roles are reversed. It is certainly more difficult to get men to take part in research on the subject. This group of men may not be typical since they were mostly engaged in helping their wives' treatment efforts, and they agreed to take part in a focus group. But what is interesting to me is that most had considered separation at some time or another, or been advised by other people to separate, and Tom was still thinking about it. The nature of the dilemma about whether to leave or to stay, the pros and the cons of either course of action, are very familiar. Familiar also is the debate about the nature of alcohol addiction as a disease or as something that is self-inflicted, the self-doubts that spouses and partners experience about whether they themselves might be to blame in some way, and the criticism that other people sometimes express towards affected family members. There seems nothing especially male about the way this group of men were talking about those questions.

Questions

1. I am inclined to think that husbands trying to cope with wives' addictions and wives trying to cope with their husbands' addictions are more similar in their experiences than they are different. Addiction trumps gender rather than the other way round. What do you think? Am I failing to appreciate some of the ways in which this is a gender issue?

2. What about assuming control of family finances, which is something that family members are often forced to do? Are male partners more likely to attempt to do that than female partners, and are they more likely to be successful at exerting such control?

3. Can you think of any ways in which being the husband of someone with an addiction problem is actually worse than it would be for a wife?

4. Are you convinced by what these men say about their aggressive reactions: that they were occasional, much provoked, now genuinely regretted? Would some of the examples have been more appropriately considered as cases of domestic violence towards their wives?

5. Wives of men with drinking problems have often come in for criticism and misunderstanding in the past. Do you think it is possible that husbands of women with drinking problems are liable for even greater misunderstanding?

6. Do you agree with John that the lack of help for family members of patients with alcohol (and drug and gambling) problems is a major fault of the health service?

7. If you were developing a self-help manual for affected partners, would one version suffice for both women and men or would two separate versions be required? If the latter, in what principal ways would the two versions differ? If you opt for a single version, how would you make it clear that you expected the manual to be useful to men as well as to women?

Exercises

- A man has come to see you wanting advice about how to cope with his wife's drinking problem. He has talked with you at length about what has been going on, which has impressed you as very typical of the experiences of family members where a close relative has an addiction problem. On your second meeting he admits that he and his partner have come to blows over it on a few occasions, which is something he much regrets. With the help of another person, role-play your response to that revelation and discuss the results with your colleagues and others in your group.

- Set up a debate amongst yourself and your colleagues on the motion (or something like it), *Coping with a partner with a drinking problem is largely a gendered issue.*

18

A Chancer by James Kelman

This is an interesting novel because it revolves almost entirely around gambling. The central character is Tammas, a young man aged about 20. The book contains numerous instances of him gambling on horses (in the book-makers), on dogs (at the track), cards (both in a casino, and privately with friends at work) and dominos (in the pub). Glasgow is the setting. The book is full of details of the betting choices that he makes, and his mixed fortunes. Sometimes he wins, on one occasion coming away with several hundred pounds, but more often he loses. He is often out of money altogether, on several occasions pawns clothes or possessions, and is forever begging cigarettes off other people. He is living with his older sister and her husband, and causes them worry because he is unreliable about coming in and going out and eating meals, they know he has pinched a small amount of money from the bowl where they put coins for the electricity meter, and he seems very unsettled as far as work is concerned. He leaves two jobs during the course of the book, the second one after only one day, partly because the work was certainly very hard but also because he had just won some money. He fails to turn up for a trip with mates to Blackpool. He leaves his girlfriend standing in the street in order to go gambling on one occasion and leaves her guessing whether he has given her up or not. He develops a

Addiction Dilemmas: Family Experiences from Literature and Research and their Challenges for Practice,
First Edition. Jim Orford.
© 2012 John Wiley & Sons, Ltd. Published 2012 by John Wiley & Sons, Ltd.

relationship with a single mother, Vi, but is unreliable about when he goes
to see her.

The book well conveys the monotony of his life, and the large part that
gambling is playing in it. A number of people are more or less aware that
Tammas is a gambler, but sometimes this is a cause for admiration at his
winning rather than criticism. The most consistently worried and critical
people are his sister Margaret and her husband Robert who from time
to time do confront him, but mostly about things other than gambling
(his treatment of his girlfriend, where he is getting his money from, not
letting them know where he has been). The book finishes on a somewhat
positive note as Tammas packs his bag to leave Glasgow to head south
for possible work in England. Gambling is certainly not presented in an
especially positive light, but nor is the book moralizing against it. The back
cover, however, carries a statement of an angle that certainly escaped me
when I read the book: 'Tammas is a gambler . . . Sometimes he wins, more
often he loses – but the gambling gives Tammas the best chance he's ever
going to get to work out what's really important to him, the only chance
that society is going to give him to discover himself.'

One of the most relevant passages in the book for our purposes occurs
about a third of the way through the story. Tammas comes back to Margaret
and Robert's house, somewhat unsteady after drinking. Margaret fries him
up sausage for a sandwich and puts the kettle on for him to make himself
some tea. Robert is sitting in the armchair and Margaret on the settee.
Tammas takes his tea and sandwich and sits next to her. The atmosphere
is tense. Tammas and Margaret try to make conversation but it takes an
uncomfortable turn as the following extract shows:

> Margaret said, Did you go to the job centre?
> No, I was a bit late.
> Late?
> Aye, I was a bit late. Hell of a long walk.
> You're a lazy bugger!
> Robert grunted something.
> Tammas paused before saying: I'll go the morrow, I'll be fine the morrow. Aye,
> different story then, get the giro and that, be able to take a bus.
> Okay! Robert had swivelled round on his seat to gaze at him. What is it? If
> you've got something to say say it!
> Tammas sniffed. I've no got anything to say.
> Bloody liar – he tried to tap me for a pound on Tuesday morning Margaret.
> You were wondering what was up with me, mind? Right? That's what was up with
> me. He tried to tap me for a pound and I wasn't having any. That's it Tammas eh!

No.

Ah ya liar ye! Robert sat back forwards again, the newspaper falling from his lap.

These things dont bother me.

Robert glared round at him but said nothing for a few moments. No, he went on, these things dont worry you – wee things, like money, they dont bother you, Only when you come trying to tap me or your sister.

I wish you'd get your facts straight Robert. I think about once in the past two years or something, that's the number of times I've tried to tap you.

Listen son . . .

Margaret interrupted. Why dont the two of you stop it! I wish you would just stop it.

Well, cried Robert, I dont know how many times he's taken it from you!

That's rent money, said Tammas.

Rent money!

He always pays it back, said Margaret.

Robert was saying: What d'you mean rent money? It's our money, it belongs to me and your sister. So never mind what the hell you call it. And as far as I'm concerned when you dont come up with that on a Friday night then it's a hell of a sight worse than borrowing. And what about that bloody meter bowl? Never a bloody tosser in it once you get through with it. You couldn't care less whether we've got enough electricity or no. O naw, nothing like that bothers you. Just wee minor details!

Aye. Tammas leaned to lay the unfinished sandwich on the teaplate, and he looked about for his cigarettes and matches. He saw the packet beneath the corner of the settee and soon was smoking; he exhaled at the ceiling. It's all coming out the night, he said.

Aye and high time too if you ask me . . . Robert shook his head at Margaret: Look at the state of him! He tries to tap me for a pound and then he can still come marching in here half drunk and looking for you to make his bloody supper!

I didn't look for Margaret to make my supper at all.

Tammas goes on to explain how he has been given some money by an acquaintance in the local betting shop who, Tammas says, has no need to work there, having won so much money in the past, but just likes to keep in touch with the game. Robert is irritated by the suggestion that money is considered so lightly by some, and the temperature rises. Tammas suggests that his betting friend has had more cash than Robert will ever see and, unlike Robert, has no need to work. The conversation continues:

. . . Robert frowned and he shifted round on his seat to be facing away from him. Away and grow up son.

I might and I might no – have to watch it in case I turn out like you.

Tammas! Margaret was staring at him.

Robert held his hand up to her. It's alright Margaret . . . he glanced at Tammas: I've got one thing to say to you: why dont you pack your bags and go. The trouble is you *have* grown up, you *are* a big boy. You just dont act like one. And I think it'd be best if you went, and I mean that.

Aye. Dont worry about it. Tammas was getting onto his feet, gathering his cup and plate and the cigarettes and matches. Soon as the time comes I'll be off, away, dont worry about that. He was at the door and he paused to add, Goodnight folks, pleasant dreams.

Robert shook his head. God, you give me a pain in the neck, so you do.

Comments

Kelman has caught in this novel the way in which an addiction like gambling can dominate someone's life, pushing other considerations into the background, and interfering with a person's relationships in the process. Gambling, in one form or another, is what motivates Tammas, and wherever he goes he seems to leave behind him a trail of broken promises and expectations. Those who are left feeling let down by him include two women friends, mates who were expecting him to go with them on a trip, people at work which he left after only a single day, and most particularly Margaret, his older sister, and her husband Robert, with whom he is living. They are experiencing the things that so many families experience: concern about where Tammas has been and what he has been doing, how he is treating his girlfriend and where he is getting his money from, and concern about whether he is paying his way and even whether he is pinching money from them. As is so often the case they are worried both on his behalf – how will he make his way in life if he cannot get or keep a job or if he treats girlfriends so badly – and on their own behalf – is he taking advantage of Margaret who is cooking his meals, or of them both by hassling them to borrow back the rent money or for cigarettes.

But one of the angles that this novel is particularly good at revealing is the difficulty that concerned family members have in confronting a problem. Robert, in particular, is harbouring upset feelings about the situation and it all comes out over tea. The atmosphere is tense and gets more so. Communication is not direct and objective but angry and increasingly full of epithets and charges of misdoing on both sides, and it finishes with Robert suggesting that Tammas should leave. Margaret's role is an important one. It is the case that elder sisters often feel this kind of responsibility for looking after younger brothers who are having difficulty with gambling, drug or alcohol problems. Not surprisingly she finds herself caught between her husband Robert and her brother Tammas. At one point she interrupts, implying that both of the men are at fault in arguing. She sides with Tammas at one point, telling Robert that he always pays his rent in the end. At another point she reacts when Tammas makes a cutting remark to Robert. Tammas himself is not short of arguments in his defence: Robert he says is exaggerating the number of times he has asked for money; he will go to the job centre tomorrow. One of the arguments, and one that often arises in the context of gambling, is that sometimes he and other people win, even several hundred pounds on occasions, and sometimes he is admired for it. He comes home with a story that someone in the local betting shop had given him money, having won so much money in the past that he can give it away: an unlikely story, but it is the kind of story that puts Margaret and Robert in a difficult position because to counter it they would have to accuse Tammas of lying.

The teatime episode, in short, encapsulates much of what goes on in families where such problems exist. The atmosphere is tense, the family members are worried, feeling concerned but also exploited, communication is difficult, family members are easily divided, arguments can escalate, and everyone is left unhappy with the outcome.

Questions

1. Do you think there might be something in what is stated on the back cover of the book – that in some way gambling gave Tammas one of the few chances that society gave him to work out what was important to him? Or is that simply another example of misunderstanding and under-estimating the destructive power of a habit like gambling?
2. Do you feel a greater affinity for Tammas or for Robert? Why?
3. If you were Margaret, would you have Tammas come to live with you and your partner? Why do you think older sisters feel that sense of responsibility?
4. In the situation described in the extract from Kelman's novel, Margaret is caught between supporting Tammas and backing up Robert's criticism of Tammas. For his part, Robert would probably have nothing to do with Tammas were it not for the fact that he is married to Tammas's sister.

Can you think of other sets of family circumstances where one member of the family has an addiction problem and others, like Margaret and Robert, find themselves caught up in conflicts of loyalty?

5. What can a family member say if a relative with an addictive behaviour problem comes asking for a loan, employing plausible arguments that the money is needed for a good purpose, will be paid back, is needed urgently, and there is no other way of obtaining it?

6. Research suggests that there are many Tammases. What responsibility does the state have, if any, for providing help or advice to the many Margarets and Roberts there must be?

7. In an ideal world, what help would be available for Margaret?

Exercises

• If older sisters sometimes feel responsible for their younger brothers, who in your family do you have that feeling of responsibility towards? Is there anyone you would take in to your home if he or she had such a problem, and if so what conflicts might that cause? What about the other way round: who in your family would feel a sense of responsibility towards you if you had an addiction problem? Discuss those questions with one other person, and ask the same questions about his or her family.

• This is an exercise in two parts. For the first part you need two people, one to take Margaret's part, the other Robert's. The two of you are concerned about Tammas but you know from experience that it is difficult to raise your concerns without coming across as critical and making Tammas uncomfortable and defensive. Your task is to plan how you will raise your worries with him over tea. Part II is the teatime episode itself with the three of them present. Find out how your planned interaction with Tammas works out in practice.

Growing Up with Parents Who Drink Excessively

Four Stories

Of the following four stories, each of the first three is closely based on one or more of the accounts given to researchers in a study in which the sons and daughters of problem drinking parents were interviewed at length about their experiences of growing up. The fourth story is based on a published account given by a daughter who took part in a study of counselling for family members affected by a close relative's problem. The reader should imagine that each story is being told by someone who is now in her or his very late teens, in some cases still living at home, in other cases having left home. You might imagine that these four young people have come together to share their stories.

Annie's story

I know that my father has had a drinking problem since even before I was born. I was aware of it as a small child. He has been a lifelong heavy drinker and everybody knew it. He drank at home and in pubs. He would start as soon as the shops opened where he would buy sherry or whisky and would

Addiction Dilemmas: Family Experiences from Literature and Research and their Challenges for Practice,
First Edition. Jim Orford.
© 2012 John Wiley & Sons, Ltd. Published 2012 by John Wiley & Sons, Ltd.

drink through the afternoon into the evening. Then he would go to the pub and drink beer. I have early memories of his strange behaviour. For example I remember him falling off a bike in the high street, presumably drunk. When I was a bit older I remember being really frightened when I found him laid out on the kitchen floor. He's never had any treatment to my knowledge although in the last few years he has only been drinking in the evening, only whisky, maybe a bottle and a half a day, and he has been without drinking at all for periods of three or four weeks at a time.

There were always financial difficulties because of the money he was spending on drink. I particularly noticed this when I went to grammar school and realized that everything I had was always homemade. I didn't have a school uniform and I couldn't go on trips abroad and my parents didn't let me stay on to do A-levels. In fact I realized my family was different in every way.

He was disgusting when he was drunk and I was disgusted with him. I would tell him straight out that I hated him and wanted him to go away. I tried to get my mother to leave with my younger brother and I, but she said she still loved him. There were a lot of arguments between them and at one time it got pretty bad. There was some violence and a few black eyes. Although there was terrible tension a lot of the time they always made it very clear that despite all the aggro they would never split up. They actually seemed a loving couple at times. But I think she made too many allowances and excuses for him. For example she'd try and get him off to bed without an argument.

She's a very good mother, a very likeable person and I did have a very good relationship with her. But she started to develop bouts of depression and my father encouraged her to drink when she was depressed. She started to drink more and more sherry and taking pills as well. Our relationship has not been so good since I became more aware of the difference between our family and others when I went to grammar school and as my mother's depression and drinking got worse.

I wasn't confident at secondary school and I felt quite lonely. I didn't tell other girls about my father's drinking and I didn't like to bring friends home, certainly not boyfriends, just in case. I did have one best friend who came round but I was always in a terrible state wanting her to go before my father came in.

I had a lot of illness as a teenager. My mother was always taking me to the doctor for a bottle of tonic as she called it. I do remember getting very shaky and I think when I was about 15, I had something like a nervous breakdown. I spent some weeks as an in-patient in a psychiatric hospital but I don't think they got to the bottom of the problem and I couldn't see the sense of the treatment. I think I was basically anxious and depressed.

John's story

My father drank throughout my childhood. The drinking was constant, the central core of his social activities, and it overlapped with his work. Although he drank huge amounts every day, market day was the worst. It was a dreadful day, everyone would get really drunk. Otherwise his drinking was just a fact of life, it was just how it was. Things got worse as time went on. He'd go off and not come back at night, for example, which he'd never done before. One Christmas Eve really sticks in my mind when he smashed a new car. It was so incredibly lucky he didn't kill someone else. He managed to drive it home, God knows how.

My parents' relationship was basically really very bad, extremely traumatic. Every few weeks there would be a terrific row followed by several days of tension and not speaking. I don't know why they stayed together. They did separate later on after I left home. The worst was when he was drinking and in a bad mood. Then it became a regime of terror. I know there was regular violence towards my mother. On occasions I could see she was bruised. He'd wear you down, make sure you couldn't leave the room and then, when he'd got you in tears, he'd let you go. I hated him but couldn't do anything about it. I was more afraid of him than anything. You had to be quieter if he was at home. The atmosphere between us children and our mother was good so long as he wasn't there. Any family activities and discussions took place without him. We had a good relationship with our mother. She was very quiet, very organized, she did everything. She tried to keep a quiet life, to keep the peace. She sent us kids off to the pictures on Saturday afternoons although she couldn't afford it. She couldn't stand up to him. I don't know how she lived with him.

I got to an age when I wouldn't cry, I wouldn't stand for it, I used to shout back. I got to be very rebellious in my early teens. By that time my elder brothers were quite big and strong and they started to step in to stop it. In fact I was worried that one of them would kill him one day.

I never had any difficulty making friends but my friendships were quite separate from my home life. I knew I had to try and make something of my life in spite of my father and I tried to have as little contact with him as possible as a teenager. I mainly went round to other people's houses and I developed a strong sense of belonging to a group who were very important to me. A lot of my friends were a number of years older than me. I couldn't relate to kids my own age. At secondary school I got into a hell of a lot of fights. I found that kids respect you more after a fight and are keen to hang around you. Sometimes people didn't seem too friendly towards me because of Dad's drinking. I started smoking cannabis when I was only 11 and drinking in pubs at 13. I spent a lot of time out. I lived for evenings and weekends. Home became just like a hotel, somewhere I just ate and slept. I tried never to speak about my home life.

Alan's story

Until I was 10 we lived abroad. Drinking was part of the social scene and my father would drink from dawn to dusk and more, drinking wherever he went, at home, others' homes and at work. I knew he could drink several bottles of gin or whisky at the weekend and that he hid bottles in the garage, in the garden or in his coat. He always needed to drink before he went out and he brought drink home with him from town. He slept a lot. In my teens, when we were back in this country, he was a sporadic attender at AA and seemed to be in and out of hospitals, sometimes with physical problems caused by his drinking.

I do remember arguments at home and they did get more common and worse as time went on. But there was always affection as well between my mother and father and I don't think there was any violence. But I couldn't say we were a close family. As a child I never felt I could really talk to my father. He was distant, even non-existent at times. I particularly remember him promising to take us to a show and being really upset that he didn't. He seemed to be able to detach himself from the family and there was little opportunity to talk. At times I hated him; at other times I felt sorry for him. Despite everything I love him. He cared about us, there's no doubt about that. He's got a heart of gold really. Mum was very good and did everything for us. She was like a leaning post in coping with our father. She got very involved with Al-Anon in later years.

Early on I felt very baffled by it. I can remember taking long walks, cutting myself off and becoming isolated from the family and even from friends. It was only later that I realized that he had been an alcoholic all the time I was growing up. Later on I used to pretend there was nothing the matter. I made sure friends kept out of the way and didn't upset him. Somehow I felt it was my responsibility to make it easier. I'd ignore him and avoid upsetting Mum. That was the way I adapted, which was very different from my sister who was much more open about it all. Sometimes I helped her pour the contents of bottles of his that we found down the drain. But I wasn't confrontational like she was. She's my older sister and in her teens she began to argue with him and take more responsibility in the family. I think she managed our father quite well by being firmer with him than our mother did. For example she told him that if he got drunk she wouldn't do anything for him and sometimes this seemed to work and he drank less for a while. I tried to keep my father's drinking secret from my friends but her friends knew all about our father's drinking. Her attitude was that people should take her as she was and she wasn't going to let it bother her.

I left home as soon as I could. I was only just 17. I have found it difficult to settle down. I left school without any qualifications and I had a number of different jobs. At one time I was out of work for 18 months. I worked for a while for a brewery and a bit later on in the local pub. Looking back I can see I was a very heavy drinker at that time. I was drinking to forget worries, mainly financial, and to relax. I was getting drunk probably several times a week and I could get nasty with it sometimes, especially when I'd been drinking cider. I'm married now and my heavy drinking continued at first. My wife couldn't handle me spending money on drink, getting drunk and being deceitful about it, and she left me for a while. But we have an agreement about it now and I no longer feel I am in danger of having a drinking problem.

Catia's story

When I was little I didn't realize what a problem my mother's drinking was. It was roundabout when I was 10 that I remember her asking me not to tell my father that she'd been drinking. I was afraid they would argue so I did cover up for her. It was later on that I realized that was wrong and I started to tell my father what was happening when he wasn't there. Now I'm grown up I feel I have to do something about it, to find some solution.

I remember feeling full of worries particularly that something bad could happen to her when she drank, maybe out in the street. She used to take money and valuables out with her and even at home she could leave the gas on. She had health problems as well, heart trouble. When I was at school I was always thinking about what could happen to her and I couldn't concentrate on my school work. I felt a lot calmer when I was at home and I could manage to get her involved in cooking and other things. I would go out socializing myself sometimes but often I didn't feel like it. I couldn't relax knowing that my mother was at home alone. I worried too about what people might think of her. It's not that I was ashamed. I just didn't want other people to make wrong bad judgements about her. I didn't want other people to get the wrong idea about her.

As a teenager I used to cry over any little thing. I couldn't stop myself. I also felt dizzy sometimes. My doctor sent me for some tests but just said that I was nervous. I remember thinking that typical teenage worries were not very important. If one of my friends confided in me about a problem with some boy or other I couldn't see that as being a very serious thing. At one time she had several months without drinking but then she started again the same as before. I had started to trust her again but then I felt it had all fallen apart and I felt really disappointed, betrayed, like being stabbed. Mostly what I felt was sad because I couldn't believe that there was nothing that could be done. What I couldn't understand is why she had relapses, why she couldn't see the difference between all the problems there were when she drank and how happy she was with herself and how calm things were when she didn't drink. If it's like a disease, aren't there places and ways to cure it?

As I got older I was very involved in doing a lot around the house and I don't know if that was a good thing. For example if I got home from school and my mother had been drinking and hadn't done things like the washing up, then I did it and tidied the house up. When that happened I often found my mother asleep or I had to put her to bed. At least when my father got home he found everything clean and tidy and so there were no arguments. Although it took me quite some time to do all that at least things were calmer and there was no fuss. But it's not as if it did any good. The problem was there just the same. Maybe if I hadn't done all that then she would have started doing it herself or at least she might have understood what she'd done.

I went through one period when I decided not to talk to her very much. By doing that I felt further away from the problem and a bit freer to think more about myself. But it didn't do any good and I was afraid that my mother was really upset by the feeling of being neglected. If we did things together I could take her mind off things and she didn't drink. That was good while it lasted but as soon as I stopped or when there was no one around she started drinking again so it was useless really. I know she got upset if I kept my distance but maybe that way she realized what was happening to other people, to me.

Later on my father and I took it in turns to stay at home and keep her under control. We felt we were doing something but we really don't know if it helped or not. One disadvantage is that my time was not my own. I didn't have time to think about myself. And the problem was not getting any better. As soon as we let her off the leash she'd start again. If you ban someone from doing something then maybe when they can they do it even more.

I see my father as a strength in this. We've been allies regarding the family problem, although we don't talk about it openly. And I couldn't rely on him when I was feeling really down. I didn't open up to him when I felt bad because I was afraid that if he saw me upset he'd end up blaming mother and arguing with me.

Comments

There are a number of similarities in those four stories and those common themes will resonate for so many youngsters who live in a family where one or more parent has a drinking problem, and for adults who can recall such experiences. Some of the commonalities that stand out are as follows:

(i) Early memories are often fragmentary but vivid. Annie remembers her father falling down drunk; John remembers market days and one particularly traumatic Christmas Eve; Alan remembers bottles being hidden in all sorts of places. Realization that a parent has a drinking problem grows and clarifies as the children get older.

(ii) As older children, a parental drinking problem has effects on the spheres of school and friends. Catia couldn't concentrate at school because she was worried about her mother coming to harm; in fact she felt better being at home in order to keep an eye on her mother. It was when Annie went to secondary school that she realized the financial effects of her father's drinking and how different her family was from others. She made sure she didn't bring friends home and if she did she was worried all the time. Alan too made sure that he kept friends out of the way. John had a strong circle of friends but he made sure he kept his home and friendship worlds well apart. Catia was worried what people would think of her mother. She was so worried about her mother that she found other people's ordinary teenage problems to be rather trivial.

(iii) For all four the whole family atmosphere was affected. Annie describes family arguments and some violence, but also believed her parents to have had a basically loving relationship. John described the most violent atmosphere with big rows, tension, violence towards his mother and a sheer reign of terror. Alan described family arguments but also affection and he described no violence. But they were not a close family. Neither did Catia describe violence but her fear of arguments between her parents was a big factor in how she coped.

(iv) All four described good supportive relationships with the other parent, a factor that some believe to be crucial if young people are to show resilience in the face of parental drinking, drug or gambling problems. Alan described his mother as a leaning post in coping with his father and Catia described her father as an ally and a source of strength in coping with her mother's problem. In John's family it was his mother who remained organized and around whom the family activities took place. Annie also described a good relationship with her mother but this got more difficult as her mother became depressed and started to drink more herself.

(v) Between them these four stories provide a good picture of the range of ways in which young people respond. Annie found her father disgusting and told him so. She tried to get her mother to leave with the children. Her mother she thought made too many allowances for Annie's father. John was another who after a certain age stood up to his father, shouting back at him. Alan represents a different but equally common way of coping: he cut himself off, remembers taking long walks, pretended all was well, and tried to avoid upset. In that respect he was very different from his sister who was much more direct in her criticism of their father's drinking. Catia's way of coping is also very common, particularly amongst girls. She was very involved, to the point of neglecting her own interests as a teenager, in doing the housework that her mother wasn't doing, tidying the place up, avoiding arguments between her parents. She was full of doubt about whether that was the best way of coping. At one stage she didn't talk to her mother and again she was unsure whether that was the right thing to do.

(vi) All showed signs of strain in one way or another. Catia cried a lot, was nervous, had dizzy spells. Annie was often ill and as a teenager had what she describes as a nervous breakdown. The boys described male-gendered signs of strain. John was out a lot, had older friends, got into fights, sometimes over his father's drinking, and started drinking and smoking cannabis as a young teenager. Alan left home at a quite early age and found it difficult to adjust to the world of work. He became a very heavy drinker which was a difficult factor in the early days of his marriage. It is interesting to note that although the two girls came into contact with health services as teenagers, with psychological symptoms, in neither case were their problems traced to their likely source in the family problem.

Questions

1. Confronting the parent, cutting oneself off and becoming self-absorbed, and being useful by taking on extra responsibilities around the home, are three common ways in which young teenagers respond to a parental drinking problem. What are the main advantages and disadvantages of each of those three ways of coping?

2. Although one source of resilience for children of addicted parents may be the strength of the other parent or another adult, in practice it can be very difficult for that person, who is also likely to be affected. How can the strength of the other adult best be supported?

3. I'm a secondary school teacher. One of my pupils has been under-achieving, has had quite a bit of time off school and is clearly upset. I have reason to believe one of the parents has an alcohol problem. What can I do?

4. I am a GP and I am worried about one of my teenage patients who has become very disturbed. Her mother, who is also my patient, has been on anti-depressants for some time. The father is a patient of one of my colleagues who has recently told me that the father has a drinking problem. What can I do for my teenage patient?

5. I am a police woman. There is a boy I am worried about on my patch. He is mixing with a bad crowd. I know from the school I liaise with that he has been truanting quite a lot recently. I can see that he is danger of heavy drinking under age and getting into drug-taking. I happen to know that his father has a drinking problem. What can I do?
6. My spouse has a drinking problem and I am worried about the effects it is having on our teenage son and daughter. What can I do?
7. I am a teenager. My parent has a drinking problem and I am very upset about it. It's affecting my school work, my friendships, and our family. What can I do?

Exercises

- You are a GP. A mother comes to the surgery with her 10-year-old daughter who is having a lot of episodes of crying, is showing signs of nervousness and has had a number of unexplained dizzy spells. You have been prescribing anti-depressants for the mother for some time. A colleague has recently alerted you to the fact that the husband/father in the family is receiving treatment in the same practice for an alcohol problem. What do you do? Try role-playing it.
- You are a teacher. You were particularly wanting to meet the parents of one boy in your class whom you are worried about. He is seriously under-achieving in his school work, has a bad attitude and has been regularly getting into fights with other boys. You recently overheard another boy teasing him because his father was a 'junkie'. Only the boy and his mother turn up. What do you do? Try role-playing it.

20

Baudelaire and His Mother in Chains

In 2004 my attention was caught by a review of a new book about Charles Baudelaire, the celebrated and much written about nineteenth-century French writer. The new book was written by Frank Hilton, a lecturer in European literature, writer of TV documentaries and dramas, and translator from French and German. He is thus eminently qualified to write yet another biography of Baudelaire. But this book has a focus that Hilton believed was missing from earlier biographies, namely Baudelaire as drug addict. What is especially interesting for us is Baudelaire's relationship with his mother which is a major theme running throughout the book. Hilton's book is called *Baudelaire in Chains*, but, as is usually the case with close family members, the chains that Hilton believes bound Baudelaire to opium extended around his mother also.

From just a few weeks after Baudelaire set up home on his own at the age of 21 to shortly before his premature death in 1867 at the age of 46, he and his mother kept up a relationship, mostly by correspondence, much of which revolved around Baudelaire's requests for money and his mother's attempts to resist, usually resulting in her eventually giving in to his request. Sometimes there were gaps in their correspondence, as for example when his mother and stepfather spent three years in Constantinople where his

Addiction Dilemmas: Family Experiences from Literature and Research and their Challenges for Practice,
First Edition. Jim Orford.
© 2012 John Wiley & Sons, Ltd. Published 2012 by John Wiley & Sons, Ltd.

stepfather was Ambassador. Depending on the state of their relationship Baudelaire would address her with the familiar *tu* or, coldly, *vous*. The manipulative style of Baudelaire's requests for money is very apparent from the examples that Hilton gives. Amongst them were the following:

> *All I need is twelve days* to finish something and sell it. If, for a sacrifice of *60 francs, representing a fortnight's peace*, you get the pleasure of seeing me at the end of the month give you proof that I have *sold three books*, representing at least *1,500* francs, and thank you from the bottom of my heart – will you regret it? . . . I can assure you I would not boast about such a feat if I had not started writing these books so long ago that the paper they're written on has turned yellow . . . *60 francs!* Is it really possible, and do I have to give up hope of finding one last kindness, even from my mother (1845, Hilton, p. 85).
>
> In spite of the cruel letter you sent in reply to my last request, I believed I had the right to approach you once more, though I know full well how much it will annoy you and what difficulty I will have in making you understand the legitimacy of this request. Nevertheless I have such a powerful conviction that it can be infinitely and definitely useful to me that I hope to be able to persuade you to share that conviction with me. Please note that when I say *once more* I mean, very sincerely: one last time . . . (1847, p. 105).

Hilton describes their relationship as one of two people, '. . . locked into a relationship in which financial and emotional need are inextricably intermingled . . .' (p. 78). Later he comments that she was unable to carry through on a policy of 'tough love', not being able to bring herself to leave her son long enough at rock bottom to see if he would be able to do anything of his own accord: 'She was what the modern jargon describes as an enabler' (p. 106). In 1851, when Baudelaire was 30, his mother, in a short gap between ambassadorial postings, found him:

> . . . in a pitiful state, his coats and shirts so threadbare that she insisted on buying him some new clothes. Laudanum and poverty had brought him once again to rock bottom. 'What a frightful state I found him in!' his mother confided to Asselineau [Baudelaire's friend and subsequent first biographer] years later. 'What destitution! And I, his mother, with so much love in my heart, so much goodwill for him, could do nothing to get him out of it!' (p. 117).

Four years later she writes to the family solicitor, authorizing a payment, saying she prefers not to renew relations with her son since he has hurt her so much and has been so rude. But she goes on to say how worried she is about his impoverished state and says she would do anything she could to relieve his distress. Baudelaire's mother, according to Hilton, is a good example of the two main schools of thought about how family members and close friends should cope with drug abusers. The 'doves', like Baudelaire's mother, showed tolerance and generosity towards the addict, arguing that addicts are unfortunate victims of bad company or cynical dealers, or that they simply cannot endure seeing their children in such a terrible state. They do whatever they can '. . . to mitigate the situation – buying clothes, paying bills, giving money for food, all in the hope that their addicts' promises to reform, take a cure, leave the bad company they are mixing with, will – this time – prove genuine' (p. 107). The doves, according to Hilton, almost always end up behaving like the second group, the 'hawks', the 'un-enablers', who believe that no help should be given, a position based on the belief that giving help will only delay the process of change, but also probably fuelled by hard-heartedness, an inability to empathize, and resentment at being taken advantage of. Baudelaire's stepfather – often referred to, using his army title, as 'The General ' – was the perfect example.

Baudelaire's half-brother, Alphonse, the son of their father's first wife, like Baudelaire's mother, receives criticism from most of Baudelaire's biographers. They portray him as taking the General's side, lecturing Baudelaire in a stupid and pompous fashion, and aiding and abetting the family's undue controlling of Baudelaire's financial affairs. Hilton considers that unfair. There is another side to Alphonse's stance towards Baudelaire. He was 16 years the elder and made efforts to keep in touch with Baudelaire during the latter's school days, being a confidante and generally acting like a father figure cum older brother. He arranged and paid for treatment of a venereal infection for Baudelaire and offered to pay off the latter's debts. Admittedly, Hilton says, when Baudelaire submitted a list of his debts, Alphonse reacted badly to the extent of them and the disorderly way in which Baudelaire presented them. Baudelaire was a young man of 20 at the time and Alphonse's letter to him, of which the following is a passage, probably would have appeared somewhat overbearing:

> Never forget that your mother, the General, your brother, have only one thought, one desire, that of making you a man and that your past faults will be forgotten the sooner you have given more thought to the absurdity of the beliefs of those who led you astray. Goodbye, brother. Write to me often. An elder brother is a sure friend, whose advice you can always count on and whose sincere affection can never be called in question (p. 73).

Their relationship was never so close again. Indeed Hilton is appalled by the fact that Baudelaire never made it to the funeral of Alphonse's surviving son who died a few years later at the age of only 21. Nor did he make it to Alphonse's own funeral a few years after that.

One of the things for which Baudelaire never forgave his half-brother was the latter's part in imposing on Baudelaire a legally appointed *conseil judiciaire* who would take control of the income from Baudelaire's remaining capital and dole it out to him in monthly amounts for the rest of his life. The role was taken by the family solicitor, Narcisse Ancelle. Financial decisions were to be made jointly by Ancelle and Baudelaire's mother. At the age of 21 Baudelaire had come into a considerable inheritance much of which he squandered within a few months. At the suggestion that legal control might be applied to his spending, he responded to his mother by writing, 'If I were to discover that you had done such a thing without my knowledge, I would leave here immediately. . . and you would never see me again' (p. 80). When, the following year, it seemed that his mother had no alternative, he wrote again to her:

> . . . I'm writing all this very calmly, and when I think how ill I have been during the last few days, caused by anger and amazement, I wonder how I will ever be able to put up with such an arrangement! . . . I would rather lose my fortune completely, and give myself up entirely to you, than submit to some legal judgement or other – one is an act of freedom, the other is an attack on my freedom . . . I beg you, as humbly as I possibly can, to save yourself this great trouble, and spare me a terrible humiliation (p. 82).

When the matter was done he wrote the next day to his mother saying, 'yesterday Monsieur Ancelle gave me the last rites' (p. 83). From then until the end of his life Baudelaire's relationship with Ancelle was an important one, at times causing Baudelaire rage at Ancelle's refusal to give him the money he asked for or his interference in Baudelaire's affairs – on one occasion he visited the hotel where Baudelaire was staying to enquire about his expenditure. But towards the end of his life Ancelle played a role, useful to Baudelaire, of someone who enabled him to deal with his publishers and creditors at a long distance.

Baudelaire's borrowing and spending did not stop, which Hilton attributes in large part to his opium addiction. Hilton believes that his mother and stepfather never knew about his opium habit. In fact the theme of Hilton's book is the way in which he believes Baudelaire deceived both himself and others about the extent and seriousness of his drug-taking. In his correspondence and writing on the subject of drug-taking (which he famously wrote about in his *Les Paradis Artificiels*) he is not open about his own opium-taking in anything like the way that the English writer

De Quincey was in his *Confessions of an English Opium-Eater* (*Les Paradis* contains a translation and adaptation by Baudelaire of *Confessions*). Even Coleridge, who kept his opium use secret from others for many years, preserved his detailed notes about his habit (see Chapter 16). Baudelaire only occasionally referred to his opium use in a few letters to his mother, Ancelle and his publisher, but then usually as something that was-medicinal and under his control. It is therefore difficult to know exactly when he started taking opium and in what quantities he took it. Hilton found it extraordinary that, despite his admiration for the writings of De Quincey and of Edgar Allan Poe, another English language writer who wrote of the state of 'enslavement' induced by opium, he never himself faced up to the devastating effects that the drug was having on his life including often his ability to concentrate on writing. There is, however, the occasional admission of harm caused by laudanum, as in a letter to Ancelle in his late twenties when he says, 'My digestion has been pretty well wrecked by laudanum; but it's not the first time, and it's strong enough to recover' (p. 114), and the very occasional reference to how much he might be taking, as in a letter to his mother near the end of his life when he writes of taking up to as much as 150 drops of laudanum a day over a period of several years in the past – Hilton is convinced that 150 is an under-estimate and that 'in the past' is a cover up.

Hilton was struck by the fact that everyone who had written about Baudelaire since then seemed to know that he used the drug, and many described him as an addict. But scarcely any had grasped the full consequences of such a condition, putting much greater emphasis, when explaining his bad health and the strokes that preceded his premature death, on his youthful syphilitic infection (doctors at the time of his death referred to a 'softening of the brain'). Only his French biographer Claude Pichois, seems to have recognized '. . . the ravages due to alcohol and laudanum . . .' as one of a number of factors responsible for his failure to write more than he did. Most of Baudelaire's biographers, on the other hand, are critical of what they see as his hard-hearted mother and interfering, controlling *conseil judiciaire*, Ancelle, along with Baudelaire's half-brother.

Hilton takes the matter to the other extreme, constantly seeing in Baudelaire's behaviour signs of a typical drug addict. And those signs are not pretty ones. Indeed it is a feature of Hilton's book that a thoroughly negative stereotype of the drug addict is referred to throughout. There is reference to, '. . . the deteriorating moral standards of opiate abusers . . .' (p. 58), to the difficulties for family members in '. . . dealing with so irresponsible and unpredictable a person as a drug addict . . .' (p. 88), '. . . the endless unfulfilled promises of the drug abuser' (p. 149), '. . . a characteristic drug abuser's cover-up' (p. 216) and to the 'Dishonesty, idleness, selfishness, indifference to others . . . monotonously manifested by opiate abusers' (p. 20). Hilton is in no doubt that it is the drug use that was responsible for Baudelaire's moral decline, as it is for other addicts:

> It compromises artistic integrity and distorts and embitters political and philo-sophical views. As time goes by and the addiction deepens, the user becomes lethargic, unreliable, unable to keep his promises or pay his debts. Eventually he neglects his appearance, blames others for his plight and demands special consideration both for his talents and for his misfortunes. He resents the suc-cesses of his contemporaries and sneers at the decency of honest and respectable citizens, including his loved ones. Because he has himself become an outcast and a pariah, he is drawn to outcasts and pariahs – though usually all the while maintaining a secret inner sense of intellectual and spiritual superiority over them (pp. 49–50).
>
> Self-deception seems to be an inherent part of the condition. Having taken over the addict – having replaced its host's freedom of action and way of life with its own imperious demands – the chosen drug seems also to have the malign power of concealing this state of affairs from the victim of its depredations . . . What is the cause of their poverty? The cruelty of the world, the heartlessness of their relatives, their friends . . . Their lack of success? The cruelty of the world, the heartlessness of their relatives . . . Their chaotic lifestyle and unhappiness? The cruelty of the world, etc., etc. Everyone gets the blame except the nightmare drug itself . . . (p. 171).

Towards the end of his life Baudelaire comes up with an unrealistic scheme to move into theatre direction, prompting Hilton to refer to this as:

> . . . the kind of unreal assessment of the outside world that all opiate addicts suffer from and attempt to promulgate as an acceptable virtual reality among their friends and relatives. The many deceptions that their families suffer in the course of their individual Calvaries, however, make eventually for a sceptical reception of the addicts' dubious propositions (p. 207).

Many years after his death Baudelaire was accused of plagiarism, again a cue for Hilton to air his views about addicts:

> Where plagiarism is concerned, however, opium addicts are automatically in a special category. For them, the dividing line between what is theirs and what is someone else's is often hopelessly blurred (p. 129).

A minor character in Hilton's book is Baudelaire's mistress, Jeanne, with whom he lived at various times. Baudelaire's mother and stepfather considered her a very unsuitable companion for Baudelaire, and Hilton appears to share that view:

> ... she was certainly not the bourgeoisie's idea of the ideal wife and companion. It was no good Baudelaire expecting regular hot dinners from Jeanne, nor a well-run household. In this respect the two other nineteenth-century writers most famous for their opium addiction – Coleridge and De Quincey – were a great deal better off than Baudelaire. Their wives were sensible, practical, sober women, both mothers to boot, who took their husbands' affairs in hand – as far as such a thing is possible ... (p. 88).

Comments

Frank Hilton wanted to bring out Baudelaire's drug addiction, apparently recognized by most of his previous biographers but scarcely ever focused on in much detail. That may have been, Hilton seems to suggest, because Baudelaire himself was secretive and devious about it. Indeed his mother, Hilton believes, may never have known about it at all. She certainly experienced the what-to-do-about-money dilemma, which is such a common one for family members and which has been a recurring theme in this book. Like so many other mothers and other family members she was regularly hassled for money, and Baudelaire seems to have been particularly manipulative in his attempts to extract money from her. She was well and truly 'humbugged' to use the expression that we learned in our research with indigenous family members in Northern Australia (see Chapter 8). Like so many mothers since, she was appalled by the frightful state that she found her son in, was desperately worried about him, and wanted to do anything she could to help him.

Frank Hilton, I believe, falls into a familiar trap by proposing too superficial a separation of family members into two camps: the dove-like, kindly enablers, and the hawk-like, not to be taken advantage of, un-enablers. Baudelaire's mother he puts in the first group, his stepfather, the General, in the latter. But these are stereotypes and are not borne out even from the evidence presented in Hilton's book. Baudelaire's mother resists being humbugged for long periods of time, and in the end carries through on her threat to appoint a *conseil judiciaire* to control Baudelaire's income. His half-brother is portrayed as hard-hearted and controlling by most of Baudelaire's previous biographers, and some of what Hilton writes about him supports that characterization. But Hilton also brings out the kindly, helpful elder brother side of Alphonse's treatment of his brother. Even the *conseil judiciaire*, Ancelle, given a controlling role in Baudelaire's life, turns out to be a helpful friend in some respects. It would have been good to know more about Baudelaire's mistress, Jeanne. She appears not to have been a very steadying influence on Baudelaire, but she remains a shadowy figure in the book.

In fact Hilton, having offered his dichotomy of family member types in an early chapter, makes little attempt to confirm it as the book goes on. His main theme is the previous failure to recognize the importance of Baudelaire's drug addiction. Unfortunately he supports his thesis by identifying in Baudelaire what he believes to be the moral failings of a typical drug addict: his irresponsibility, unpredictability, dishonesty, laziness, selfishness, deviousness, blaming everyone and everything else apart from himself, even plagiarism. Family members, whether appearing to be doves or hawks, are seen as victims. It is the addict who is condemned as morally despicable. From the point of view of someone trying to understand the experiences of family members, that is an unhelpful position to take. In fact it is rarely how family members themselves see things, and they mostly find it unhelpful if other people take that view. Unless they are completely at the end of their tether, and want nothing more to do with the person whose addictive behaviour has caused them so much distress, family members do not want other people to take sides. They do not find it supportive if other people condemn their loved ones, suggest they are beyond help, or recommend that the family member turn her or his back on the addicted relative.

Questions

1. Do you like the metaphor of the 'chains' that may have bound Baudelaire to opium extending also around his mother? What do you think that metaphor implies? Can you think of an alternative, better one?
2. The biographer describes Baudelaire and his mother as 'locked' in a relationship. Family members have sometimes been described as 'co-dependent'. What do you think of that term? Does it imply that the family member is as much an addict as the person he or she is concerned about? Does it even imply that the family member's behaviour is as much responsible for maintaining the problem as is the addict's behaviour?

3. Do you think it is helpful to divide family members into hawks and doves?

4. Baudelaire's biographers have generally criticized the family's *conseil judiciaire* arrangement for being heartless and controlling. What do you think? Imagine a mother, stepfather and elder brother of a man, now aged in his late 30s, who has had an addiction problem since his teens, is chronically short of money, often ill-fed and from time to time homeless. They are concerned about his future and would like him to benefit in the best way possible from his share of the family inheritance. But they have learned that simply giving him money results in him squandering it very quickly, doing him no good and making him feel even worse in the process. What are their options and the pros and cons of each option?

5. What do you think of the proposition that family members mostly find it supportive if other people show understanding both of their own experience and of the experience of the addicted relative they are concerned about?

6. How do you react to Hilton's very negative depiction of 'drug addicts'? Is there any truth at all in it?

7. Do you think Baudelaire would have been better off with a wife like Coleridge's or De Quincey's? Does every man who has a drinking, drug or gambling problem need a firm, supportive wife? Does every addicted person need a sound, steadying influence?

Exercises

*   You have a younger brother who has developed a drug problem and you are very worried about him. You are several years his senior and you feel a responsibility to do something. You decide that writing him a letter is the best way. Compose the letter that you might write.

*   Imagine that you have the opportunity to speak with Hilton, Baudelaire's biographer. You enjoyed the book he wrote but you believe his very negative, blaming attitude towards people with a drug addiction was very evident in the book. You have someone in your own family who has had such a problem so you feel some obligation to put him right about this. Get someone else to play Hilton while you try to explain to him that criticism and blame are not appropriate towards someone who is experiencing an addiction.

21

Fever Pitch by Richard Brooks

J.W. Dement devoted a whole book to the way problem gambling is treated in films: *Going for Broke: The Depiction of Compulsive Gambling in Film.* He reviewed no less than 151 films on the subject that appeared between 1908 and 1998. He picked out *Fever Pitch* as one of a small handful of films providing detailed and accurate portrayals of problem gambling. He had strong views himself about how problem gambling should be portrayed, and was particularly concerned that a number of films, including *Fever Pitch*, had 'dishonest' or 'unrealistic' endings showing the gambler having a big win. Otherwise he rated *Fever Pitch* highly, believing that everything leading up to the ending was informative and valuable on the subject. It appeared in 1985 and was directed by Richard Brooks who had written and directed such classics as *Elmer Gantry* for which he was awarded an Oscar for his screenplay adaptation of the novel. He later focused his attention on what Dement called 'message' films, including *Fever Pitch*. The message of that film, according to one reviewer cited by Dement, was, 'Gambling is big, and gambling is bad'. Several notable experts on problem gambling were recruited as technical advisers to the film, including Dr Robert Custer, the first author of one of the early classic books on the subject of compulsive

Addiction Dilemmas: Family Experiences from Literature and Research and their Challenges for Practice, First Edition. Jim Orford.
© 2012 John Wiley & Sons, Ltd. Published 2012 by John Wiley & Sons, Ltd.

gambling, *When Luck Runs Out: Help for Compulsive Gamblers and Their Families*, which also appeared in 1985.

The film's central character is Steve Taggart, a prize-winning sports reporter for the Los Angeles *Herald Tribune*, earning a good salary which he is gambling away. In Dement's view Brooks did an excellent job of depicting Taggart's preoccupation with gambling, beautifully illustrated in an early scene between Taggart and his daughter. He rarely sees his daughter but has taken her to an amusement park for a birthday celebration. He is preoccupied with studying the racing news in his paper, and the scene shows her trying to get his attention while she enjoys a ride on a merry-go-round – that she is riding a horse Dement finds to be a nice touch in view of Taggart's preoccupation with horse racing. He has one eye on his daughter and the other on his paper. She is disappointed that he seems not to be sharing her enjoyment, and that he then seems to want to cut the trip short.

> 'Well, I'm working on a story. If I don't get going . . .', he lies.
> 'That's Okay. We understand'.
> . . . She has the knowing look of someone who has been through this before, the look of someone hoping a loved one will change his ways, only to find that he has not.

A later scene, that Dement believed to be key in demonstrating the effect that living with a compulsive gambler has on a spouse, involves Flo, a woman Taggart meets while working on a story in Las Vegas. He visits her late one night after losing practically all of his money, wanting to borrow from her so that he can win back enough to pay off an accumulated debt amounting to several thousand dollars. In turns out that Flo is familiar with this scenario, having experienced it with an ex-husband. Dement describes the scene as follows:

> This scene is one of the most powerful and effective in the film. The power comes from the raw emotional pain that Flo conveys. The encounter with Taggart brings back the pain she felt when she was married to another man who was a compulsive gambler. Over the course of the scene, her buried feelings rise to the surface and explode . . .
>
> Taggart goes to see Flo at the casino where she works. She is seated as he approaches her from behind. Reaching over her, he places a yellow rose on the counter in front of her. Happy about receiving the rose, she quickly turns around and looks at him. Her mood changes when she sees how worn out he looks. Sympathetically, she asks, 'Rough night?' He does not answer her, managing only

a sarcastic laugh. She understands the meaning. 'That bad', she says. Again, there is no response from Taggart. 'Had anything to eat?' she asks. Again, nothing from Taggart. She hands him a bottle of liquor, which he accepts. Her indignation is growing now with every question. 'How much you lose?' He does not reply. 'That much?' she asks. Again, nothing. 'Flat broke?' Still nothing from Taggart. Flo pauses, gathering her thoughts. 'And you expect me to bail you out? Just a small loan though, right? Which I'll get back in the morning, right? You'll even pay 5 per cent interest even 10 percent, right? Eleven hundred for a thousand, right?'. Flo pauses again, briefly, before continuing . . .

'Do you know what I see here? I see my second ex-husband. Always looking for the big win, the big score. I hate to think of the times that I bailed him out. Down on his knees, begging, crying, swearing . . . "No more, Hon. Never make another bet". And me, dumbbell, believed him every time! No! No! Sorry, no money. Not for one of you guys; not for what you want it . . .' .

Frustrated and upset, she begins to walk away. He stops her, finally speaking. He asks her for money. She says no. He tells her he loves her. She walks back to where he is, leaning against the counter, and slaps him across the face. She asks him if it hurt, and he says that it did. She apologizes and slaps him again, even harder this time. Slapping Taggart's face – as she does twice – is an accurate and powerful analogy to the pain a spouse must feel. It must feel like a slap in the face to be repeatedly promised that the addict will quit gambling, only to find out later that his gambling has resumed.

Comments

This is another fictional account, in film form in this case, that tries to get across some of what it is like to have a gambling problem and to be in the shoes of other people witnessing it and trying to respond appropriately to it. Preoccupation with gambling, and the difficulty of attending fully to other life demands – Taggart taking his daughter on an outing for example – is poignantly illustrated. Failure to join in family activities, keeping other people waiting or failing to turn up altogether, are things that children and other family members often feel most bitter about.

The scene with Flo is interesting because it shows, yet again, how difficult it is to take a clear, kind but firm position in the face of desperate requests for money. Despite Flo's familiarity with such a scenario, she becomes indignant, it reminds her of similar occasions with her ex-husband, it makes her frustrated and upset, she responds emotionally, speaks aggressively, and finally is violent, slapping Taggart across the face.

As Dement explained, *Fever Pitch* is a message film, using technical advisers who are convinced of the importance and significance of compulsive gambling. Dement approved of films that, in his view, took a realistic and informative position on the subject. The line the film takes, excepting the ending that Dement objected to, is very different in tone to James Kelman's book, *A Chancer* (see Chapter 18), which avoided 'moralizing' on the subject.

Questions

1. What do you think of a 'message' film like *Fever Pitch*? It is out to make a point, part of which is how painful a problem such as compulsive gambling is for family members and others. Do you think that helps an understanding of the family issues involved, or hinders it?
2. Feeling that you are taking second place to the object of the relative's addiction is a common experience for affected family members. Can you think of other analogous sets of circumstances in which family members might feel much the same thing? Does thinking of analogies help in understanding how family members affected by addiction might feel?
3. What do you think are the risks for children with parents with problems such as Taggart's? Would you be worried about his daughter?
4. Do you find yourself applauding Flo for the way she handled Taggart when he came to the casino hoping for a loan? How would you have responded if you were Flo?
5. Is violence towards an addicted relative ever justified do you think?
6. Gambling has been the addiction in several of the chapters in this book. Are you persuaded that gambling addiction is in all respects like substance addictions in terms of its effects on family members? In what respects might it be different?
7. It has been difficult enough to raise awareness of substance addiction problems in frontline services such as primary healthcare and social work. How might we raise consciousness of gambling addiction in such services?

Exercises

- Sketch an outline for a film on gambling addiction highlighting the effects on the family. Share ideas about this with others and see if you can agree on what would make a good film that would get across the reality of gambling addiction as experienced by partners and children.

- Flo has been married to a man with a gambling problem. She reacts emotionally to Taggart's request for money. But supposing she was invited to speak at a community forum about the harm that gambling can do to the family – assume that members of the forum are interested because of a proposal to build a large casino in their area. She has been given 10 minutes to speak. Plan what she might say, covering effects of problem gambling on partners such as herself, and on children such as Taggart's daughter in the film. If you have time try giving the talk for real to a group of your colleagues.

I Only Had the Baby's Welfare at Heart

Concerned Grandmothers

Two of the themes that have been constantly with us throughout this book have been (1) the worry that family members experience in the face of their relatives' addiction problems, and (2) their dilemmas about what to do about it. These take a particularly acute form when members of the extended family see young children apparently being put at risk. One group who are increasingly being recognized as family members in that position are mothers of daughters or sons with problems of drug addiction who themselves have started to have a family. The mothers, now in their role as grandmothers, have started to speak about the dilemmas they face. This has been the subject of research by Marina Barnard and her team in Glasgow. A whole chapter is devoted to it in her book, *Drug Addiction and Families*. The following examples are taken from that chapter and, in the first case, in a modified form from our own research files.

Doreen

She is back living with us again but she's not my daughter, she lies constantly, she's completely changed. She's depressed. She sits watching TV all day,

Addiction Dilemmas: Family Experiences from Literature and Research and their Challenges for Practice, First Edition. Jim Orford.
© 2012 John Wiley & Sons, Ltd. Published 2012 by John Wiley & Sons, Ltd.

doing very little for the little boy. He sleeps badly and I'm finding it hard-going looking after the two of them. I get really tired. She says I'm interfering and trying to take the baby away from her, but it's not so, I'm simply looking after him until she's better. She started taking drugs again just before Christmas, although she denies it. I think it was because her partner had just come out of prison. He used to send her threatening letters when he was inside. He's a thoroughly bad sort. She would then go out for hours at a time and her mood changed and things started disappearing from her room. I found methadone pots still full up so I knew she wasn't taking it. My husband's away working most of the week and doesn't really want to know about his daughter's drug use. The two of us had planned to go away at Christmas but we were worried about leaving her on her own and what might go missing from the house. My main concern is the baby's welfare. He had a minor operation recently. Although my daughter and her partner were at the hospital it was me they called in order to soothe the baby when he was given his pre-med.

Things really came to a head a few weeks after Christmas and we had a big bust up. My daughter and her partner were then living in a flat very close by. The flat was boarded up and they had no electricity. Her sister had tried to get in but they wouldn't let her. So I went and banged on the door and shouted until I was let in. I found her partner taking drugs and the baby lying on a dirty mattress. I took the baby home and called social services. They let the baby go back to his mother two days later. My GP was amazed they'd allowed it. I know I should have called social services or the police first but I only had his welfare at heart and I couldn't think of anything else to do at the time. Sometimes I wonder if I am too over-protective or clingy about my grandson. Deep down I know that's not true but my daughter's behaviour and harsh words do make me wonder sometimes. I know she gets very angry with me. She thinks I interfere all the time, that I'm too wrapped up with the baby and that I don't think she's a good enough mother. She's accused me of trying to take the baby away from her. She's even said horrid things to me such as I'm the villain of the piece or that I'm evil. I don't know what to do next.

Pearl

I knew there was something wrong but I just couldn't put my finger on it. My brother went up to visit my daughter one time and he seen needles so then I started going up all the time and my daughter would stay in the bedroom with her partner and I noticed then that my grandson wasn't properly looked after. He wasn't up and dressed and out and about … I mean he was clean and things but he just seemed lost and living on crisps and biscuits and things like that so I noticed it and I didn't know what to do. I think I actually spoke to social workers saying that I was a bit concerned, so by then she had a social worker appointed to them and they helped her to get the kids to nursery and different things.

One day social work contacted me at work and said … did I know that my youngest grandson had been burnt … I rushed home in a state and I couldn't find my daughter so I phoned social work up and I said to them 'I want these children if they are going into care'. … so about half nine that night they brought the two children. So, I had no access to the children's clothes or toys or anything. I couldn't get into her home. I had no keys. The children came with what they stood in.

Oh my God, they were all fighting and carrying on. Ben, he's the oldest [grandmother's oldest teenage son], he didn't want them here because he couldn't get his rest and his pals was coming up and all these weans were running about. Logan complained because he lost his room because he's not got a room of his own now … That was the worst part, trying to get them to accept that the children were going to stay here. They were all arguing. Ben didn't want them here. He would say, 'How is it our lives need to get disrupted?'

Sometimes she was granted access but she didn't turn up. They would be standing with their faces at the window waiting for her, so they were disappointed, but that happened so many times that I had to pick up the pieces and explain, you know, that maybe something had turned up, or maybe she got the days mixed up.

Mrs Lennie

They were using but not too severe. There wasn't that much abuse at the time that we really would have took much notice of. They coped with it and they were looking after the kids and things like that at that time. It wasn't until Jessica was born that the drugs really got out of hand …

… my two sisters and I went down one day and I was so mortified with the place. I wouldn't let a pig live in it. My sisters and I just lifted black bags and threw every single thing that was in the house out. Their clothes were covered in maggots and the food . . . They had been bringing sandwiches back from the food kitchen and they were all lying in bags and they were all full of maggots and this is what these weans were living in. The cupboards were all full of syringes so we just threw everything out. That is when I took the weans away.

As I says to [social worker] the reason why I don't ask them for anything is that I don't want them thinking that I've only got these weans to get money off the social work. That's not why I've got these weans, I've got these weans because I want to have them. They're my grand weans and I'd rather have them than see some stranger with them. But as [social worker] says, 'That's not the point, they should be helping you. They should have helped you long before now'.

It's a shame, it's the weans that suffer. It's the weans that suffer all the time.

Viv

I thought I'd went round all the issues that would be, but the funny thing I never thought on was money . . . know, 'how am I going to manage?' but all of a sudden it was like I had these two extra to feed on a daily basis, I had to buy them like different things, socks and shoes and school bags . . .

And what I think feels even worse, is because you have the guilt that it's your child that's caused this . . . It's like because you feel responsible.

Edith

I ended up in rent arrears. I always kept plenty of food for the kids. I bought them clothes. I had to buy prams. I thought, something's got to give and if it means my rent, then, so be it. I can't say, 'well, I won't buy food for them', that would have been crazy, or clothes, they would have been back in care. So, I thought, 'they are not doing without. Why should they? I'll give them everything they need, the rent can remain unpaid and if it goes to court, I'll tell them why', which I did . . . but it was the embarrassment . . . I'd never been in court. I'd never been in trouble.

So when I got it fixed with the social worker she [daughter] wouldn't give me the money. She still gets their money. It's still in her name but I've accepted that. I mean, she gives me it now. I've got the cards and that for the child benefit and her social money. I get that now. I feed them, I buy them clothes. I never ever took it off her before because I felt that was taking the weans away. I never ever wanted to take them away from their mother as such.

I mean I'm rotten with arthritis, this hip's bad, this one's worse; I need operations on that. I've got arthritis more or less from my head to my toes and there's days I could scream with the pain, and that's being quite honest with you. But again, what can I do? I've got to think on the kids.

Esme

Most of the time I had him because she was away wandering looking for drugs and she wasn't turning up with money and all the money was getting used for drugs, as you know. So I decided; 'I'm keeping him Meg. I'm not letting you keep him.'

And I loved her to bits and I tried everything. I just couldn't understand how she couldn't get involved with her own two weans you know.

I'm not unhealthy or anything like that but if I fall not well then I make myself really, really ill. I panic if something happens to me and I get myself into a terrible, terrible state. If I get ill what's going to happen to them? Because there is nobody else that I can talk to or turn to, family-wise, because every one of my family are all junkies.

Comments

These grandmothers were facing a very special kind of dilemma arising in the context of drug addiction. But, for all the agonies associated with this particular conflict, I would argue that what we are witnessing here is simply one example – albeit one of the most stressful types – of the dilemmas that all family members struggle with in the face of a close relative's addiction. What these concerned grandmothers were demonstrating can be seen as fitting in with one common way of trying to stand up to addiction in the family.

Rather than detaching from a daughter or son's drug addiction which, at least for the moment, is not showing any signs of improving, and getting on with their own lives, they were engaging themselves in active coping. The way they were coping falls under the general heading of 'protecting self, family and home'. Family members who take steps to control family finances to prevent too much leakage from the family coffers, or family members who make family rules about bringing drinking or drug-taking friends home, or who keep children out of the way of drinkers and maintain positive family activities, are all doing similar things. They are all forms of 'harm minimization'.

What more important form of harm minimization could there be than protecting the health and safety of small children who may be at risk because of a parent's drug addiction. In several instances these grandmothers were taking on childcare responsibilities despite being financially stretched themselves and in some cases not being as fit as they had once been. They were also acting out of conviction that it was their responsibility to do so as grandmothers, but often also in the face of criticism and resistance from their grandchildren's parents. A big additional complication, which of course makes the situation even more fraught, is the involvement in many cases of the authorities in the form of social services. But again these are not the only addiction-related circumstances in which family members face the dilemma of whether to involve outsiders who will be seen as controlling or worse. In this book we have met numerous examples of circumstances in which family members have debated whether to involve treatment or public order authorities.

Questions

1. Where do your sympathies mostly lie in reading what these grandmothers had to say? Do you think they were doing the right thing? Or do you sympathize more with the daughters or sons who may feel their roles as parents are being undermined?

2. In her book, *Drug Addiction and Families,* Marina Barnard expresses awareness of the danger of further stigmatizing an already stigmatized group – young adults with drug problems. This is a controversial area. She tends to the view that, unless drug-taking is very well controlled, drug dependence and good parenting are not compatible: while

drug-taking remains uncontrolled, children would be better in the care of other people. She is critical of the view that drug-taking should not be seen as necessarily incompatible with adequate parenting. Do you have a view on that controversy?

3. When assessing the risk of harm to the young child living with a parent addicted to drugs, and deciding what action to follow, should the authorities always focus on the child's needs above all others and recommend removal of the child from the home if there is any doubt?

4. In their 2011 book, *Parents who Misuse Drugs and Alcohol*, Forrester and Harwin produce evidence that social workers are not well prepared to work with families where children are thought to be at risk because of parental alcohol or drug addiction. Think of a professional group – it might be social work or your own profession or one you have come into contact with. Are those working in that profession well prepared to work with families affected by addiction, do you think? If not, what kind of preparation do you believe they need?

5. If you were a grandparent and you discovered your grandchild living in what you considered to be squalid and unsafe conditions, would you contact social services? If not, what would you do?

6. Would you take your grandchildren in, even if it meant inconvenience and extra financial strain for you and the rest of your family?

7. Families coping with addiction are generally doing so in isolation. Can you see any prospects for collective action, like grandmothers, for example, getting together to combat addiction? Are there any prospects for families jointly campaigning for their rights or for their relatives' rights?

Exercises

• Debate the motion, *Drug addiction is always incompatible with good child caring.*

• Based on what you have read in this chapter, set up a role-play exercise starting with just two parts: mother (holding baby) and grandmother (the mother's mother). The grandmother is very concerned about the baby and has in her mind the possibility of contacting social services. The baby's mother is defending her ability to be a parent and thinks her mother is interfering. Later on try introducing a third part, the baby's father. Then introduce a social worker. Try the exercise once in order to get a good picture of how each of the parties might be feeling and what their responsibilities are. Try a second time with everyone making an effort to seek a way forward that represents a 'win-win solution' for everybody.

Further Reading

The Alcohol, Drugs and the Family Research Group: A. Copello, A. Ibanga, J. Orford, L. Templeton and R. Velleman (2010) The 5-Step Method: A research-based programme of work to help family members affected by a relative's alcohol or drug misuse. *Drugs: Education, Prevention and Policy*, 17:Suppl. 1.

> This special journal supplement describes a method that our group has developed for helping family members affected by a close relative's addiction. The papers included in the supplement cover the stress-coping model on which the method is based, a summary of the background research, the method itself and its effects, and policy and practice issues related to it.

Copello, A., Orford, J., Hodgson, R. and Tober, G. (2009) *Social Behaviour and Network Therapy for Alcohol Problems.* London: Brunner-Routledge.

> This publication is in the form of a manual for professionals wishing to use Social Behaviour and Network Therapy (SBNT) in the treatment of alcohol dependence. Central to SBNT is the identification of concerned family members and friends who can be engaged to help in the efforts of a person wishing to overcome his or her drinking problem.

Orford, J., Natera, G., Copello, A., Atkinson, C., Mora, J., Velleman, R., Crundall, I., Tiburcio, M., Templeton, L. and Walley, G. (2005) *Coping with Alcohol and Drug Problems: The Experiences of Family Members in Three Contrasting Cultures.* London: Brunner-Routledge.

In this book are described parallel research projects carried out by our group in England and our colleagues in Mexico and in Australia. In each case family members affected by relatives' addiction were interviewed in depth. The book begins with a summary of our own and others' theoretical positions on the subject and a review of previous research, and ends with discussion and integration of the findings.

Velleman, R., Copello, A. and Maslin, J. (eds) (1998) *Living with Drink: Women who Live with Problem Drinkers*. London: Longman.

The accounts given by each of six women who lived with problem drinkers are given in detail in this book, followed by a series of chapters by academics or professionals, each of which comments on the six accounts from a different theoretical perspective.

Velleman, R. and Orford, J. (1999) *Risk and Resilience: Adults who were the Children of Problem Drinkers*. Amsterdam: Harwood.

This book is a summary of a detailed interview study of a large sample of sons and daughters of problem drinking parents and a comparison group.

Index

Addiction Dilemmas: Family Experiences from Literature and Research and their Challenges for Practice,
First Edition. Jim Orford.
© 2012 John Wiley & Sons, Ltd. Published 2012 by John Wiley & Sons, Ltd.